Drawing upon their combined decades of personal and professional experiences, Janet Farrar and Gavin Bone take us on a journey through the past histories and present incarnations of Witchcraft. But as the true pioneers that they are, they then forge ahead taking us with them into a future where Witchcraft is both an evolutionary and revolutionary spiritual force that can change the world.

The key to the future of Witchcraft may indeed lie in its past. But as Janet Farrar and Gavin Bone point out with much wit and wisdom in Progressive Witchcraft, *this might not be exactly the same version of "the past" that you were taught!*

A refreshingly honest look into the Witchcraft of the past with a visionary eye focused firmly upon its future.

A truly visionary work. Janet and Gavin prove once again why they are among the most respected and widely read authors of our time.

What Witchcraft was is not as important as what it will be. As Janet Farrar and Gavin Bone take us through and then beyond the controversies surrounding our Witchcraft/Wiccan roots, a truly evolutionary vision of the future begins to unfold.
                                    —The Witches' Voice.

Progressive Witchcraft is required reading and an important contribution to the powerful, anti-dogmatic, and evolutionary leap occurring within modern Wicca and Witchcraft. It is a wise, inspiring, and useful guide for all those seeking the real and holy magic of union with the Divine, the true purpose of this profound spiritual path.
            —Phyllis Curott, esq. Priestess and author of the
            bestselling *Book of Shadows* and *WitchCrafting.*

PROGRESSIVE WITCHCRAFT

SPIRITUALITY, MYSTERIES, AND TRAINING IN MODERN WICCA

By

Janet Farrar

&

Gavin Bone

NEW PAGE BOOKS
A division of The Career Press, Inc.
Franklin Lakes, NJ

PROGRESSIVE WITCHCRAFT
EDITED BY NICOLE DEFELICE AND LAUREN MANOY
TYPESET BY EILEEN DOW MUNSON
Cover design by Cheryl Cohan Finbow
Printed in the U.S.A. by Book-mart Press

To order this title, please call toll-free 1-800-CAREER-1 (NJ and Canada: 201-848-0310) to order using VISA or MasterCard, or for further information on books from Career Press.

The Career Press, Inc., 3 Tice Road, PO Box 687,
Franklin Lakes, NJ 07417
www.careerpress.com
www.newpagebooks.com

Library of Congress Cataloging-in-Publication Data

Farrar, Janet.
   Progressive witchcraft : spirituality, mysteries, and training in modern wicca /
by Janet Farrar & Gavin Bone.
      p. cm.
   Includes bibliographical references and index.
   ISBN 1-56414-719-3
      1. Witchcraft. I. Bone, Gavin. II. Title.

BF1571.F346 2004
299'.94—dc22   2003066474

Dedicated to:

Twilight Circle, Temple of Bast, Star Circle,
Coven Clannad, Jonathan's Coven,
The Water Dragons,
Earth Central, and Callaighe.

And in remembrance of a passing generation of Witches and trailblazers:
Doreen Valiente,
Eleanor Bone,
Louis Martello,
Jesse Belle,
Chris Gosselin,
Ellen Cannon-Reed,
and our beloved Stewart.
May they meet and laugh in the Summerlands.

Table of Contents

Introduction

God(dess) grant me the serenity to accept the
things I cannot change, the courage to change the
things I can, and the wisdom to know the difference.

—Reinhold Niebuhr

It has been more than 50 years, bridging two centuries and a millennium, since the witchcraft revival began. This is quite an achievement for a new religious movement, which one of its founders believed would only manage to survive another decade. According to Doreen Valiente, Gerald Gardner, the "father" of modern witchcraft, said to her in the early 1960s: "The problem with this religion, Doreen, is that it has too many Chiefs and not enough Indians." He strongly believed that this would be its downfall and that it would not survive as a religious path beyond the 1970s. Luckily for many of us, he was wrong. He failed to take into account one of the most important factors that has allowed witchcraft to survive: its ability to change with the times, to evolve and adapt culturally and socially. There is, of course, a scientific word for this type of change: evolution.

It is for this reason that we have entitled this book *Progressive Witchcraft*. We are not the only ones within Wicca who have used the term *Progressive* to describe themselves. The term *Progressive Wicca* was used, as far we know, for the first time in the 1980s to describe a diverse, eclectic movement originating in the United Kingdom. Others may call it eclectic, but it is the nature of evolution to encourage diversity and variety. A look at its history shows there is nothing more eclectic than Traditional Wicca, with its blend of Italio-Etruscan, Ceremonial Magic, Masonic, and possibly even Sufi origins! For us, the use of the term *Progressive* does not indicate a specific tradition, but a way of seeing the spiritual truths that underlie all nature based religions—especially the truth that they must be able to adapt if they would cater to the spiritual needs of the individual.

Witchcraft is a religious movement with its roots in nature and of course, natural law. Evolution is at the core of its philosophy whether its practitioners have realized it or not. It is important to note that evolution affects not only physical and social development, but also spiritual growth. This is reflected in almost all of Wicca's practices: the use of magical energy to affect positive change, the Wheel of the Year; the cycles of the sun, the moon, and the seasons, and, of specific importance with reference to this book, change within the self—initiation and the mechanisms that cause it. In the spiritual cultures of the ancient past, these came to be called the mysteries.

In the last few decades, we have come to see many changes in the way witchcraft has been viewed, both publicly and internally. What was once a small group of individuals secretly trying to recreate the past has now become a large movement trying to embrace the future. Because of this, witchcraft has become more noticeable. Witchcraft was once viewed by the public with suspicion; the word *Wicca* was unknown and rarely appeared in the lurid stories of witchcraft that appeared in the tabloid press. Now the word *Wicca* appears regularly in all the media as a modern, fashionable kind of witchcraft, which has become one of the fastest growing spiritual practices in the world.

Witches embrace positive change, and when this change does not occur spontaneously, they create it. This has always been the role of the witch, going back to the medieval village and forward to the modern day. For this reason, witches have always been irrepressible rebels by nature; they challenge the status quo, not just within their own sphere of practices, but also in the wider world. This is why witchcraft was seen as a challenge to established authority, particularly the Christian Church. It was for this reason witchcraft was labelled as sinful and had to be eradicated, as it promoted the idea that everyone had access to the power of The Divine through it's manifestation in nature, not just the politically motivated Priesthood of Christendom. Now, in the 21st century it is the corporations and governments that have become the authority to be challenged by the witch. These institutions put materialism over spirituality, threatening the environment. Witches know that both materialism and spirituality need to be in balance if there is to be a positive future for both ourselves and the planet we live on.

Materialism has seen a market in witchcraft, and herein lies the paradox of this book. The market has been flooded with books on witchcraft due to the increasing need and desire for a spirituality that challenges the doctrines of consumer society; the paradox is that now spirituality can be purchased, just like fast food, from your nearest book shop. Or this is what modern society would like to have us believe. Many of these books contain substantially the same information, rewritten and regurgitated for mass consumption. But witches are rebels and know differently; they know that true spiritual connection comes from the soul, and that books can only give us ideas and, of course, the experiences of the author. This is a book about ideas on how to change, and for this reason, much of the material is subjective, drawn from our own experiences over the years. This is a book about the quest for the spiritual experience that is the path of witchcraft, but it is not the quest itself, only a guide to help the seeker along this path.

The word *revolution* originates in the word *evolution:* to re-evolve. Since the 1950s, witchcraft has reinvented itself several times because of the need of those within it to revolt against the dogmatic practices that have seeped into it. Such dogmas and doctrines go against the true nature of the witch; there are and always have been rebels and there always will be. This was the factor that Gardner, a rebel of his time, did not pencil into the equation when he made that statement to Doreen Valiente (see page 9). Without the rebels, Gardner's prophecy would have come to pass, for change, evolution, and revolution would not have happened.

We were both part of this process. Janet in a more direct way, by being involved with the King of Wiccan rebels Alex Sanders, and Gavin by being part of an organization that rebelled against the doctrine that one could only be a witch if one was part of a traditional lineage. We were both rebels, as was Janet's late husband, Stewart. Likewise the need to rebel against dogma encouraged other authors such as Starhawk, Ray Buckland, Phyllis Curott, and Raven Grimassi to put pen to paper to cause change, and to cause Wiccan evolution to take a leap forward.

People face change in different ways. Witches are no different. As we try to show in this book, witchcraft has never been slow to accept the inevitabilities of time. Evolution and the will of the Goddess eventually win. A true witch knows that time, evolution, and spirituality are indivisible, so witchcraft as a spiritual path will always embrace these changes as they occur. Unfortunately, there will always be those who feel differently. These are the people who are comfortable where they are or are scared of the effect change might have on the personal power that they have obtained for themselves. For them, the leap across the void of the mysteries is too large a journey to contemplate. They sit in spiritual stagnation. They are not—regardless of a string of initiations, validated lineage, and heritage—witches.

The Mysteries, the central theme of this book, are about change. They are about the transformation of the self for the benefit of all. When you change the self, you change the world. This is inevitable; the macrocosm (the whole of the world) and microcosm (the individual self) are intertwined like the two snakes on the staff of Hermes. This is a book about changing witchcraft into a spiritual path for this new millennium. Microcosmically, this is done by changing the individuals who call themselves witches. This can only be done when change is first accepted as inevitable, and the strength for this change comes from spiritual connection.

The need for spiritual union is at the core of all true spiritual paths. Somewhere along the line, for many within Wicca, this was forgotten. The form of ritual became more important than its actual purpose; words became more important than intent. It is time to right this. It is time that Wicca took its place where it belongs alongside the other contemporary spiritual paths that encourage connection and union with the Divine, such as Santeria, Voudon, Hinduism, Buddhism, and Shinto.

Over the years, we have also changed. We have embraced the need to look at new philosophies as part of our spiritual growth. We have looked into the past, into the Celtic, Norse, Anglo-Saxon, and Greek worlds for inspiration. We have drawn what we can from them, but in recent years, have found more inspiration from living religions rather than the fragmented remains of dead ones. Others feel the same. We have noticed that many witches have become drawn to contemporary spiritualities, particularly Voudon and Santeria, which are alive and vibrant and offer one-on-one spiritual connection. This is because some Wiccan practice has become lacking in this connection. It is our hope that we can encourage such witches to take their experiences of such living religions and infuse them into Wicca, to boost the next evolutionary leap forward in its development. Wicca can become a vehicle for the return of the old gods and goddesses not just into circle, but into the everyday life of the witch, both mentally and emotionally.

When you approach Wicca from this direction, you come to a realization, an epiphany, if you will. As Wiccans, we like to say that "all religions are paths to the same truth." If we truly believe this, we must accept that much of the ceremonial aspect that we are taught in Wicca is simply "icing on the cake," a way of enticing you to experience the truth of the spiritual experience. The ritual and the systems associated with it are nothing more than a tool to bring you to god/goddess and your connection. They are tools to change you and the way you view the world you live in. There is no right or wrong, either in the way you do things or the way you think, so long as you seek the guidance of Spirit in the quest for the experience of the mystery. What we wish to do here is help the reader access the mystery in the term Mystery Tradition. The irony is that one cannot write about the individual spiritual experience in an objective way, as there are no words to convey the impact such experiences have. We believe that the purpose of any true Priestess or Priest of witchcraft in the modern age is to encourage, inspire, and guide the individual to experience the secrets—the mysteries—for themselves.

If witchcraft is to survive the next millennium, then it must now come of age and accept the importance of its core of spiritual beliefs in the scheme of things, which can unite true religions of healing in understanding and tolerance. It must also accept the truth of its origins as a new religion based on old wisdoms, rather than a surviving remnant from the Middle Ages, if it is to truly become a spiritual path for a modern world. This is not a book telling you what to do or think. It is a book telling you that it is okay to do what you are already doing as long as it is done with the guidance of Spirit.

There are some points that we need to emphasise regarding our use of the words *Wicca* and *witchcraft*. We use the term Wicca to describe modern traditions of witchcraft, stemming from Gerald Gardner, Alex Sanders, and their contemporaries. The word witchcraft is used to describe general practice and may also apply to older, more historical practices such as Stregheria, the Italian practice of witchcraft that still survives today.

We have attempted to create aspects of a system of Wicca useable by all, regardless of whether they are solitary or in a coven, that can easily be applied to already existing traditional practices. We easily could have just subtitled the work "A Modern Coven Handbook" or something similar, but the reality of Wicca is that many practitioners are solitary and at the end of the day, individual witches have the task of teaching themselves. It is not our intention that the practices within this book should be dogmatic or even doctrinal. This book simply offers ideas to guide the reader, as all books about witchcraft should do.

For the previously discussed reasons, we do not claim within this work to be publishing ancient knowledge, secrets, or archaic occult techniques, although much of what we have written has its origins in past occult practices that we have synthesized for the modern world. All of the practical exercises are ones we have created ourselves and have used successfully; they were not created purely for this book, as some writers have done in their works. They are drawn from our work with our magical training group, and from a series of intensive workshops called *The Inner Mysteries*, which we started back in early 2002, and have since been held in Europe, the United Kingdom, the United States, and Australia.

Our thanks go to those who attended these workshops, encouraging and inspiring us to write this book. Our experiences with you have changed us, just as they should. We would also like to thank several others for their assistance in creating this book: Adam for his graphical professionalism, Cathbad for his philosophical insight, and of course, the members of our coven for being patient guinea pigs for many of the magical exercises. Our thanks also go to all the staff at New Page, especially Lauren and Nicole, our editors, for their patience in overcoming our grammatical shortcomings.

Janet Farrar and Gavin Bone
Herne's Cottage
Ethelstown
KELLS
Co Meath

August 2003

Chapter 1

In the Beginning:
From Witchcraft to Wicca

Study the past if you would define the future.

—Confucius[1]

First, we must look at the true origins of witchcraft, those hidden in the mists of time. This is a subject that has been written about many times by many authors. This, of course, may be quite repetitive to those who have been involved in the modern witchcraft movement for several years, but they must bear with us as this book is just as likely to be picked up by those who are making the first steps in the sometimes confusing world of the Neo-Pagan movement. It is our hope that we have given some different viewpoints to its origins that have not been covered before in our own or other literary works.

Witchcraft's Origins in Shamanism

The first magical practices of mankind came about when the first Homo Sapiens began to move east and west from central Asia. Their magic was simple; it revolved around the most basic instinct of mankind—survival. Imagine the scene: In a fire-lit cave, a man dresses in deerskin and dons an antlered headdress. He begins to chant; the chant grows into a grunt; the grunt turns into the recognizable "hurnnn" call of the rutting stag. He slowly circles the fire, and out of the darkness come the other male members of the tribe; each grasps a stick tightly as though it was a spear; and in a moment, they lunge on the figure in frenzy, symbolically killing the stag. By doing this form of magic, they see themselves as successfully procuring meat for the tribe on the following day's hunt.

A division of sexual roles was noticeable in these societies. It was not sexism, but came out the reality that men were more capable of defending and hunting due to physical build and strength. Men were therefore responsible for defending their communities and providing meat, while women cared for the young and the old. During the hunt, the women of the tribe gathered berries and nuts to supplement the tribe's diet, and importantly, from a magical perspective, had the opportunity to gather herbs for the sick. As we have seen, the male mysteries revolved around their role in the preparation for the hunt. Here we see the female mysteries in the treatment of the sick, and for caring for other women during pregnancy. As they were healing the sick, they also found themselves dealing with the spirits that caused the illness. We still see this division between the sexes today in hunter-gatherer communities, such as the aboriginal peoples of Australia. Within this culture, you see a strict division between "men's business" and "women's business" when it comes to the male and female mysteries. It is this division that was probably responsible for mistrust of the old feminine magical ways during the medieval period and the development of the feminine descriptive word *witch*.

It is in both male and female forms of magic that we see the roots of what we call Shamanism and its development into what we now call witchcraft. As humanity developed and settled into an agricultural way of life, the tribal magic-worker evolved. It became a family affair with the skills of one generation passed down to the next. Here we see the idea of "hereditary witchcraft" first appearing, but it should be remembered that at this time, *all* trades and skills were passed down through the family. Within the village/tribe specific families would have been responsible for the skills handed down, such as metal working, torch making, farming, etc. This is the origin of such descriptive surnames as "Baker" and "Smith." In a harsh world, specialization, with each member learning specific skills, is more conducive to survival than a strategy in which everyone is "a Jack of all trades but a master of none." The magical worker became the Priest and Priestess of the village, and although they were not considered more important than any other trade, they were respected. Their roles would have included being responsible for keeping track of the seasons and performing the seasonal rites. This would have involved making offerings to the local gods and Spirits for good crops and good hunts. These were important rites in an agricultural society, and to do them the Priesthood had to understand the cyclical nature of the seasons and be the keepers of the mysteries of birth, death, and rebirth. They looked after the sick with the herb lore they had accumulated from generation to generation; they were responsible for the banishment of malign spirits, which caused disease. Here again, we see the underlying reason for the existence of the magical practitioner—survival—but now the need was more important. The roles within the village/tribe had become more specialized, and the death of one of its members would threaten the well-being of the whole tribe. Here we see the idea of the witch at its purest, without any of the preconceptions put on it by Christianity and the 20th century.

Origins of the Word *Witch* and the Mediterranean Cults

With the spread of Celtic, Germanic, Italio-Etruscan, Greek, and other cultures across Europe, we see the next development within witchcraft, that of taking on cultural symbolism, including language. We see the origins of the word *witch* in Anglo-Saxon culture, and other words evolved in other cultures to describe the tribal magical worker. The word *witch* in old English has its origins in the word *wicce*. It would be wrong to say that witchcraft is of purely Anglo-Saxon origin just because *witch* is an Anglo-Saxon word. Witch is a modern descriptive word that crosses cultural barriers, and this is important to remember. It has several interpretations. It can mean "to bend and shape" (as in the forces of nature); others say it means "wise." Of course, this is the feminine declension of the word. The male, being *wicca,* is the word that became adopted by the modern witchcraft movement in the early 1950s, but it's meaning is intrinsically no different than the word *witch*. This is important to remember as in recent years some in the Neo-Pagan community have felt it necessary to define these words differently (more on this later in this chapter). It is Christianity that turned the word *wicce* into *wych,* then *wytch,* and finally into our modern word, *witch*. The use of the feminine word rather than the masculine came about because of the underlying misogyny of the early Christian Church. Women were seen to be at the root of all evil ever since Eve took the apple of the Tree of Knowledge. The idea of women being in prominent, responsible positions and dealing with spiritual forces was repugnant to the Church. It is not surprising that they adopted the feminine rather than the masculine word, as they considered all female mysteries to be inherently evil.

Similar words for witch exist in other cultures. The Old Norse used the word "vitki," a word that obviously has similar etymological roots as the words wicce or Wicca. The Italians use the word *strega*. According to Raven Grimassi, a noted author on the subject of Italian witchcraft, its origins are very different than those of the word *witch*:

> "The word Strega is derived from both lore and language. The cultural roots extend back to the Latin word *strix*, which indicates an owl (and particularly a screech owl). In archaic Roman religion there was a mythological creature called a striga. The striga was a type of vampire woman that could transform into an owl. The death of infants in their sleep (as well as the disappearance of babies) was blamed on the striga. This brought a supernatural connection to both words, and so *strix* and *striga* came to be interchangeable. In time the Latin word *striga* evolved into the Italian word *stregare*, which means to enchant. Then, over the course of time a female witch came to be called a *Strega*, literally an enchantress."

Raven has also recently discovered that there is a relationship between the earliest known word for a witch, the Greek word *pharmakis*[2] (an herbalist who prepares potions) and the Italian word *strigare*, which means "to extract." He believes that the word *strega* may, in fact, have had its origins from this word rather than the word *strix*. This, of course, seems to link Italian witchcraft directly back with the origins we mentioned earlier in this chapter.

We once believed that there was no such thing as hereditary witchcraft, as we had seen no proof, but our contact with members of the Strega tradition have convinced us otherwise. The survivals of witchcraft into the modern era in the hereditary form are very much linked to the early days of Christianity and its absorption of three other cults in the Mediterranean. Within the Roman Empire, during the early part of the first millennia a new cult appeared in Rome: Mithraism. It has its origins in Persia and, ultimately, in Zoroastrianism. Mithraism was a mystery religion that believed in an entity of Good and an entity of Evil who were in conflict with each other on the spiritual plane, and who manifest as the personalities of Mithras and Ahriman. It was widely adopted by Roman military officers and spread through the empire; a Mithraic temple has even been found and excavated in London. As the Roman officers settled in the new provinces of the far-flung empire, they became traders and the cult changed from being militaristic to one of business. It is not surprising that many aspects of modern Freemasonry have similarities to Mithraism. The new,

Mithras

young, and open Christianity absorbed the idea of dualism from the older cult. This was achieved because many of the converts in Britain and mainland Europe were settled Roman officers who were already practising Mithraism. But the biggest challenge to early Christianity was from another cult that would be difficult to absorb.

The cult of Artemis/Isis was centered in Ephesus in Asia Minor, which is now known as Turkey. Its rituals and practices are some of the best recorded ceremonies of ancient times. Visitors there describe a haze of incense that permanently settled as fog above the city. It was truly the Pagan Vatican of its time, with pilgrims coming from all over the known world to worship and pay homage to the "Great Goddess." The cult had begun to develop into a more structured multi-national religion absorbing many of the other principle national goddesses that existed around the Mediterranean basin: The Egyptian Isis, the Assyro-Babylonian Ishtar, the Roman Diana, Selene, and others all became identified as one Great Goddess, their symbolism absorbed.[3]

This cult remained a thorn in the side of Christianity for four centuries. Women in Greek, Roman, and European culture generally refused to give up worship of the Great Goddess, and there was no replacement within

Artemis

Christianity. The misogynistic views and teachings of St. Paul of Tarsus made it difficult for Christianity to absorb it. The problem was finally resolved in 440 A.D. at the Council of Ephesus, when the doctrine of Panagia Theotokos—the All-Holy Virgin Mother of God—was declared, thereby incorporating the Great Goddess into Roman Catholicism and the Greek and Russian Orthodox Christian religions. Unknowingly, they had planted a seed that allowed the survivals of goddess and Pagan practice under the very eyes of the Christian hierarchy right up until today, allowing the survival of hereditary witchcraft. Some authors and historians have pointed to the idea that witchcraft has its very origins in the Goddess cult of Artemis/Isis, and we would not argue this point with them.

Witchcraft Survivals in Christianity and Their Similarities With African Diaspora Religions

The first act of established Christianity was to discredit the existing Pagan religion. They destroyed the temples and statues dedicated to the old gods, while at the same time absorbing Pagan symbolism into their practices, just as they had absorbed some of the philosophy of Mithraism earlier in their history. The old gods became saints, their festivals and feasts became holy days, and the placing of churches on sacred Pagan sites was encouraged to bring the existing Pagans into Holy Mother Church. It was these very acts that allowed the village witch to survive. The old

Pagan Priesthood of the community actively adopted these changes for its own survival while teaching those they trusted the Pagan symbolism hidden within the new Christian practices. As time went by though, many of the origins of these magical practices were diluted and became lost, particularly by the time of the Protestant Reformation.

In Roman Catholic Ireland we have seen folk magic continually practiced under the guise of Christianity. We once discovered a "prayer" attached to a fairy tree at a holy well close to where we live. It was a piece of paper folded up in plastic and attached by twine to one of the boughs of the tree. The contents read, as closely as we can remember, as follows:

> "Blessed Holy Saint Martha, I ask of you to intercede on my behalf to Holy Mary Mother of God, and her Son Jesus Christ. Bring wealth, health, and prosperity to my family. If such blessings are not forthcoming I will refuse to light candles to our Lady in the Chapel, and will not pray for the soul of _____ . I ask this in the name of Holy Mary and her son Jesus Christ."

I doubt very much that the person placing this in the tree would consider herself a witch and, being a good Christian soul, would have little knowledge about the fact that the tree is of Pagan symbolic origin and that the holy well was originally dedicated to the Pagan god Lugh![4] Raven Grimassi told us that such practices are still common throughout Italy, as much as they are in Ireland. He recounts practices that involve the threatening and cajoling of saints, including the practice of turning statues of the Madonna on their heads if the petitioner does not get her way. From travelling in Greek Orthodox Crete, we can also report that the survivals of Pagan magical practice are common there, too. We have in our collection a small beaten brass plate depicting a leg used as an offering for healing. It is noticeable that survival of folk magic and witchcraft seem to be more prevalent in non-Protestant countries such as Greece, Ireland, and in the Afro-Caribbean.

When slaves were brought from the West Coast of Africa to the Americas during the 16th and 17th centuries, they brought with them their own spiritual and magical practices. These practices continue today with several names. The pure form still practiced in West Africa is known as Ifa, but in the Caribbean and in the American state of Louisiana, it has developed into two distinctly separate forms. When the slaves were brought to the colonies they were, of course, converted to Christianity, and like early Christian Europe, refused to give up their Pagan practices easily, hiding their magical practices and beliefs behind the culture that had enslaved them. In French colonies such as Haiti and New Orleans, this was less of a problem as the French had a much more *laissez faire* attitude to religion. Here we see the development of what is known as Voodoo, or more correctly Voudon, which has always been linked in the popular imagination with witchcraft. The old ancestral spirits, the *loas* of the West Africans, were quickly absorbed into existing French culture; a good example of this is Baron Samedi (Lord of Saturday), popularised by the James Bond film *Live and Let Die.*[5] Originally the old West African spirit of death, Ghede and his black and white, top-hatted face remains one of the popular icons of Voodoo in people's minds. Saturday is the last day of the week and is ruled by Saturn, the planet and classical god who rules death.

In the Spanish colonies, Christianity was less forgiving. It became necessary for the slaves to hide their deities behind saints, just as the Pagans did in Europe. This practice is commonly known as Santeria, and its mystical practices bear striking similarities to the Catholic folk magic practices we have found in Ireland. There is one major difference though: The practitioners of Santeria are still very aware of its Pagan origins, and know whom the saints represent. One should bear in mind that only 300 years have passed since the Christianization of their practices, as opposed to more than 1,000 years within Europe, but by looking at Santeria and Voudon we can possibly see what hereditary witchcraft, minus the cultural overlays, would have looked like up until 12th and 13th centuries. What is also interesting is that its practitioners still consider themselves Priests and Priestesses, just as we do in modern witchcraft. This seems to confirm the idea that magical practitioners were always considered Priesthood. Within Voudon and Santeria, the idea of the spirit of the deity or loa possessing ("riding" as it is commonly known) the Priest or Priestess seems to be reflected in the process known in modern Wiccan ritual as Drawing Down the Moon, in which the Priestess allows a deity to speak through her. Again, we see that Voudon, Santeria, and the other African Diaspora religions survived within prominently non-Protestant areas of the world, but we see no survivals in such areas of the Americas that were strongly Protestant, such as Georgia or Virginia, even though they had a large West African slave population.

Catholicism, Protestantism, and the Witch Hunts

It is the rivalry between Roman Catholicism and Protestantism that is the key to understanding the nature of hereditary witchcraft in Western Europe because Protestantism systematically went about trying to destroy Pagan survivals. From the writings of the time of the Reformation, it is clear that Protestantism's main aim was to remove the remains of Pagan practices from Christianity. Martin Luther's main argument with Catholicism was that such survivals existed within its system of indulgences, relics, and saints, and that these were unholy and against God. The result was that many a Catholic went to the fire or was hung as a witch by Protestant inquisitors. It also goaded the Catholic Church into having its own witch hunt to try to clear its name, as well seek out Protestant heretics. But of the estimated 300,000 witches who were executed during this period (and some put the figure as unrealistically high as 9 million) it is probable that the majority were good Christians and that hardly any would have practiced witchcraft, let alone considered themselves witches.

In Britain, the real witch hunts did not start until the Stewart King, James I of England, the VI of Scotland, came to the English throne, even though Britain had rejected Roman Catholicism two monarchs earlier in one of the bloodiest periods in English history. James was paranoid about being poisoned by witches and therefore commissioned the rewriting of the Bible to reflect his paranoia. For example, he changed "thou shalt not suffer a poisoner (of wells) to live" to "thou shalt not suffer a witch to live." Even though there were few witch trials in England, there appeared to be many in his home country, Calvinist Scotland. When the English Civil War erupted, Mathew Hopkins, the infamous Witchfinder General, set forth from Cambridge in England, and it was no coincidence that he headed towards the fen lands of East Anglia, an area known not only for witchcraft, but also for its Roman Catholic population. It must be remembered that Hopkins did this during a conflict very much fuelled by the antagonism between Roman Catholicism and English Puritan Protestantism, dating back to the Tudor King Henry VIII. In modern witchcraft history, which we will discuss later, East Anglia comes up again as one of the supposed birthplaces of Wicca. This is important to note.

An interesting paradox occurs in the modern history of witchcraft. Protestantism almost completely eradicated its survivals in the United Kingdom, Germany, and the other countries of that faith, or they forced it so deep underground that it almost disappeared completely. It survived in Catholic countries but was slowly absorbed into Catholicism, so its origins became unknown; a few folk practices continued to be performed as part of that faith. We are not trying to say here that the Neo-Pagan movement or even that hereditary witchcraft has its origins in Roman Catholicism. We are saying quite the reverse: From one perspective, the origin of many Catholic practices is witchcraft and Paganism! So here is the paradox: If you look at the rise of the modern witchcraft and modern Neo-Pagan movements, it is most prominent in Protestant countries. Why has this happened?

The fact is, even though some witches might dispute it, modern witchcraft has its origins very much in *rebellion* against the established Protestant monotheistic culture rather than the Catholic. In the United Kingdom, many who come into Wicca and Paganism do so because they are looking for the magic in their spirituality, which they find in the ritual practices offered in Wicca. In Catholic countries such as Ireland, Spain, Italy, and Portugal, the situation is a bit different. Ever since childhood, members of the Roman Catholic faith are brought up with the high ritual, mysticism, and other magical elements that Protestantism rejects. The result is that when they reject the Catholic Church, they reject these aspects, too. This makes them far less likely to embrace a ritualistic tradition such as modern Wicca. The result is that when they reject the Catholic Church they reject these aspects too. While in Protestant countries Neo-Paganism is one of the fastest growing religions, in Catholic countries, we have found traditions such as Zen Buddhism growing rapidly. Of course, this situation is now changing as the Roman Catholic Church loses social power, and Catholic countries are now starting to develop growing Neo-Pagan communities.

Gerald Gardner and the Reconstruction of Witchcraft

It was in the early 1950s that we saw the rise of modern witchcraft, or Wicca as it is called today. In most people's minds, this came about mainly because of one man, but this is not the only history that exists. It is from this point on that we first see the first-named traditions within witchcraft occur. This not only a modern idea, but also came out of acrimony between a self-professed hereditary and the followers of Gerald Gardner, the man often referred to as the father of modern witchcraft. Of course, there are those who avoided such labels, and in recent years this has included us. To understand the argument you have to understand some of the history of modern witchcraft related to Gerald Gardner and the New Forest Coven.

In 1936, Gerald Gardner retired from his duties as a planter of tea and rubber trees and a Customs official and moved back to England to be with his wife, Donna. His interest in folklore and the occult had been sparked while living in Malaya. This area of the world has always been a melting pot of cultures, and, prior to his retirement, Gardner had already started to work on his book *The Keris and other Malay Weapons,* which was published in 1936. It is not surprising that he choose this time to move back to England. The Japanese had already invaded China and everyone was expecting a war in the Far East between the armies of the Rising Sun and the Colonial nations. Of course, by the time Gerald and his wife settled in the New Forest, war with Germany was imminent.

He was a well-read man on the subject of magic. His interest in Malaysian folk magic made him look carefully into its European equivalent, witchcraft. After reading Margaret Murray's *The Witch Cult in Western Europe* (see bibliography), he became convinced that her central hypothesis that witchcraft had survived the Middle Ages was correct. It spurred him on to read more on the subject, including Charles Godfrey Leland's *Aradia or the Gospel of the Witches* (see bibliography), which claimed in its introduction that its contents originated from a hereditary Italian witch, or strega, named Maddelena.

It was during this period that Gardner supposedly first made contact with what he claimed were surviving witchcraft traditions. He first met several Rosicrucians through the Rosicrucian Theatre in Christchurch. It soon became obvious to him that there was more there than met the eye. He was introduced to the members of the Fellowship of Crotona, formed under the guidance of Brother Aurelius and Mrs. Besant-Scott. Her mother, Annie Besant, had been an active figure in the Theosophy movement. According to his story, it was through them that he met several other people, including Dorothy Clutterbuck, and it was she who initiated him into the surviving witch coven in England. Of course, there is much more to the story, which has been told, retold, and reinterpreted several times. It is, in fact, the most analyzed story of modern witchcraft, but bear in mind that, as we said earlier, it is not the only history. More information of the history of modern witchcraft and Gerald Gardner can be found in Doreen Valiente's *Witchcraft for Tomorrow* and *Rebirth of Witchcraft,* as well as in our Janet and Stewart's book, *The Witches Bible,* and Stewart's *What Witches Do* (see bibliography). The most complete work we have come across is *Wiccan Roots*[6] by Philip Heselton. This is a subject that has been written about to the point of exhaustion and remains the central myth of the modern witchcraft movement.

From the beginning, Gardner claimed that the origins of what he practiced were hereditary, although the material he produced in his *Book of the Art Magical* and then *Book of Shadows* (BOS) (the main liturgy of Wicca) was anything but! His story is that he was initiated into a coven that originated with an East Anglian gentleman known as George Pickingill. There are several problems with this story, the main one being that Pickingill never claimed to be a witch. He was often referred to as "the Cunning Man," but in his own words was a self-confessed Satanist. It is fascinating that East Anglia comes into the picture again, as it is an area renowned for its survivals of witchcraft.

We will probably never know whether Gardner really found a genuine coven or not. We believe that those he referred to as witches probably never referred to themselves as such, or considered their working group to be called "a coven." There is plenty of evidence to support that the group he is talking about is in fact the Fellowship of Crotona, a Rosicrucian group whose ritual practices included those originating from the French Lodge of Masonry (*Grande Loge Symbolique Ecossaise Mixte de France*).[7] This was very different from English Freemasonry; it was Co-Masonic, allowing women members, and was more Gnostic in its approach, incorporating elements of Cabalistic ritual magic in its practices. We base this belief on two claims, the first being that the degree system used by Gardner is patently Masonic, even down to some of the ritual practice. The second is that the word *witchcraft* had a broader meaning at the time of Gardner than the way it is used today within the Neo-Pagan movement. During this period, any form of magic was referred to as witchcraft, as was Spiritualism and even Theosophy. From this perspective one could even argue that Co-Masonry is really a survival of witchcraft. But note that many hereditary practitioners stated that they never originally described themselves as witches, as we mentioned earlier regarding Pickingill. What we have here is a problem with the definition of the word witch.

Gerald Gardner wrote several books including *High Magic's Aid* and *Witchcraft Today* (see bibliography), some of the first books on the subject of Wicca. He claims he was thrown out of the original coven for betraying the secrets in his books. He therefore became the first known banished witch in the history of modern Wicca. It is more than likely the real reason was that the group got fed up with being referred to in a term they likely found insulting. Gardner went on to form a coven in the early 1950s, and over the years, initiated several High Priestesses, including Doreen Valiente, Eleanor (Rae) Bone, Madge Worthington, Patricia Crowther, and Monique Wilson. All went on to initiate more modern witches and create more covens. This resulted in Wicca spreading not only through Britain, but also into the United States. It was Doreen Valiente who first pointed out some of the inconsistencies in Gardner's claims regarding the origins of the witchcraft he practiced or wrote about. The young Doreen was a well-read person when it came to the occult, and she quickly picked up on the fact that much of the material scribbled into Gardner's *Book of Shadows* was from published sources. When she challenged him about this, his reply was that this was necessary, as much of the material had been lost. Gardner had introduced large amounts of Western magical tradition into *Ye Bok of Ye Art Magical*[8] and his later *Book of Shadows*. Most obvious is the use of passages from Leland's *Aradia,*[9] but there are also passages from the Carmina Cadelica.[10] There are even claims that elements of the teachings of the infamous Aleister Crowley[11] are present (see

Valiente

pages 46–47). Regardless, it was a viable magical system for its time; it fulfilled the needs of those practising it, and more importantly, it worked.

Gerald Gardner's absorption of material from several sources, mainly published works, has been cited as proof for his creation of modern witchcraft. Although this can be seen as an argument as to why Wicca is not an ancient tradition, there is one factor ignored in it: Witchcraft has always used magical techniques "to get the job done." It saw magical practice in its past as a tool for survival, in the forms of tribal healing and sympathetic hunting magic, rather than for the creation of a religious doctrine. Like all crafts, it has always updated its methods and used what was available at the time. Exchanges of ideas between craftsmen to update their skills is a common practice, for after all, the aim at the end of the day is produce quality work. This is no different for the witch. The method of magical practice is only important in that it produces a quality outcome for the person for whom it is done. The aim and intent has always been more important that the form that it takes. Gardner and his followers integrated the magical technique of their time, Ceremonial Magic, rather than trying to historically recreate those of the past. By doing this, they unwittingly continued the *real* tradition of witchcraft: "If it works, use it!"

Initially, Gardnerians did not describe themselves or their practice as "Gardnerian." There is actually no noted use of the term Gardnerian in any of Gardner's works or in the literature on witchcraft of the time; the term simply wasn't in use. In a 1965 copy of *The Pentagram* magazine, we find the term first used in a rather condescending article called "'Ancients' and 'Moderns'" by an anonymous figure calling himself Taliesin. It reads as follows:

> "The report of Mrs. Valiente's talk at the *Pentagram* dinner, together with Mr. Cochrane's article in the same issue, make fascinating reading, and could be said to represent the two extremes of the Craft—Witchcraft Ancient and Modern, so to speak. From the former, one gets the Gardnerian atmosphere of sweetness and light coupled with good clean fun, all under the auspices of a universal auntie!"
>
> —Taliesin, *The Pentagram*,
> March 1965.

Not surprisingly, a rebuff followed from Arnold Crowther, the husband of High Priestess Patricia Crowther, particularly as a following article by Taliesin attacked Gardnerians for cloak and dagger initiations. In Arnold Brwther's rather curt reply, it is important to note that he uses the term *Gardnerites*, not *Gardnerian*. It is likely that those who were initiated by Gardner originally thought that only they possessed the true survivals of witchcraft in England. They felt no need to label themselves in any way. To be rebuffed by others who also claimed hereditary origins would have been a shock.

In the final interview prior to her death in September 1999, Doreen pointed to Robert Cochrane as the originator of the label Gardnerian, and probably the real identity of the anonymous figure, Taliesin:[12]

"He (Cochrane) claimed to be a hereditary witch and detested those whom he called 'the Gardnerians.' In fact, I believe he invented this word 'Gardnerian'—originally as a term of abuse."

—Doreen Valiente's interview with Sally Griffyn in
Wiccan Wisdomkeepers

Prior to 1965, Gardnerians were referred to as "followers of Gardner." This division by Taliesin was meant to outline the difference between self-professed hereditaries (if their claims were even really true) and those following the modern tradition of witchcraft embodied by Gardner's teachings. Inadvertently, he sowed the seeds of the idea of "tradition" in the witchcraft movement by his attack on the new wave of Paganism that was occurring. Even Robert Cochrane, "the Magister" as he is often referred to, found it necessary to label his practices "1734 tradition" to separate them from Gardner's. He also didn't use the term *witch* until the public use of it by Gardnerians, and he stated that none of his family used it, either. Prior to this, there is no evidence from the past that witches separated themselves into specific traditions. What does appear are natural traditions dictated by culture and language. The ancestral tribal magic worker may not have used the term *witch* to describe him or herself; it may have been a label used by the Christian culture around them. Its use today is most definitely a modern reclaiming of the word. More on this is covered by Margot Adler in *Drawing Down the Moon: Witches, Druids, Goddess-Worshippers and other Pagans in America Today.*[13] She dedicates a whole section of one chapter to "that vexing 'w' word," discussing whether it should be used by modern witches at all. We feel that whether we like it or not we are stuck with the word and should therefore make the best of it. For many, the use of the term Wiccan was one of convenience, a way of avoiding witch, which had too many overtones for people who were influenced by the Christian concept of the word. The use of the word Wiccan allowed people to reply with "what's a Wiccan," thereby creating dialogue.

Alex Sanders and the New Traditions

It is apparent that when the Gardnerian form of witchcraft appeared, its practitioners were considered to be "the New-Age fluffy bunnies" of their time (if you'll excuse the detestable term) by many of the hereditaries, as well as Britain's general occult community, something the Gardnerians themselves were to accuse others of in the future. This is important, as a pattern soon seemed to appear within the tensions of the mainstream Wiccan traditions, which reached its height with the appearance of Alex Sanders in the mid- to late-60s.

Pat Kopinsky, a renegade Priestess of Patricia and Arnold Crowther, brought Alex Sanders into Wicca. She did not actually initiate him, but introduced him to Medea, her initiator, and passed on the Gardnerian *Book of Shadows* to him. This was done without the Crowther's permission, although recent letters show that Kopinsky was in contact with Gerald Gardner and that it is also likely that Gardner and Sanders had been in contact with each other:

> "Dear Dr Gerald,
>
> I have just had a letter from Alex Saunders who I gather has been writing to you… she (Medea) finally made her mind to initiate him (Saunders) on the 9th of March with me as his sponsor…I have five members in my coven at the moment, counting Alex who comes now and again."
>
> —Abridged letter from Pat Kopinsky to Gerald Gardner, 5th September 1963[14]

Alex Sanders' claim that he was a hereditary witch initiated by his grandmother[15] to gain acceptance from the wider occult community was hardly surprising. Hereditary origins have been claimed by those wanting acceptance as witches ever since Gardner, and have included many false claims. Its causes lie very much in the arguments we mentioned earlier and the continuing need for validity through the idea of lineage, something we examine more fully in Chapter 2 (see page 42). Initially, Sanders did not use the term *Alexandrian* to describe the way he worked. There are several stories surrounding how this description came into being. One is that the name was a creation of Janet's late husband, renowned Pagan writer Stewart Farrar. It was suggested that Stewart coined the term *Alexandrian* during the writing of *What Witches Do*. During an interview with Alex in 1969, Stewart asked him how many witches recognized him as "King of the Witches." Alex's reply confirms the origins of the word *Alexandrian*:

> "O, yes. Probably all of them, apart from Gardnerians… Gardnerians, and those that don't want publicity, tend to refer to my witches as 'Alexandrians'".[16]

So here we have it, "from the horse's mouth," so to speak. Regardless of origins, Alexandrian soon became a name for the new tradition of witchcraft created by Alex Sanders and his wife and High Priestess Maxine, and the concept of *tradition* was compounded even more.

It was into the Alexandrian tradition of Wicca that Janet and Stewart were first initiated. To quote Stewart, Alex had a "scatter gun" approach to initiation. The standing joke was that if the milkman were to hang around the front door too long he'd find himself initiated! His approach paid off: By the early 70s, the Alexandrian brand of Wicca had reached the United States and was gaining ground from the Gardnerians. The Gardnerians refused to accept the Alexandrians, and the literate battles in Pagan periodicals seemed to be at their most prevalent in the United States. This situation continued until the 1980s, when they finally realized that they had more in common with each other, particularly as new traditions started to rise out of the United States from the early 70s onwards. Alex Sanders' contribution to the modern witchcraft movement was two-fold: He caused growth by initiating so many into Wicca, but more importantly, he introduced the idea of a system of training within Wicca (more on this in Chapter 6), certainly within the United Kingdom.

It is Raymond Buckland[17] who can be credited with the next stage of development within Wicca: the open creation of new traditions, often referred to as "reconstructionalist Wicca." In many ways there was more honesty in these traditions, as they made no false claims of lineage. Ground was initially broken with Buckland's *The Tree: the Complete Book of Saxon Witchcraft*, which was the ritual liturgy for a whole new tradition, Seax-Wicca. Buckland had lived in the United States since the early 80s and had become very much influenced by its more liberal occult culture. Seax-Wicca was almost completely researched from the literature of the time, the most obvious work being Brian Branston's *Lost Gods of England*. Here, Ray Buckland explains his reasons for creating it:

> "I started it at a time when I realised that Gardnerian [craft] was not totally satisfying for me—this after about twelve years of it! There were things about it—about the make-up of the rituals, specifically—that didn't work for me... I decided to construct a tradition that was exactly right for me, as an individual...I did not pretend, and never have pretended, that I was reconstructing anything ancient; this was new and I just wanted something right for me that had

an ancient flavour to it. I most certainly did NOT start it as a joke, as has been erroneously reported... I would hardly give up Gardnerian and devote my life to a joke!"
—Ray Buckland, 28th November 2002[18]

Seax-Wicca also introduced another idea into print that was completely against the grain of the other main traditions: It was acceptable to self-initiate. This concept was followed by the publication of Doreen Valiente's *Witchcraft for Tomorrow*, which also contained a self-initiation ritual, and by our own arguments for it in *The Witches Way*. Gardnerian and Alexandrian Wicca had maintained the dogma of "only a witch can make a witch," even though it seemed to contradict the Craft law that there is only one true initiator. The origins of the idea of lineage are not from hereditary witchcraft as one first might suppose. As mentioned earlier, Gardner had adopted rituals from the Co-Masonic-influenced Fellowship of Crotona, and one of these rituals was the passing of power at initiation. This rite was in fact of Christian Gnostic origin, rather than Pagan, and was based on the idea of apostolic succession[19]. The same rite can in fact still be seen today in the modern Catholic and Protestant Churches at ordination.

Original witchcraft teachings were passed down in a generational learning process (see Chapter 6) from parent to child. They would happily adopt and train others if they showed promise, but this was not lineage. The reason it was kept "within the family" as a secret was purely a mechanism to survive what modern witches often refer to as "the burning times," the period of repression. If you couldn't trust your family, because your family would undoubtedly face the same fate as yourself, then whom could you trust? In recent years, many have challenged whether lineage, which is of Christian origin, has any place in modern witchcraft. We count ourselves among this group.

Witchcraft, Feminism, and the New Age

The 1970s saw the rise of Dianic (women only) forms of witchcraft coming out of the feminist movement. These reached their height in the 1980s with the publication of books by Starhawk[20] (*The Spiral Dance*) and Z. Budapest (*The Feminist Book of Light and Shadows*). The feminist witch movement sought to reclaim the word witch as a word of feminine power. Their non-hierarchical, eclectic approach clashed with the English Traditional (Alexandrian and Gardnerian) approach of a fixed doctrine.

Their works and views heavily influenced the development of Wicca, both in the United States and in the United Kingdom. Feminist Wicca also assertively pushed the ideals of environmentalism as being an integral part of Pagan spirituality, as well as political involvement in the anti-war movement. This was considered not only desirable, but also compulsory (many in feminist Wicca had been activists at the time of the Vietnam War).

By the time Gavin joined the craft in 1986, *The Spiral Dance* had become compulsory reading with its ideas of "power from within" rather than "power over" (see page 154) from those who had bad experiences with the more dogmatic covens. This resulted in the first Pagan contact networks in the United Kingdom—Pagan Link—which rejected "Wicca" as "old hat." Regardless, there were those who stayed true to the ideas of Wicca but in a non-traditional way, questioning the systems of training, the need for degrees, and the hierarchical structure that had sneaked through the back door from Freemasonry into witchcraft practice.

One of the most obvious things in this short history is the importance and influence of *books* in the growth of modern Wicca. Gardner would never have got the new movement off the ground with out them. The main reason for this was that up until the 1990s, information on witchcraft was hard to come by. When Janet joined the craft in the early 70s, there were less than a dozen books specifically about Wicca and modern witchcraft. Some books claiming to be about the subject were in fact about Ceremonial magic or even demonology. By the mid-1980s, we saw a change. A more liberal attitude towards religion meant more books were being published on the subject, but still there were few. Gavin remembers having to specifically order books, and the mainstays were Gardner's, Valiente's, and the books by Janet and her late husband, Stewart. There were, of course, other works, such as *A Book of Pagan Rituals*[21] by Ed Fitch and as previously mentioned, *The Spiral Dance*. Most other books were heavily Cabalistic in their influence. Technology would soon change everything.

The rise of modern witchcraft is noticeably riddled with paradoxes, but there is power in paradox (see Appendix III). The major influences on the Neo-Pagan movement and Wicca in the 1990s was not only the same film companies and media that had been portraying lurid images of witchcraft since the 1950s, but also something that had come out of the United States military industrial complex, the very thing feminist witchcraft was aimed at bringing down—the Internet.[22] While books were available forms of information, the Internet—first through bulletin boards, then e-mail, mailing lists, chat rooms, and Websites—offered a two way, easily accessible form of communication and information for witches that cost almost nothing. It was also completely anonymous if you wanted a free exchange of ideas without fear of reprisal, regardless of age, an important point we come to later. Shortly thereafter, the terms *Cyber-witch* and *cyber coven* began to appear. This resulted in a boom of interest in witchcraft, something quickly noticed and exploited by the producers and film moguls of Hollywood.

The growth of Neo-Paganism, with interest from a younger generation combined with an increasing number of books on the subject, caused the media to look at ways of exploiting this new trend. Initially, it was rather badly portrayed, in films such as *The Craft*, then represented on television with good witches such as *Sabrina the Teenage Witch* and mentioned as a positive spiritual tradition in *The X-Files*. Unfortunately, the urge to turn the witch character Willow into something evil became irresistible to the producers of *Buffy the Vampire Slayer*. There had of course been positive portrayals prior to these, such as the film of John Updike's novel *The Witches of Eastwick*, which, if you examine carefully, is a pro-feminist statement of the reclaiming of women's power. But the link between witchcraft, rebellion, and teenage angst had been firmly made by the film and television producers. By the end of the 1990s, witchcraft had become the new outlet for teenage rebelliousness.

The result was a sudden growth of interest caused by media and the Internet. The interest from a younger generation, particularly from under-18-year-olds, caused Wicca to reel as it tried to cope with the influx of teenagers asking questions about what witchcraft is. This became a difficult period for many of us who were brought up with the idea that you had to be age 18 or older to be a witch, particularly when encountering a 16-year-old running a coven from the school playground. It also begged a question: If Christianity can teach it's young, why can't we? The issue is still being debated today as many Wiccans try to put into place mechanisms for dealing with these future witches.

Now that we are into the new millennium, witchcraft has started to enter its own renaissance. It has moved from the tribal village to the online communities of the World Wide Web. We are now seeing a new breed of witch not influenced by the figures of the immediate past, but the culture of the present. This has left witchcraft facing several questions that need to be addressed before it moves on. Is it a religion or a craft? Is it old or is it something new? Where is it going, and more importantly, why has it become resurrected in this new technological age? We try to answer these questions in the next chapter as well as the question of why it is important that Wicca should realize its past failings, if it is to evolve and survive into the new millennia. We will also show that the future of Wicca is already here if we but look.

Endnotes

1. K'ung Fu master (Latinized as *Confucius*) born in the state of Lu in 551 B.C. and died in B.C. 479. Chinese philosopher and reformer; teachings known as Confucianism and compiled as "Analects."
2. A more thorough explanation on this can be found in *The Witches' Craft* by Raven Grimassi, page 15 (*see* Bibliography).
3. R.E. Witt's, *Isis in the Graeco-Roman World* (*see* Bibliography).
4. St.Kieran's Well, Castlekieran, Kells, Co. Meath, is a Lughnasadh site. One myth related to the site is that the evening before the annual Lughnasadh festival held there, a salmon (the symbol of the god Lugh) swims up the river along side the site.
5. A surprisingly accurate portrayal of Caribbean Voudon ritual is shown. This is due mainly to the fact that Ian Fleming spent many years working in this area of the world for MI5. He also had strong occult connections, being a friend of occult writer Dennis Wheatley.
6. Chapter 4, pages 52–63. (*see* Bibliography).
7. This is according to *Wiccan Roots* by Philip Heselton (*see* Bibliography) a book we highly recommend.
8. This was his second book. A ritual book predating even this exists in the care of Doreen Valiente's estate.
9. Doreen Valiente is responsible for converting *Chapter 1, How Diana Gave Birth to Aradia* into *The Charge of the Goddess*, the central rite of any Wiccan ritual.
10. The Carmina Gadelica is a collection of folk prayers from the Hebrides of Scotland in the late 19th century by amateur folklorist Alexander Carmichael. "Queen of the moon, Queen of the sun..." used in the consecration of the cakes at the end of ritual derives from this source.
11. There is little doubt that there was communication between Crowley and Gardner; Gardner held the rank of Philosophus 4=7 in Crowley's Ordo Templi Orientis (OTO). Evidence can be found in the original copies of *High Magic's Aide* (*see* Bibliography).
12. Confusion remains over whether they are the same figure, as Cochrane never admitted to the deception.
13. This remains one of the most complete and scholarly books on the development of the Pagan movement in the United States to date (*see* Bibliography).
14. Circulated copy of a letter originating from Gerald Gardner's Castletown collection.
15. This claim first appeared in June Johns' *King of the Witches: The World of Alex Sanders* (*see* Bibliography). It has since been refuted by Maxinne, Alex's High Priestess and ex-wife.
16. From an unpublished interview between Stewart Farrar and Alex Sanders in 1970, in the authors' collection.

17. A formerRoyal Airforce officer initiated by Monique Wilson in Perth, Scotland, before moving to the United States in the mid-1960s and initiating his wife, Rosemary. He is a prominent figure in the American Wiccan movement and a renowned author.

18. Personal correspondence, following a discussion between Gavin Bone and Ray Buckland at Witchfest New Orleans in 2001.

19. Apostolic succession traces its lineage back to St. Paul, the first Pope, who was physically touched by Christ; therefore the power of Christ is passed on from one Pope to the next, and down through the hierarchy of the Church.

20. Starhawk was originally initiated into Victor Anderson's Faery tradition.

21. This book is listed as authorless. Fitch originally wanted it to be freely available to the Pagan community and without copyright.

22. The Internet was originally a network created between research Universities, defense contractors, and the Pentagon in the 1970s.

Chapter 2

Into the New Millennium: Progressive Witchcraft Evolves

When we blindly adopt a religion, a political system, a literary dogma, we become automatons. We cease to grow.

—Anaïs Nin (1903–1977),
The Diary of Anaïs Nin, Vol. IV[1]

What is Progressive Witchcraft? During the writing of this book, we came across witches who had adopted the term *progressive* to describe themselves and their method of working[2]. It is not our intention to create yet another new tradition of Wicca claiming ancient roots. For us, the use of the term Progressive Witchcraft does not imply a tradition, but a way of thought, belief, and practice related to being a witch. After this book is published, some may adopt the term; this will not make us unhappy! We understand it is in human nature to need collective labels, and we have created such a label. But we have done so, we hope, in a positive way.

From a historical viewpoint, it would be easy to suggest that the origins of modern Wicca come from a group of misfits, desperate for recognition as witches, not only editing published material and passing it off as proof of ancient survivals, but also creating their own material with the same intent. We would like to put forward the point of view that this is not the right approach to take. Instead, we see a growth process, just as when a child learns to walk, modern witchcraft has, on many occasions, fallen over and grazed its knees. Modern witches need to look at the past and realize that its failings are an evolutionary process at work, returning witchcraft to its original roots. A danger of "building a house on sand" comes about when the mistakes of the past are not recognized. This results in no evolution or growth, just as we have seen in the contemporary monotheistic religions that have replaced spirituality with dogma.

The Death of Dogma and the "Cult of Personality"

It is important for people to realize that Gerald Gardner, Alex Sanders, and all those trailblazers who came before have made positive contributions to the development of what we have today, but they were human beings with failings like everyone else. The way they worked and saw witchcraft was appropriate for their time, but not necessarily for ours. If they had made any serious mistakes in their approach, Wicca would not have survived to today. It must be remembered that all of them added something new that was needed at the time, and dropped out those things that were redundant and hindering its growth. We saw this occur in the United States from the 70s onward, but it didn't happen in Britain until the 1980s.

Something also happened at the end of the 1970s and beginning of the 1980s within the modern witchcraft revival: We saw the end of the cult of personality, which had played a dominant part in the development of Wicca. This is common in many new religions as they begin to establish themselves. A central figure becomes the focus of the movement and is responsible for its direction. We see this in religious cults and taken to extremes in the monotheistic religions where the founder is deified. Until his death in 1964, Gerald Gardner fulfilled this role, and it was taken over by Alex Sanders within years of Gardner's death. It is interesting to note that these were male figures rather than female ones; again, this relates to the fact that witchcraft had not really managed to discard the old Christian values of the culture in which it evolved.

When Alex Sanders died in 1988, the Elders of the Alexandrian tradition in the United Kingdom issued the following document:

Statement of the Council of Elders
of the Alexandrian Tradition

A meeting of the Elders of the Alexandrian Tradition was held on Thursday 12th May 1988.

The Law of the Craft has always been that a King is chosen by the Craft when the need arises. After due consideration, a unanimous motion was carried that there is no need for a King of the Witches.

This is fortunate, as there is no one properly prepared for the role.

Alex Sanders led the Hidden Children of the Goddess into the light. It was a task well done and it was his last and most earnest wish that they should continue their work into the light.

This officially ended the idea of Kings and Queens of the witches within the modern witchcraft revival, which the majority of us were not sad to see go. It is important because it marked within witchcraft the end of this cult of personality with its inherent risks. There were, of course, others who tried to wear the crown. Even today some have tried to claim to be the legitimate "King" or "Queen," but they have generally been ignored or have had to face ridicule from the majority of rational witches. What replaced it was not one, but multiple leaders who surfaced within the witchcraft community. They neither claim to be hereditary, or to be initiated by their grandmothers, nor have they courted the press as both Sanders and Gardner did. Instead, they have attempted to pass their wisdom on through writing and action. Instead of one, there are now many leaders of the movement to reestablish witchcraft—mostly, but not exclusively, authors. It is interesting that this very much reflects the change within Wicca regarding traditions and the move towards a truly polytheistic doctrine. Such examples are Raymond Buckland, Ed Fitch, Starhawk, Vivianne Crowley, and a host of new writers such as Fiona Horne and Phyllis Curott, to name a few. But it is not just writers that are now shaping Wicca. There are also those who are active in networking and in creating the idea of community, such as Fritz and Wren Jung, who run *The Witches Voice* Website. We would rate the work of the Cyber-Witch as equally important as that of writers, if not more so, as they provide the anonymous individual witch a voice. To this end, Wicca has become a "republic," as we like to put it, with individual witches collectively giving a consensus of direction to the movement, rather than one leader, as in the past.

Fitch

Books have had much to do with the development of Wicca. We have given the principle reason towards the end of Chapter 1, but there is also another reason. Monotheistic cultures have their norms and values rooted in the religions of the book, Christianity, Judaism, or Islam. In these religions the book is "the word," the book is always right or "righteous." It is inevitable that when being brought up in such a culture, even if you reject the predominant religion, these influences will remain part of you. Therefore books outlining sacred ritual practice were treated with similar reverence, as were the predominant sacred books of the culture, be it the Bible, Torah, or Koran. Initially this caused problems with the way the main liturgy of Wicca, the *Book of Shadows*, was seen and treated. Many saw it as sacred, treating it on a par with the Christian Bible; its origins were therefore not to be questioned.

At the end of the day, the *Book of Shadows* was and is nothing more than a collection of rituals, rites, and information cobbled together by Gerald Gardner and Doreen Valiente. As time went on, it was expanded with material from books whose ideas were also not questioned. It must be remembered that most people in rural areas in Britain didn't learn to read until the late 1800s, so the idea that it was ancient is quite ludicrous from a historical viewpoint. Even the name *Book of Shadows* may have origins in Eastern Sufism rather than Western European occult practice.[3]

It was not until the early 1990s that the *Book of Shadows* origins were really seriously questioned, and this of course was done again in a book: *Crafting the Art of Magic (Book 1)* by Aidan Kelly.[4] Janet and Stewart had, of course, questioned its origins in *The Witches' Way* (and in the combined edition of *A Witches' Bible*) with the help of the mother of modern witchcraft, Doreen Valiente. Kelly's eventual conclusions were correct: It was a created work put together over a period of time by Gerald Gardner and Doreen Valiente. To date, we have seen many copies of the *Book of Shadows*. We know that there are at least three distinct phases in its development, scrupulously catalogued and dated by Aidan Kelly. There are also five root copies, each with differences, related to Gardner's High Priestess who all changed material after hiving off from him. Plus, there are Alexandrian Books of Shadows and other ritual books created by Alex Sanders that have no relationship to Gardnerian practice at all, such as his *Book of Planets*.

The *Book of Shadows* was never intended to be dogmatic. We strongly believe Gardner intended it to be something that witches added to in an organic fashion. It was suppose to be more like a witches' notebook reflecting their ongoing development, rather than a Bible or ancient Grimoire of magical secrets. One story that came from an original Gardnerian initiate is that he actually changed material around in one version to make his initiates think for themselves.[5] Unfortunately, this didn't work out the way he expected, so there is now a Gardnerian line where one of the main Sabbat rituals is obviously in the wrong place.[6] This is one of the dangers of dogma taking hold and why fixed traditions are facing the issue of adaptation or extinction.

The Questioning of Tradition

It is important to understand what tradition is. A tradition is a set of workable ideas, philosophies, and practices that are passed down from one to another over a period of time. The process of transmitting a tradition over several generations often results in inspiring reverence for the tradition's content. Sometimes the reason why the actual tradition is passed down is lost. This doesn't necessarily mean that the tradition is no longer valid or is obsolete. It may still work, particularly in occult practice. But a tradition with a lot of reverence placed on it by the users can be hard to change if the situation changes and the material no longer fulfills the original role it was created for. The people might say, "It's traditional; we've always done it that way." The tradition becomes an end unto itself.

Progressive witchcraft adapts the idea of tradition into something more tenable. This is where a coven, be it of Gardnerian, Alexandrian, or of self-initiatory origin, has developed its own system, and then members hive off to develop their own covens. A good example of this is an American tradition called Blue Star. According to an article written by Cat Castells and Amy Douglass:

> *Blue Star Wicca is a centuries old Pagan tradition founded in the mid-1970s. Originally established as a single coven in Pennsylvania, Blue Star evolved over the next decade or two into a collection of more than a dozen covens all across the U.S., all working in what is essentially the same framework and therefore recognizable as a tradition.*

> —Castells and Douglass, *The Witches Voice*,
> 26th May 2001

We first encountered Blue Star when Janet and Stewart met Ziporah and Kenny Klein in 1991. It was the Kleins who went on to develop Blue Star into a viable system of training.[7] We have since met many of its members and can honestly say that we find their approach to Wicca one of the most refreshing we have come across. First of all, there are no claims of heredity. In fact, they are very proud of their modern origins and see this as no hindrance to being a system of witchcraft. They also see evolution as an important factor, and actively encourage each hived-off coven to develop its own way of doing things rather than sticking to dogmatic tradition, while maintaining the core beliefs unique to Blue Star that keep them a coherent and recognizable system. Most prominent of these is their code of conduct related to the Rede and their system of training and education. They consider themselves as having one of the most strenuous training regimens of any Wiccan tradition—hardly surprising, as Blue Star has its origins in The Pagan Way and the Alexandrian traditions, which both pioneered the idea of fixed training systems within modern witchcraft (see page 114). We have come across several other similar coven-based traditions out there and have regular contact with many of them. We see this, rather than the inflexible monoliths of the past, as the future of tradition within modern witchcraft.

Evolution, Cultural Selection, and Lineage

History shows that witchcraft is an adapting, evolving tradition. You can easily apply the ideas of Charles Darwin to its development, and witchcraft's religious and philosophical beliefs certainly do not disagree with the ideas of Darwin. In fact, the infamous "Darwin Fish," which mocks the Christian religion's refusal to accept evolution, is commonly found as a bumper sticker on the fenders of cars owned by modern witches. This isn't surprising, as at the core of witchcraft is its reverence for Nature and the belief that we are not separate from it—an idea the monotheistic religions have tried to discourage. What is happening in modern witchcraft is cultural selection.[8] If something contributes no positive benefit within witchcraft, then it is rejected. If this rejection doesn't happen, then the tradition that maintains the non-contributing element becomes dogmatic and eventually disappears. The most obvious example of this is the differences between the development of Wicca in the United States and in the United Kingdom. The culture in the United States is much more open in its approach to religion, as the First Amendment of America's Constitution protects the right to religious belief. However, while in some areas of the United States (for example, California) you can have an open, public Pagan festival, in other parts, where alternative religions face daily prejudice (such as Alabama), we see that individuals and magical groups still have to remain highly secretive. Because of this, witches in these areas will have very different outlooks about what they are doing.

In California, we have seen more openness toward Wiccan practice, which includes outer courts or circles in covens that welcome visitors and newcomers. This has, in turn, resulted in a more progressive attitude towards Wicca and acceptance of the questioning of its structures and doctrines. This is not a bad thing in our eyes. But in other states, the situation is very different. From conferring with Wiccans in the heavily Evangelical southern states, we know that heavy vetting of those who come looking for Wicca and strict abidance by rules of secrecy and tradition has resulted in a very closed approach to Wicca. We believe neither approach is wrong: They are requirements in that specific environment for witchcraft's survival. We have also witnessed situations where a coven with its origins in Gardnerian tradition has more in common with a local Alexandrian coven than the coven it originally sprung from in a neighboring state. Here we see cultural selection at work: Nature (and thus the Goddess) loves diversity, and it is this diversity that has allowed witchcraft to survive.

One of the effects of this evolutionary growth has been the questioning of what has been (for some) the cornerstone of Wiccan practice: *lineage*. The current interpretation of lineage has now become a burden, stunting the growth of some of the traditional lines due to its inflexibility. It has been misused as an excuse for elitism and a rationale for being insular—which separates the witch from the real world around him or her, including the Pagan and witchcraft movement. In the worse cases, it has become a method of control over coven initiates. In a time when information on Wicca is freely available, lineage has become an anachronism. The result is that a new type of witch has appeared, one who rejects the concepts of lineage and tradition. Many have decided just to label themselves *witches* rather than *Wiccan* because of the word's associations with these twin dogmas. We should point out that lineage does have its positive side: For many it gives a sense of security in what they are doing, knowing that they can trace their teachers' origins and that they have had at least some sort of spiritual instruction. It offers a sense of belonging and membership in something larger than oneself and immediate surroundings. The need to be accepted and to belong is quite high in Maslow's hierarchy (see page 116). It is perhaps time for the concept of lineage to change its meaning, significance, and function in Pagan culture, rather than be simply dismissed. For this reason, we do feel that this rejection is unfortunate, but also agree that it is perhaps time for Wicca to realize that spiritual training must take precedence, as apostolic succession is actually alien to Pagan practice. Here we not only see evolution at work, but also a cycle; Wicca is returning to many of the old values of the village witch, and seeing its practices as a spiritual path rather than that of a secret society influenced by pseudo-Masonic practices.

The Witch Versus Wiccan Debate

We, personally, do not actually believe there is any difference between the words *witch* and *Wiccan*. The two words meanings, as we have shown, come from the same root source (see page 17). The differentiation of *witch* from *Wiccan* originated in the 1960s when Sanders first faced rejection from the Gardnerians and went his own way. It came about as a result of the non-acceptance of those who were not seen as correctly initiated or having correct lineage. The two main traditions refused to accept those from outside their traditions as Wiccan or even as "real witches." For many years, this divided the witchcraft movement into two camps and has blurred the meaning of the words *witch* and *Wiccan* purely for the sake of political expediency. This division has been perpetuated with the statement "All Wiccans are witches, but not all witches are Wiccans." Some of us who have been around for a while find this amusing, as we remember when the statement was "All witches are Pagans, but not all Pagans are witches!" We, with many others, realized the divisive nature of this situation early on and have always refused to accept these artificially created divisions. As time has gone on, these divisions have broken down due to the need for communication within the Pagan community. This interaction has now resulted in the majority of the old traditions accepting that you can be self-initiated, or be from reconstructionist traditions, and also be a witch. Some have even accepted that you can be classified as a Wiccan, resulting in the term "Initiatory Wiccan" to define those of Gardnerian or Alexandrian origin.

Of course, what is really going on here is the continual cycle of need for the new generation of witches to prove themselves to their perceived elders before being accepted. "Second degree syndrome" can also be a factor in this cycle (see page 74). We have no doubt that, as the new generation of young witches strive to assert their own way of doing things, new semantic divisions will occur until they are also finally accepted, just as the reconstructionists and self-initiates found in the past. For this reason, we continue to believe that Wiccan is the more correct way to define anyone who is following the modern spirituality of witchcraft, but it does very much depend on your individual view and whether you believe Gardner and Sanders really found any survivals of ancient witchcraft.

The Predominance of Training and Ethics Over Doctrine

While witchcraft remained underground within a culture that did not accept religious differences, it was necessary to have the ideas of lineage and fixed traditions, and the resulting attitudes toward initiation. These doctrines allowed it to remain a coherent practice while keeping it secret and out of public view, but with the opening of attitudes these doctrines have now become redundant and only exist for "tradition's sake." The two most important doctrines that have kept witchcraft from degenerating and loosing cohesion as a spiritual path are its system of ethical principles (the Wiccan Rede) and its system of training. If these systems didn't exist within Wicca, someone would create them, regardless of whether tradition or lineage continues as a prevalent factor or not.

The Wiccan Rede ("Eight Words the Wiccan Rede fulfil; an it harm none, do what thou will") has origins with Gerald Gardner, and many have noticed its similarity with Aleister Crowley's "Do what thou wilt is the whole of the Law; Love is the Law, Love under will." As discussed in Chapter 1, we know there was communication between Gardner and Crowley; the first editions of Gardner's book *High Magic's Aide* referred to his attainment of Philosophus degree in Crowley's Ordo Templi Orientis (OTO). The occult writer Francis King goes further, suggesting that Crowley wrote much of the original *Book of Shadows* for Gardner, and a substantial financial sum was exchanged for his services:[9]

> *He [Gardner] accordingly hired Crowley, at a generous fee, to write elaborate rituals for the new 'Gardnerian' witch-cult and, at about the same time, either forged, or procured to be forged, the so-called* Book of Shadows... *but betrayed its modern origins in every line of its unsatisfactory pastiche of Elizabethan English.*
>
> —Francis King, *Ritual Magic in England*:
> *1887 to the present day*

Yet again, like the Rede, we see elements of practice absorbed into Wicca from another system, and although it is unproven, there is little doubt that there are strong elements of OTO ritual styles in the original *Book of Shadows*. Its origins, though, are irrelevant. What is important is that it worked, and gave Wicca a ritual and ethical base as all other genuine spiritual paths have. The Rede has become the central defining ethical tenet for nearly all witches regardless of tradition, which not only reflects the "golden rule" found in almost all other religions, but should also be seen as an ethical imperative, which encourages witches to learn and train so that they do no harm. It has remained the main focus of modern witchcraft's philosophy and is always the first statement used when witches face the ignorant and discriminatory accusation of being evil. We have even heard it being used by those who are quite adamant that they are Pagans and not witches, as no other ethical principle fits the Neo-Pagan movement so well. If the glove fits, why not wear it?

Secrecy has remained one of the main precepts of Wicca, and in the Gardnerian initiation ritual it is very prevalent. In the first-degree rite, initiates are pushed into the circle in a particular way, so they do not see their initiator. An argument levelled at Alexandrians by hard line Gardnerians is that some witches are "not real witches" because this act was not part of their initiation rites.[10] Secrecy within witchcraft would have been necessary in the Middle Ages, during the times of trial and persecution, and even in the 1950s when there was still serious prejudice. But even the founder, Gerald Gardner, continually broke the rules of secrecy, as did Alex Sanders, to seek media exposure for the growing craft of Wicca.

Strange as it may seem, without this rule-breaking, there probably wouldn't be a Pagan movement today, nor the amount of interest in Wicca.

Secrecy exists within witchcraft for three reasons:

1. To protect the individual members from suffering discrimination outside of circle.

2. To prevent information about coven meetings and magical practices of the coven from becoming available to non-members.

3. To stop "the secrets of the Craft" from being passed on to those outside of the coven or even those within the coven who are not prepared for them.

Although we see good reasons for the first two points, the last is now considered an anachronism made by many Wiccans because of the amount of published material available. Within our coven, we still maintain secrecy from the outside world. To quote Doreen Valiente, "witchcraft doesn't pay for broken windows." Even in a world with a more liberal attitude, there are still those in our society likely to cause problems for self-professed witches. As for the second point, what goes on in our coven is nobody's business but the members', and more importantly, an outsider's awareness of the rites you practice can dissipate the rites' energy. It is the third reason for secrecy we have the most problem with and that we have been accused on numerous occasions of breaking in the publication of our books.[11] Janet and Stewart found it interesting to be accused of breaking oaths by writing about rituals they had researched and created themselves. One reason for this was that some individuals didn't want to be perceived as ignorant about this material. The very idea of a "tradition of secrets" has degenerated Wicca into a second rate form of Freemasonry in many people's eyes.

Witchcraft: The Mystery Tradition

Some of Wicca's origins seem to be in the concept of a mystery tradition (see Chapter 3). This means that the mysteries or secrets are *experiential*. This is important if you are going to understand the true nature of witchcraft. Many people have given away the secrets; it started with Gardner, continued with Sanders, and continues today. There is not one element of original Gardnerian or Alexandrian practice that has not been published somewhere, be it in a book or the Internet, but these secrets are meaningless, as they are no more than words. You have to experience them to understand them, as they cannot be conveyed in language; they are the very spiritual essence that is sought in the pursuit of ritual and magical practice to create communion with The Divine. This is the important spiritual truth within Wicca. If someone explains what is going to happen to you when you go on a roller-coaster ride, describing how the roller-coaster works and then how it feels, does it detract anything from your experience? Of course not, particularly because the person describing how it feels is describing something subjective, and your experience will be very different from theirs. The same applies to the mysteries. It is the idea of experiencing spirituality, which is one of the main causes of interest in those seeking witchcraft. In a world governed by logic and science, where every question is answerable with a mathematical equation, it is not surprising that we seek a return to magic. From this need, a romanticism about the past can sometimes develop, a nostalgia, which has been channelled into the idea of hereditary witchcraft or the idea of witchcraft's continued survival throughout the Middle Ages and up to the present day. It's a nice image but unlikely to be true in way that some expect. Yes, there are hereditary survivals, but there are no dusty Grimoires or secrets from the past that aren't already known.

If this romanticism is directed properly, we can see the links with our own ancestors through culture, such as in Celtic, Norse, Egyptian, or Anglo-Saxon symbolism. This is reconstructionism (see page 24), which is highly creative and expressive in its form and has helped to guide Wicca back to its spiritual origins. In essence, this is all that Gerald Gardner did when he put Wicca together with Doreen Valiente as a viable system, taking material from The Fellowship of Crotona, Aleister Crowley's OTO, and several pieces of literature of the period, including the accounts of Isobel Gowdie's witchcraft trial[12]. The only difference is that he claimed it was hereditary and was of ancient origin, which he considered necessary to gain acceptance in a critical occult world. This has led the writer Raven Grimassi to suggest that Wicca's origins are in Strega, as the only real hereditary witch material present was from Charles Godfrey Leland's *Aradia or the Gospel of the Witches*. From a practitioner of Strega's perspective he is correct, although others may disagree. What is often overlooked is that any true hereditary or traditional material would have been about Anglo-Saxon magical practice, as the New Forest is situated in the way old English Kingdom of Wessex. Perhaps, without realizing it, Ray Buckland stumbled on an important truth with the publication of *The Tree: The Complete Book of Saxon Witchcraft.*

We have always strongly believed in the free-flow of information about Wicca. It is this very process, along with the Rede, that has kept Wicca a thriving spiritual path. One of the triumphs of the modern Neo-Pagan movement is its progressive attitude to new technology. It would have been easy for Wicca to have become a religion of Luddites, but it did not. Wicca has embraced the computer revolution; our *Book of Shadows* became a *Disc of Shadows* in 1995 and continues to grow to this day. Since the 1980s, one of the "pre-Christian values" that witchcraft has returned to is the absorption of that which works and aids the belief structure of the individual. This can be seen as far back as the Middle Ages when witches first encountered ritual magic and integrated it into their practice.

Buckland

Within our own coven, we do not keep secrets from members of the coven, including information about the origins of the material we have in our *Book of Shadows*. The exceptions are information from private conversations and, when it comes to initiation, the initiate is kept from knowing exactly what is going to happen to assist the suspense. We strongly believe that people will understand what they're taught when they're ready. As we have previously mentioned, the mysteries have to be experienced. Initiations, rituals, and magical practices are, in this context, tools to assist in the spiritual experience of the initiate.

Freemasonry and the Origins of the Degree System

Another doctrine that has come under scrutiny is the degree system. There is no doubt about the origins of this system, as it clearly has ritual magic and Masonic overtones. It certainly isn't a system that you could imagine being used in a hereditary witchcraft family of the Dark Ages. Again, Crowley's relationship with Gardner comes into the picture. One suggestion we have heard many times is that Gardner attempted to align his system of Wicca with that of the OTO via a charter granted by Crowley.[13] The first degree of Wicca can be seen as equivalent to the first three degrees of the OTO, the second degree to the next three, and so on. The other possibility is that the degree system is purely Masonic in origin. After talking to practising Freemasons, we consider this to be more plausible showing the Co-Masonic influence. But if the former is true, then you can certainly understand Gardner's reasoning behind this. It goes back to the need for acceptance. Perhaps he felt that by doing this he could gain universal acceptance amongst the fickle middle- to upper-class occult community of Britain at the time, although he was probably a bit optimistic about how this alliance with "the mad, bad, and dangerous to know" Aleister Crowley would be taken.

The main criticism of the degree system is its hierarchical nature. We couldn't agree more, but it has not stopped individuals from adapting it. A good example is the system used by the incredibly non-hierarchical Neo-Pagan Church of All Worlds.[14] Although not Wiccan, it has a system of "circles" through which its members pass as they head towards scion or clergy status. It was created because there are good psychological reasons for a system of levels (which are covered more fully in Chapter 6). In the 1990s, even we attempted to finally do away with the hierarchical degree system. Initially, we adopted an organic system based on the ideas of dedication, initiation, and eldership. We hoped this would result in a one-initiation system. It sounded good on paper and seemed much more like a method that would have been used by the village witch. The problem was that our initiates continued to refer to themselves as "first," "second," and "third." They were familiar with this system and felt secure with it. In the end, instead of having one initiation, we ended up with a system that has four levels: dedication, first, second, and third. We have come across other adaptations—Alexandrians with five-degree systems and Seax-Wiccans using three degrees, even though Raymond Buckland's book had only one initiation. At the end of the day, the degree system should not be hierarchical, but a reflection of the competency and spiritual experience of the initiate. We feel it is up to individual covens and witches to decide whether they should use this system. There is no reason why it cannot be adapted to suit specific needs. It is a system, a tool, and should not become dogmatic. It certainly should not become a system of hierarchy with individuals achieving a higher status than any other member of the craft. This is stated clearly (but seldom heeded) in Gardnerian law by the phrase: "All members of the Craft are equal." Somehow, the Orwellian *Animal Farm* joke, "but some animals (witches) are more equal than others," crept into the older traditions of Wicca, but we believe we have found one other reason for its existence and continued use in modern witchcraft, and that is its unquestionable link with the mysteries.

Defining the Modern Witch

We now come to one of the most difficult questions to answer: What are the modern definitions of *witch* and *witchcraft*? This is a question that has been debated ever since Gardner appeared in the 1950s. In the 1990s, the terms were pretty much interchangeable, before the new trend appeared that we mentioned earlier. This is, of course, the same rebellion against dogma that we have seen all the main figures of Wicca go through since Gardner's expulsion from the first coven. As we've seen, it isn't a path based necessarily on its doctrines (lineage, tradition, or secrecy). What seems to define it is its belief structure. The first obvious thing is the presence of deity in some form. The principle forms in witchcraft are the God and the Goddess. There are two approaches to them: the duotheistic "all gods, one god; all goddesses, one goddess" and the polytheistic belief that the Divine has many faces that manifest as the many gods and goddesses of the different cultures around the world.

Duotheism within Wicca actually has its origins in the work of Dion Fortune, and it is she who made the often-quoted statement previously mentioned. Dion Fortune was not a witch, but a follower of the heavily Cabalistic-influenced Western tradition of occultism.[15] In the 10 sephiroth of the Cabalistic Tree of Life, duotheism is found in the sephira of Binah, the Goddess principle (sphere 3, Mother, understanding, outer intellect) and the sephira of Chokmah, the God principle (sphere 2, Father, inner intellect, wisdom). These sephiroth with the first, Kether (Crown), make up the supernal triangle. Kether is the androgynous fusion of Binah and Hocma. What we have in duotheism is a heavily Judeo-Christianized idea of what the Divine is (see Figure 1 on page 52).

From the perspective of Cabala and the Western tradition, polytheism is the descent down this tree. These two principles split into a myriad of forms and personalities, gods, and goddesses. Thus, polytheism and

Polytheism, Duotheism, and the Lightning Flash

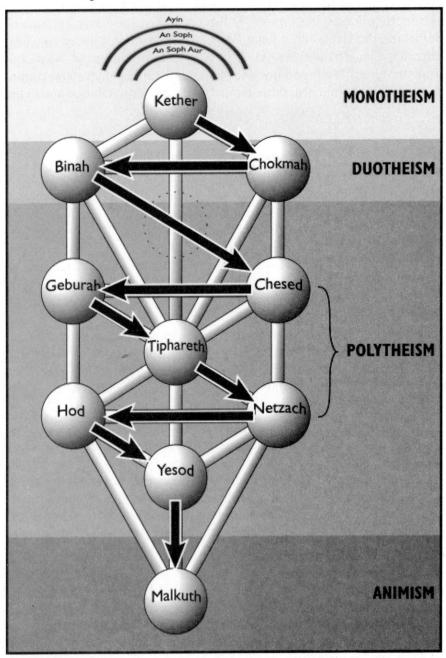

Figure 1

duotheism are not exclusive of each other. In fact, one could argue that polytheism is the eventual goal of duotheism. The idea of polytheism in the modern witchcraft community seems to be gaining ground on duotheistic ideas. It is hardly surprising then that modern witchcraft has started to become more spiritual in its perspective, as it is successfully bringing the "lightning flash," the power of the Divine, down into its practices and the world in general. The eventual conclusion to this process would be the embracing of animism,[16] still found today in contemporary Shamanic practices—a practice only understandable if you live a lifestyle close to the Earth, something that few modern witches are capable of doing. But embracing polytheism is important for another reason. With it comes the idea of "many truths," the acceptance of the many different paths to Spirit within witchcraft. The increasing acceptance of polytheism has resulted in the realization that it is spirituality that is important, not the form used to reach it. This embracing of polytheism is a result of the fact that monotheistic religion is no longer taught in schools the way it used to be. In the first years of the new millennia, the first generation of truly non-Christians who have an innate understanding of the nature of Pagan spirituality is emerging.

Any definition of witchcraft must therefore be related to the Divine, and the role of anyone who brings Spirit to Earth. In Wicca we can see this symbolized in the process known as Drawing Down the Moon, which is the most important sacrament in Wiccan practice (see page 200). Witchcraft therefore must be a Priesthood by its very nature, and the Priesthoods of ancient Paganism have always been mystery schools (see page 63). All Priesthoods must serve; it is their nature. To be a witch is to serve the Divine, not in a slavish way as we see in monotheism (which is also implied in duotheism), but in a joint partnership with the Divine for the good of the witches' community (see page 193). There should be no overblown ego when it comes to being a witch. We see this in the ancient forms of witchcraft and Shamanic practice, which we have mentioned in Chapter 1. Therefore, magic can be seen to be principally about healing.[17] To heal is the only truly ethical reason for performing magic, and the Priest/Priestess works to heal the world in some form. Magic therefore ceases to be about controlling natural forces (a principle of ceremonial ritual magic). Instead, it is about working in synergy with nature, flowing with the divine energy of the universe (see page 154).

At the beginning of the new millennium, the stage at which modern witchcraft is can be likened to the self-awareness children develop in their teens as they strive to understand their world. They begin to question their parents and their values and, like many obstreperous teenagers, they enter into a period of rebellion. Witchcraft has rejected the old doctrines, lineage, tradition, and even the old rules related to initiation, regardless of parents' protestations. By doing so, it has rejected the root causes of many of the problems that have created arguments in witchcraft in the past. Quite simply, the older generation of witches continued to hold on to the Christian values of their time because they were so deeply ingrained. This included the monotheistic doctrine of "one God, one truth, one way" without them realizing it. True polytheism believes in the idea that there are many truths, and therefore many ways to Spirit, Deity, or whatever names you choose. By definition, this encourages acceptance of others' paths, as well as diversity of practice within one's own.

Where else do the seeds of the rebellion lie but in the Woodstock generation of the 1960s? It was a generation whose main catch phrase was "question authority." When individuals set themselves up as self-professed "authorities" on witchcraft, it was inevitable that they would be questioned. Feminist Wicca, the "reconstructionalist" traditions and their authors, and even we have our origins in this generation. The idea that just because someone was old didn't necessarily mean they were right began to permeate the blossoming witchcraft community. This rebellion was connected to the very origins of ancient tribal witchcraft and the initial cause for its creation: survival. The return of this imperative is at the very roots of why an ancient practice has returned to a modern world.

So what has changed since witchcraft first began to disappear during the Middle Ages? We just have to look at the history of the 20th century to understand why; World War I, World War II, the nuclear cold war, and now potential environmental disasters have threatened the world since the 1900s. For the first time in humanity's history, we are capable not only of making our own species extinct, but also of reducing the whole planet to a pile of rubble. It is a hardly surprising that some of the main doctrines of modern Wicca are reverence for nature and the pursuit of world peace. These values were incorporated into witchcraft from that 1960s generation, who rebelled against the materialist values of the previous generation that caused these situations to arise. The role of witchcraft now is not just to help the tribe or clan to survive, but the whole of humanity and the world in which we live. Spirituality has always been a strong driving force for change throughout the history of mankind.

So now we're going to do something that few people would dare do, as it has always been so controversial. We are going to try and give our definition of a modern witch or Wiccan. As magical workers in a community setting have always been referred to as Priesthood, we therefore define witchcraft as:

An evolving, magical, nature-based Priesthood with service to its community as its main role. A witch is also therefore a craftsperson with attained magical skills, with an emphasis on religious and spiritual practice.

This definition is also, of course, a cross-cultural definition easily including Voudon practices, Strega practices, and those of other cultures.

Spirituality and Progressive Witchcraft

As we have seen again and again, witchcraft is in a continual growth process subject to evolution. It is adapting to its environment and evolving, and in some cases, aspects of it are becoming extinct as they cease to have any purpose. It is, quite simply, dynamic as all true spiritual paths are. It does not remain still; it is continually changing and going through cycles. Witches see this all the time in nature, in the natural cycles of the seasons, what is referred to as the Wheel of the Year (see page 179). Many witches have now begun to realize that these very cycles appear in spirituality itself, obeying the occult law "As above, so below." These are principles found in Shamanism, an area neglected by many in modern witchcraft in favor of Western ritual magic, ignoring the fact that ancient witchcraft and Shamanism are no different. Witches with a progressive outlook have come to realize that witchcraft is dynamic and cyclical to its very core, which has resulted in the creation of mechanisms to allow witchcraft to survive its harsh history of oppression and to evolve into what it is today. To try to hold back these forces, which are evolving witchcraft into a new form of spirituality, would be like the story Gavin was told as a child about the Old Danish King, Canute of the Dark Ages, who tried to hold back the sea at high tide. There will always be some that will try to hold back the sea of change for the sake of tradition, or rather for the sake of their positions of power and ego, but they will ultimately fail. This realization comes from the conclusions drawn from a process of understanding Wiccan history. We have deemed to call the results of this process Progressive Witchcraft.

In this chapter, we have tried to sum up what constitutes Progressive Witchcraft and Wicca. We have done this in a system of tenets.

The Tenets of Progressive Witchcraft

1. *Progressive Witchcraft* is not a tradition, but a name describing the evolution of modern witchcraft into a coherent magical and spiritual path for the next millennia. Those following this path may not necessarily even name themselves as such, and may classify themselves as belonging to one of the many traditions of Wicca that exist; it is their actions and beliefs that dictate their belonging to it.

2. Evolution is an important aspect of this path, particularly in the understanding that all that has come before Wicca has been part of its growth process, whether perceived as negative or positive. Because of this, progressive witches believe that there are no "good" or "bad" experiences, only experiences that can be learned from.

3. Spirit is at the core of any belief structure. Those who are progressive witches realize that spirituality must be at the center of Wiccan belief, training, and practice. Therefore the emphasis is on connection with the Divine, Deity, God, Goddess, or by whatever names It is called. For those on a true spiritual path, connection and union with the Divine is the ultimate goal of being a witch.

4. With connection to the Divine comes the realization that we are servants of Spirit, not the masters. The terms *Priestess* and *Priest* are therefore put into their original context, and the implications put on them by 2,000 years of hierarchical abuse of the words are thrown aside. Within progressive witchcraft, a Priest/Priestess is someone who has union with Deity for the benefit of society, humanity, and the world around them. They also see their role as to assist others with this connection, realizing that there is no monopoly on it as there has been within the monotheistic religions. There is no room for *ego* within the words *Priestess* and *Priest*; they are a description of what someone does, not a hierarchical title to be bestowed.

5. Progressive witches do not feel that initiation has to necessarily take place in a "properly prepared circle." Individuals may have initiatory epiphanies outside of circle—the result

of divine intervention. There is only "one true initiator" to quote an old Gardnerian Wiccan law: This is understood to mean that it is not a Priest or Priestess who initiates someone into Wicca, but the Divine as God or Goddess, or even "the higher self." The doctrine of lineage is therefore seen to be irrelevant, and the term "self-initiation" misleading, as Deity will always manifest at a true initiation if the person has reached the right level of spiritual growth, even if only he or she is present.

6. Although much can be learned from books and from word of mouth (in formal or informal teaching situations), progressive witches know that Wicca is a mystery tradition and that experienced knowledge is the most important form of spiritual growth. They also know that it can never adequately be explained by word of mouth or written word as it touches the individual's very soul. It is therefore impossible to give away "the true secrets of the Craft."

7. Like all true spiritual paths, it is essential to have a firm ethical and moral base. Anthropologists often refer to this as "the Golden Rule." In Wicca there is the Wiccan Rede: "Eight Words the Wiccan Rede fulfil, an it harm none do what thou will." This is not just a law, but a philosophy of ethical living, as you can do harm by inaction as well action. By implication, this means, to obey this law, you must strive to be the best that you can be by accumulating knowledge and experience as a Priestess or Priest if you are going to do your best to avoid doing harm in any of your actions, be they magical or mundane.

8. Spirit is seen as immanent in nature with its many faces. There is therefore an inherent polarity within existence: day/night, growth/decay, life/death, etc. In Taoism this is referred to as the ideas of Yin and Yang and in Wicca as God and Goddess. Although we refer to God and Goddess in a duotheistic fashion, we are by nature polytheistic, believing that the Divine has many faces manifested as individual deities, be they ancestral, of nature, or of human skill.

9. Those who follow the path of Progressive Witchcraft seek that which is best for all, both from nature and from themselves. "Good" and "evil" are recognized as human concepts,

alien to nature, that come about by imbalance. They seek to balance themselves and the world around them. For this reason witches are intrinsically healers in all aspects of their work who see magic, ritual practice, and the use of psychic skills as nothing more than tools to achieve this goal.

The next chapter covers in more depth the subjects of initiation and the spiritual experience mentioned in the fifth tenet, because it is such a large and important subject in the evolution of witchcraft. We will do the same for the subject of training (see Chapter 6).

Endnotes

1. U.S. (French-born) author and diarist (1903 –1977). Generally known for her works of erotic fiction, such as *Delta of Venus* and *Little Birds*
2. We discovered that Ariadne (Karen) Rainbird and David Rankine published *Magic Without Peers: A Course in Progressive Witchcraft for the Solitary Practitioner (Capall Bann Publishing,* 2002*),* during the writing of this work. They had been using the term Progressive Wicca since 1989: "Progressive Wicca is not organization as such because of its considerable diversity but rather reflects an attitude towards the craft. A Progressive Witchcraft Foundation has been set up through the Cylch y Gwyllt a'r Rhydd coven to provide information and training." (From *Witches: An Encyclopedia of Paganism and Magic,* by Michael Jordan.)
3. The *Book of Shadows* in Sufi practice is a method of divination, involving taking a measure of head, chest, and height. The measurements are then compared to notes within the book. As noted by Ron Hutton in *The Triumph of the Moon,* there was a Sufi among Gardner's circle: Idries Shah, author of *The Way of the Sufi.* Wicca is mentioned in his introduction as one of the many spiritual traditions of the west influenced one way or another by Sufism.
4. Much of the Kelly's suggestions on origins have since been questioned, although his basic conclusion, that the *Book of Shadows* was a creation of Gardner and Valiente is considered correct.
5. The originator of this story, Fred Lamond, has since published this with more detail in an article entitled "Gerald Gardner's Teachings" in the U.K.-based *Witchcraft and Wicca Magazine* (Beltane to Lammas 2003).
6. Evidence of this can be clearly found in Lady Sheba's *Book of Shadows,* where the Beltane Sabbat has been placed on the Summer Solstice rather than on May Eve.
7. Blue Star was originally formed in 1971 by Frank Duffner. At this time Ziporah Klein (then Katz) joined the coven, married Frank, and met Kenny Klein, who was to become her second husband.
8. Darwin's idea of "Nature red in tooth and claw" was rejected long ago as it was found that cooperation and mutual altruism are equally capable of enabling not "survival" as such, but *reproductive success.* This idea of *cultural selection* has been proposed by anthropologist Marvin Harris in his book *Our Kind: Who We Are, Where We Came From, Where We Are Going* (page 127). In this system, the criterion for

success is, as Harris puts it, "well being." In short, a new variation in the way individuals think and behave is propagated if it enables the individual, or group in which the individual exists, to obtain more of the good stuff in life: more food, better shelter, more sex, more leisure time, more fun, more intellectual or emotional stimulation, more power, more access to resources, and so on.

9. First published in *Ritual Magic in England: 1887 to the Present Day* (1970), pages 179–180 (*see* Bibliography).

10. Stewart Farrar was once informed by Monique and Scotty Wilson that he was not a real witch for this reason.

11. Many people are unaware that all the material from the Sabbats that Janet and Stewart published in *Eight Sabbats For Witches* and *The Witches' Bible* was in fact not traditional and created by ourselves from sources of literature. The ritual framework and Drawing Down the Moon ritual was Gardnerian, not Alexandrian, and was published by permission of Doreen Valienta, the co-author with Gerald Gardner, of *The Book of Shadows*.

12. In four separate confessions made in 1662, Isobel Gowdie gave what amounted to a resume of popular beliefs about witchcraft in Scotland. The Encyclopedia of Witchcraft and Demonology by Rossel Hope-Robbins (*see* Bibliography). Material useful to anyone researching Witchcraft and clearly sourced by Gardner.

13. Francis King's *Ritual Magic in England*, pages 179–180.

14. The Church of All Worlds was founded in 1961 and has based its theology on Robert A. Heinlein's science fiction novel *Stranger in a Strange Land.*

15. Dion Fortune (1891–1946) was a highly published writer of her time (*see* Bibliography) and founder of the Society of the Inner Light, which was based on Christian Gnostic and theosolphical principles rather than those that were Pagan.

16. Animism is the belief that everything in the material world is alive and sentient on a spiritual level—the Divine Spirit made manifest universally.

17. For more on this idea, see our previous work, *The Healing Craft* (*see* Bibliography).

Chapter 3

At the Heart of Witchcraft:
Spirituality and the Mysteries

*And thou who thinkest to seek for me, know thy
seeking shall avail thee not unless though knowest
the mystery; that if that which thou seekest thou
findest not within thee, thou wilt never find it
without thee.*

—Doreen Valiente,
The Charge of the Goddess

This chapter is about the spiritual experience of witchcraft. Spirituality is a word we have found so often missing when people talk about Paganism and witchcraft. In this chapter, we try to explain the origins, both ancient and modern, of the mysteries within modern Wiccan practice. We also try to explain what the mysteries are. Because experience of the mysteries is subjective, the best way we have come across to try to explain the mysteries in words is with adjectives and descriptive nouns. This explains why storytelling in Paganism—the role of the bards and their Northern equivalents, the skalds—was so important to ancient cultures. To quote Brendan Myers, research associate of philosophy at the National University of Ireland, Galway:

"If you think about the mysteries you will find that, while it is certainly the case that everyone's experiences of the mysteries are their own, nevertheless the mysteries are their own entities, 'out there' to be experienced by every seeker who finds them. The mysteries themselves may be indefinable in words but the experience of the mysteries is describable. Also since the mysteries are eternal, immutable, and immaterial, one (that is, each mystery is a unity in itself, not the sum of its parts), therefore they are the same for everyone. Thus, people's spiritual experiences can be compared with each other, and one person's vision of an otherworldly landscape or figure can usually be confirmed by another person's vision."[1]

It is for this reason that some of the material in this book is anecdotal. We will, of course, give more objective information regarding the rites and rituals we went through to attain these experiences and some of the psychology behind them, but these (as we have so clearly stated) are not the mysteries. We hope that this chapter guides the reader in how to have his or her own experiences as an integral part of the spirituality of witchcraft.

At the heart of the spiritual experience within modern witchcraft is the idea that Wicca is a mystery religion. Although this is true of modern Wicca, there is little evidence of it before Gardner and the 1950s. The mystery practices of modern Wicca seem to have been drawn from the Mediterranean, specifically the Greek and Egyptian cultures and their established Priesthoods, rather than any form of Northern or Western European village or tribal magical practice whose mystery practices would have surely been more Shamanically inclined. Rosicrucianism and Co-Masonry follow mystery cycles from these cultures, with heavy Christian Gnostic[2] influences. Gardner, of course, was originally a member of the Rosicrucian Theatre and a member of the Fellowship of Crotona, and therefore was heavily influenced by Co-Masonry. This is important, as R.E. Witt points out in his work, *Isis in the Graeco-Roman World*, that Freemasonry was the natural successor of these mysteries, and of course Co-Masonry took an even more esoteric and Gnostic path:

"The affiliation of Freemasonry with the rites of Isis and and Osiris was recognized years ago by the percipient genius of Mozart in *The Magic Flute*. When Tamino and Papageno are led within the temple for their initiation into the mysteries of Isis they must be thought of from two standpoints. They typify modern Freemasonry. They also follow in the steps of their ancient brethren, the Cabiri, and Isis who in search of the slain Osiris, or met the same god, no longer a corpse and resurrected as the god Ptah, the Lord of Life, opening and closing the day, creating 'with his heart and tongue,' superintending architects and masons at the building of temples and pyramids, ordaining that the house should be established firmly, and holding the *djed* column as his emblem of stability."

—R.E. Witt, *Isis in the Graeco-Roman World*[3]

It can hardly be surprising then, that Gardner incorporated the form that the mysteries took within the Fellowship of Crotona and the Rosicrucian Theatre into Wicca. This was also probably his reason for incorporating the Masonic style three-degree system into it, which acted as their vehicle. Like Witt, he saw Co-Masonry and the Rosicrucians as the successor to these mysteries, and for him, these mysteries were at the core of what he considered witchcraft to be. He may have been right. From examining the myths of cultures closer to hand—the Celts and the Norse—we have seen parallels with those of the Greeks, Romans, and Egyptians. It is probably not that the mysteries did not exist within these cultures, but that the evidence for their existence was trampled underfoot by Christian-influenced Roman and Greek thinking. The question is not whether Gardner was right, but *whether the* mysteries *still belong at the heart of modern witchcraft*. We still believe that they do and that they have an important place within Wicca as a vehicle for the spiritual experience. The developments of the mystery schools within Greek and Egyptian culture are no more than the evolution of the Shaman's journey into the Underworld and his or her experiences there, and it is in Shamanism that witchcraft ultimately has its origins. The only major difference is the form of practice used to experience the mysteries, but the mysteries remain the same. By reintroducing the mysteries from Co-Masonry into witchcraft, Gardner had returned them to their origins, fulfilling a cycle.

The First Thing that Magic Changes Is the Self

One of the first things we are taught as witches is "The first thing that magic does is change the self," and we feel this should still be taught first.

An understanding of psychology is essential to understand the processes in magical practice and correct interpretation of the mysteries and the spiritual experience. It is the theories of the psychologist Carl Jung that have been the mainstay of such thought, because he analyzed both myth and the occult experience. The theories of importance to the witch are related to Ego, Id, Shadow, and the Anima/Animus complex. You may ask what the theories of a scientist have to do with the mysteries. Jung's theories are important and relevant for a good reason. His outlook was Gnostic, as were the origins of his psychological theories.[4]

Jung's concept of the Ego was adopted directly from Freud. Freud believed the human personality consisted of three components, the Super Ego, the Ego, and the Id. Jung discarded the concept of the Super Ego, but retained the concepts of the Ego and Id. These terms are Latin and mean, respectively, "I" and "It." In everyday life, we normally refer to ourselves in the context of the semiconscious Ego, hence we refer to ourselves as "I." If we become controlled by our instinctual impulses—hunger, thirst, and our sexual and aggressive instincts—then we fall under the control of our Id. When this happens we may very likely refer to these forces as "It." In a normally adjusted individual, the function of the Ego is to serve, and, to a certain degree, to control the instinctual Id. Therefore, we are prevented from taking off all our clothes in a public place in hot weather by our Ego, which will fear ridicule. This is a good example of the Ego defense mechanisms that develop in an adult. But in a child, the Ego has not yet developed, so a child may very likely do such things without fear. This manifests the control function, but an example of the serving function is when we are hungry: The Id only knows the hunger and the demand to be satisfied, but the Ego knows how to open the can of food!

When the Ego finds itself trying to cope with over-demand from the Id, which is only interested in satisfying itself, the Ego defense mechanism copes by using several strategies. It may push the unwanted impulses, thoughts, and ideas into the unconscious. This is called repression. It is also responsible for projecting these impulses and ideas on to others, so sometimes what we most hate in others is what we are trying repress within ourselves. It may also displace the unwanted impulse, for example by taking out our anger for the way we are being treated on someone who is not connected with the cause of this anger. We may try to intellectualize and rationalise these impulses by developing elaborate excuses for our behavior when we succumb to the demands of the Id. Other ways of coping with the demands of the Id are to regress to a childlike state where the

Ego is less demanding, to consciously deny the cause of an impulse (whether it be fact, feeling, or memory), or sublimation (the channelling of unacceptable impulses into acceptable everyday behavior). Many sports perform this function by channelling unwanted aggression. While the Ego remains partly conscious, these methods of Ego defense always remain unconscious.

Jung differed from Freud, for he believed that we develop a Persona at the outer edge of our functioning Egos. This is a mask, a compromise between what the Ego aspires to be and the limitations and social functions imposed upon it. If there is no compromise between the Ego's aspirations and the social limitations, then the Persona becomes a rigid, stereotyped mask. In a balanced state, it is supple and pliable, able to adjust to life's everyday situations.

The Shadow is the antithesis of the Persona. Just as the Persona lies in front of the Ego, the Shadow hides behind it. It is the unacceptable face of the Ego, the part that has been rejected. This concept has appeared in mythology and literature for centuries. In Norse mythology, Odin's shadow is Loki; in Egyptian, Osiris's Shadow is Set. Biblically, Satan can be seen as Yahweh's Shadow, and in modern writing, the concept is typified by the characters of Dr. Jekyll and Mr. Hyde. Because of the Ego's rejection, the Shadow is often portrayed as evil in nature, as can be seen from the examples given previously. This is an oversimplification because, unfortunately, when the Ego sublimates some of its aspects, it may sometimes "throw the baby out with the bath water," so to speak. For example, if aggressive aspects are sublimated, individuals may also lose their ability to be assertive and make decisions. Sometimes exploration of our Shadows (an essential aspect of many forms of occultism, but particularly Shamanism) can restore these lost aspects and complete the wholeness of the individual's psyche.

The Anima is the buried feminine element in a man, and the Animus the buried male element in a woman. The neo-Jungians believe it can be found in the area they call the Bright Shadow. This is best symbolized in the fairy tale called *Sleeping Beauty,*[5] which features the beautifully draped room where Sleeping Beauty (the Anima) sleeps, surrounded by the dark ominous castle (the Shadow). It is here that positive, repressed aspects of the individual can also be found. Apart from fairy tales, they are often found, like the Shadow, in art, literature, and, of most importance to the witch, in mythology. In Welsh tradition, the Arwen is the female soul-spirit of the poet and artist, and in Irish, the Leannán Sidhe fulfils the same function. Arthurian Nimue is the Anima representation within Merlin.

Many male Pagans relate to the Goddess principle via their Anima, as do female Pagans to the God principle via their Animus. When we first fall in love or have "crushes" on the opposite sex, we tend to fall for this soul image, unconscious of the fact that we are falling in love with ourselves. The results can be disastrous if we remain unaware of what is really happening, as with Lancelot and Guinevere within medieval Arthurian mythology. (The original Guinevere was a very different woman, but that is another matter.) If recognized and harnessed, the soul-spirit can act as an inspiration and a guide.

There are inherent dangers to this process, for example in the Welsh bardic tradition where the Arwen comes to claim the bard's soul. Perhaps within this myth there is a veiled warning that the exploration of the Anima can go too far, eventually destroying important parts of the individual's persona. A similar concept appears in Norse myth, with the Valkyries coming to claim the souls of the warriors, and within the Celtic myth of the Morrigan, the crow goddess who claims Cuchulain. Even the myths revolving around various Pagan deities show the importance that the Anima/Animus concept has played in the formation of the human psyche.

In the Greek myth of Theseus and the Minotaur, we see all the above aspects of personality come together. King Minos, who tries to deceive Zeus and deprive him of the offering of the white bull, represents Ego. Interestingly, the bull is given to Minos by Poseidon, the god of the sea. Water and the sea are traditionally associated with the unconscious mind. As punishment, Zeus makes Queen Pasiphäe, wife of Minos, fall in love with a bull and conceive the Minotaur with it. The Minotaur is placed in the labyrinth because he is so hideous and dangerous: The Minotaur represents the Id and the labyrinth, the Shadow area of the mind. Seven boys and seven girls are brought regularly from the Greek mainland to Crete as punishment for the death of Minos's son Androgeos at the hands of Aegeus, the son of King of Attica. They are thrown into the labyrinth to be devoured by the Minotaur: This represents the Ego suppressing and forcing down not only unwanted impulses into the Shadow, but also those of a positive nature. It is Theseus who challenges this process and seeks the mysteries. In the myth, he represents the personality on a journey of discovery. He travels from Athens with the others and is thrown into the labyrinth to await his fate. While there, Ariadne, the daughter of Minos, sees him through the bars of his cell, and they fall in love. She is clearly the Anima, which is one of the first aspects anyone venturing on the journey of discovery must find. She tells him how to beat the Minotaur by

finding him before he wakes and killing him: This represents the unconscious mind controlling the Id. She gives him a ball of golden thread,
which he must unreel so that he can find his way back out of the labyrinth.
This act is of importance, as it clearly shows the dangers of embracing the
Shadow without first seeking the Anima/Animus complex. Not doing so
could result in becoming lost in the labyrinth of your own mind. Theseus
does triumph, defeating the Minotaur just as it wakes.

We see a similar myth enacted in the second-degree rituals of both
the Gardnerian and Alexandrian traditions of Wicca. This is *The Legend
of the Descent of the Goddess*, which is most probably based on the myth
of Demeter and Kore. Unlike the myth of Theseus, there is an agricultural
aspect related to the Wheel of the Year,[6] (see page 184) as well as a
psychological one. This is important as the fertility rites of the community
which related to birth, death, and rebirth echoed the deeper mysteries of
the soul; the occult law "As above, so below" seems to come into play
again in the mysteries, and this is also found in the Egyptian mysteries
related to Isis and Osiris:[7]

Legend of the Descent of the Goddess

*Now our Lady the Goddess has never loved, but she would solve all
the mysteries, even the mystery of Death: And so she journeyed to the
Underworld.*

*The Guardians of the portals challenged her: "Strip of thy
garments, lay aside thy jewels; for naught mayest thou bring with
thee into this our land."*

*So she laid down her garments and her jewels, and was bound,
as are all who enter the Realms of Death, the Mighty One.*

*Such was her beauty that Death himself knelt and kissed her
feet, saying:*

*"Blessed be thy feet, that have brought thee in these ways. Abide
with me; but let me place my cold hand on thy heart."*

*She replied: "I love thee not. Why dost thou cause all things that
I love and take delight in to fade and die?"*

*"Lady," replied Death, "'tis age and fate, against which I am
helpless. Age causes all things to wither; but when men die at the end
of time, I give them rest and peace, and strength so that they may
return. But thou! Thou art lovely. Return not; abide with me!"*

But she answered: "I love thee not."

Then said Death: "An thou receivest not my hand on thy heart, thou must receive Death's scourge."

"It is fate—better so," she said. And she knelt and Death scourged her tenderly. And she cried, "I feel the pangs of love."

And Death said, "Blessed Be!" and gave her the Fivefold Kiss, saying:

"Thus only mayest thou attain to joy and knowledge." And he taught her all the mysteries, and they loved and were one, and he taught her all the Magics.

For there are three great events in the life of man: Love, Death, and Resurrection in the new body; and Magic controls them all. For to fulfil love you must return again at the same time and place as the loved one, and you must remember and love them again. But to be reborn you must die and be ready for a new body; and to die you must be born; and without love you may not be born; and this is all the Magics.

This myth teaches reincarnation, particularly for those who have learned to love. The process of life, death, and rebirth, which the observant will see in nature all the time, is an important part of Neo-Pagan belief, but the experience of passing through this process as a mystery also gives those experiencing it the feeling that they have passed through death itself. This is one of the effects of passing into and facing your own Shadow—the death of the old personality as you come to understand your own Ego.

The second degree is the most important rite because it is the time when initiates actually encounter the mysteries and face their greatest challenge—the embracing of their own Anima/Animus while descending into their own Shadow. The first degree can be seen as no more than a preparatory initiation leading to this process, while the third degree is the initiation marking a witch who is capable of taking an initiate through the process. These levels are no different to the system of degrees found in the traditional Isis/Osiris mysteries mentioned earlier in this chapter. In these mysteries, Isis governs the first degree and Osiris the second.[8] It can be no chance then the first-degree sigil in Wicca, the inverted triangle, is a goddess symbol; the second-degree symbol, the inverted pentragram, is a symbol of the resurrected horned god of nature.

The Shamanic Revival and the Mysteries

In the 1980s, Shamanic practices started to be revived in the general Pagan communities of both Britain and the United States. The major influences for this were the fiction of Carlos Castenada, the academic works of anthropologists Mircea Eliade, Joseph Campbell, and more importantly, Michael Harner, an American anthropologist who had travelled extensively in South America. His interest was such that he began to do seminars and then workshops on the practices of the Conibo and Jivarí Indians whose Shamanism practices he had been involved with. He eventually published *The Way of the Shaman* in 1980, the first practical guide to Shamanic practice. For modern Shamans, Michael Harner can be considered the equivalent to Gerald Gardner.

In the magical communities of that time, Cabalistic ritual magic was being rejected in favor of more ancestor-based magical systems. To a certain degree, the mysteries within the more dogmatic traditions of Wicca had been lost in meaningless, complicated ritual, and many who were initially attracted to Wicca rejected ritual dogma in favor of the spiritual trance experience of Shamanism. Many witches, including Gavin, began to look at native forms of Shamanism for this reason. Here we saw the new witchcraft movement coming of age by rejecting dogma that it found outdated and of no use. If you have an understanding of Shamanic practice, then you realize that the reintroduction of Shamanism has not caused the mysteries to disappear. In fact, quite the reverse. Shamanism is, in fact, an earlier form of mystery-tradition, less shrouded in symbolism, and therefore, more relevant to today's generation of witches.

The first mystery in Shamanism is the reconciliation of the personality with the Id, the power animal (we would like to point out that the totem animal is very different from the power associated with the Ego, see page 64). It is believed that the power animal comes to you in traditional Shamanic practice. It is the Spirit of the Id itself, which connects you with the animal side of your nature. One belief of ours is that animals, like humans, have their own collective unconscious or Astral Plane. The result is that the animal, be it bird or mammal, connects to you across a bridge from their Astral Plane to yours. In the mysteries of Greece and Egypt, the animal was an important symbol for the Id. Their equivalent of the power animal was the psychopompous. Anubis is a perfect example, having the head of the jackal; while in Greek it was Hermes Trismegistus, the cloven-hoofed son of Pan. At a later date, they were combined within the mysteries of the Cabiri as the figure of Hermanubis.[9] In both traditional Shamanism and the Greek and Egyptian mysteries the role of the psychopompous and the power animal is the same: to escort and protect the seeker of the mysteries (for more see page 142).

Hermanubis

The second stage in Shamanic practice is the retrieval of the soul, which in some cultures is believed to manifest as the previously mentioned Anima/Anumus complex and hidden in the Bright Shadow. The Anima/Animus must be retrieved with the protection of the power animal, the Underworld Guide—this is the hunt for the soul or soul retrieval. In the traditional Greek and Egyptian mysteries, this is the connection to the Goddess for the male seeker and God for the female. Again, the same process is at work.

Finally, there is the third challenge: the facing of death. In Shamanism, the practitioner must go in to the Chthonic Shadow Realm, the Ancestral Realm of Death itself, and return. To do this they must be challenged by the guardian of the gate of death—the Guardian of the mysteries. This closely follows the previously mentioned Legend of the Descent of the Goddess, indicating that this is the same process found in the mysteries of Greece and Egypt.

Survivals of the mysteries can be found in the Northern cultures of Europe. Myths related to the descent into the Underworld can be found in both Celtic and Norse. Northern myth is particularly full of psychological analogy; Odin's hanging on Yggdrasil, the world tree, can be seen as the Shaman's decent to find the mysteries. He looks down into the Well of Urd or Wyrd (fate) at the base of the great tree and sees the runes after being close to death; the word "rune" itself means "secret" or "mystery." He then takes on the form of the psychopompous, escorted by his two wolves and two ravens, to guide others through the same process. It is no mistake that his name was given to Wednesday, Woden's day, as this day is also equated with Mercury, the Roman equivalent of Hermes Trismegistus.

Spiritual Initiation over Ritual Initiation

As every Wiccan knows, initiation takes place in a circle. Or does it? We have come to question this idea. It was toying with the concept of "walking the tight rope" that triggered Gavin's initiation. To walk the tightrope is to balance the right brain and left brain functions, which both Janet and Stewart had previously written about in several of their works. Gavin realized that it was in fact a dynamic process: We swing between these influences. Although there is some debate by neurologists and psychologists today whether these sides of the brain actually are separate in function, at the time, this was the prevalent theory, and it is relevant to the magical process regardless. The general theory is that the functions are divided into two hemispheres: The left brain is primarily concerned with logical thinking and speech, and the right brain with instincts, intuition, and feelings—the two halves complementing each other. In our society, emphasis is put on logic and the scientific process (the left brain); for our ancestors, more emphasis may have been on belief and emotional relationships (the right brain). To connect with deities, you must have an emotional relationship with them, know them to be real personalities, and understand their nature (for more on this see Chapters 4 and 10). But you must also realize the psychology with which we experience them and recognize them as numinous Archetypes within the purview of left-brain function. This is like balancing on a tightrope as you shift your weight, trying to reconcile both concepts being true at the same time. If you don't, one of two things can happen: Either you cannot connect with deity, forcing the Ego to control your spiritual practices, or you develop an unbalanced obsession with deity, which is what fundamentalism in the monotheistic religions is. This does, of course, relate to the concepts of polytheism and monotheism (see page 51).

We feel that the personal connection to deity should be the goal that the witch needs to achieve after the first-degree initiation (see page 120). This process also results in the discovery of the individual's Anima/Animus, their contra-sexual self, which is normally hidden. This is the Muse in Greek myth or the Arwen of the Welsh tradition. Both are said to inspire creativity and art. It is our society and its division into female/male role models that represses the Anima/Animus. In the male, those aspects that are considered feminine are repressed by the Ego and pushed into the Shadow. Men are therefore expected to be unemotional, detached, etc. For example, the idea of men kissing is considered a minor taboo, although it is acceptable for women. In some Shamanic traditions, particularly Norse and Anglo-Saxon, the Anima/Animus is considered to be your very soul. In the Priesthood of Frey and Freya, both men and women were expected to embrace the contra-sexual aspects within themselves in the practice of Seith: Men had to embrace Freya, while women had to embrace Frey. Hence, the gods and the individual's Anima/Animus became the same. Seith is a Shamanic tradition that the Norse considered witchcraft, making this process even more relevant to the modern witch. The same practice occurs even today within the Hindu Tantra or Shaktism.

Gavin's first experience with his Arwen was not quite what he expected. His first meeting with her was during a past life regression with a Buddhist counsellor, and he assumed that she was one of his past lives. For some time after, she began to appear in his life in different forms. The most shocking were the several occasions when his face shape-shifted into hers. This was, to say the least, somewhat disconcerting for those he was with at the time! Several witnesses were able to describe her after this, and confirmed that it was the supposed face of the past life. Janet, being an artist, has drawn her several times when she manifested. Initially this left Gavin with a conundrum: Was he manifesting a past life, or was he manifesting his contra-sexual self? We've come to the conclusion that it is possible for both to be true and that the soul from the previous past life can take on this form in the next. It was this past life experience that began to make him look at his ancestry from a magical viewpoint.

In all things, there is balance, and we would like to point out that there is a dark side to this process. This is found in Irish myth as the Leannán Sidhé, the fairy woman who inspires young men in art and music, and then at the height of their fame, destroys them. Here lies a warning of the dangers of allowing our Anima or Animus to dominate our lives, an act that can be seen to be ultimately self-destructive for the personality.

It has been our experience that the magic practitioner who has been able to manifest and balance their Anima/Anumus is more in touch with their psychic abilities, their emotions, and their true nature. This does, of course, make the old argument against homosexuality in Wicca, that is is a magical practice based on male/female polarity, redundant, as it has been our experience that most (but not all) homosexuals who join the craft are normally already in balance with these aspects and are quite capable of assuming either sexual polarity related to energy. The argument against this has come from those in the past that have held on to the female/male role models (as well as the ethical models of Christianity) and have not come into internal balance themselves via this process. Many of the older members of witchcraft, including Patricia Crowther, the late Doreen Valiente, and Janet's late husband, Stewart, have all spoken out against such discrimination.

Gavin's experience of initiation is very different than the one you see written in books about Wicca. He believes his "true" initiation took place outside of circle when he went through a difficult phase of his life. Leading up to this, he had been exploring a particular magical aspect of his own ancestry and had found himself being pulled towards one specific goddess. He actually had done his best to try to avoid this form of magical working, Anglo-Saxon and Norse Runes, because of their associations with the magical practices of Nazi Germany. Regardless, the attraction wouldn't go away, and he describes finding himself being pulled towards using them. In the past, when he first became involved with Wicca, he had tried to be fashionable by taking on the practices of Celtic magic and particularly Arthurian symbolism, even though he was originally initiated into Seax-Wicca. Much of this was related to the associations of his name with one specific character. For a while he had worked that Archetype and discovered that every Archetype has a negative as well as positive aspect. It led him into lots of trouble, resulting in several confrontational situations. It seemed strange to him that he should now embrace its historical polar opposite!

Gavin finally gave into the pull of the Northern magical practices and this specific goddess, as she was now beginning to invade his dreams. He went about preparing for a dedication ritual to her, and finally, one night, gave himself to her as Priest. It was then he learned an important lesson: Be careful what you ask for, as you may get it! His life turned upside down for the next year while she gave him the lessons he needed to learn. Gavin often describes this time as an epiphany, a series of awakenings and understandings of the nature of spirituality and Wicca itself. One of the things he did was face his own inner demons, taking responsibility for his actions. He actually went about apologizing to those whom he perceived as doing him wrong. He had come to understand that he was ultimately responsible not just for the hurt they had caused him, but for putting them in the position where they could cause such hurt. In Cabalistic terms, this is recognized as the tipharethic experience, when the initiate passes through the sphere of his essential nature. He became acutely aware of his own failings and the faults in his personality, and entered a "dark night of the soul." The initiatory question, "Art thou willing to suffer to learn?" took on a whole new meaning for him during this time. For Gavin, this was his initiation, one that occurred in everyday life, not in the pomp and ceremony of a magic circle. It was this experience that he believes made him a Priest of Freya—not lineage or tradition, but one-on-one contact with a face of the Divine Goddess.

What actually happened to Gavin is the experience the initiate should go through at the second degree within Wicca. It is during this that Ego, Id, and Shadow are recognized by the individual within their personality. You become aware of your faults and failings. By accepting their existence, you are hopefully able to change them, or at least learn to live with them. If this process doesn't happen, several things can occur, particularly within a coven setting.

We have coined a term for something we have seen regularly happen within Wicca and within everyday life, for that matter: *second degree syndrome.* Over the years, we have noticed a trend within covens: Witches rebel against the leaders of their covens and leave on acrimonious terms. Our theory is that it is not so much the student's fault as the teacher or the method of teaching employed, particularly when there is no under-standing of the processes involved. It is a by-product of dogmatism. If the High Priest/Priestess of the coven claims to be all-knowledgeable and infallible, then the inflated Ego of the High Priest/Priestess becomes recog-nizable to the initiate, along with his own Ego, after this initiation. If the student initiate does not go through the process properly, recognizing his/her own Ego, then the student will become an imitation of the teacher and will very likely enter into competition with the leaders of the coven. Whatever happens, the initiate will leave the coven, either rebelling early on and going his own way, or, in the case of the latter, leaving and carrying the process on, replicating it like a virus. In such groups, the attainment of status over-rules achievements of spiritual discovery. This is one of the reasons we no longer use the terms High Priest and High Priestess to describe ourselves: We feel they encourage the Ego. We still use the term Priest and Priestess, but we use them as a job description rather than a statement of status. It is not that we feel that everyone should drop these titles, just that they are no longer right for us. We feel that it is up to the individual to decide whether to use them, but they should be aware of the dangers to their Ego.

One problem for Wicca is that such spiritual experiences are so subjective; it is hard to judge their validity. A High Priest or Priestess can only really take any such experiences voiced to them on face value. This is a problem when you have an inflexible system still based on dogmatic ritual rather than a spiritual process. How does a coven cope with a new member who has already been through such an experience, but doesn't necessarily have a good deal of knowledge about Wicca? Training systems within Wicca must be based on both the attainment of practical and academic techniques for the attainment of spiritual knowledge, while having a flexible framework for initiation. Ritual initiations only have value if they stimulate a spiritual change, a true initiation, or if they recognize that an individual has already been through such an experience.

Gavin does point out one thing that is of importance. He became aware that there is very little difference between real spiritual initiation in witchcraft and the experience an Evangelical Christian goes through when they are born-again. They are the same experience of the death and re-birth of the individual's Persona as a spiritual experience. The only difference is that most Wiccans are trained or encouraged to be aware of the processes involved. Although most Wiccans are not necessarily encouraged to look beyond Western Paganism at the experiences of those following other faiths (such as Buddhism, Hinduism, or Shintoism), we have come to realize that this level of spirituality goes beyond the normal ancestral and cultural boundaries. There are big gaps in much of the training in Wicca regarding spirituality and how to deal with and comprehend spiritual mystery, which can now only be addressed by looking at contemporary Pagan and post-Pagan cultures in the East. For a long time, Wicca has been very insular in its approach to culture, looking at only the current Cabalistic-influenced Western magic tradition to base its practices on, or attempting to reconstruct those going back beyond 1,500 years. Eastern culture has been generally ignored on the grounds that you "mustn't mix traditions" (another dogma from Western magic). There were, of course, those who broke the rules. Aleister Crowley was one of them. The fact that this dogma ignores that Hinduism has origins in Assyro-Babylonian and Persian religion seems to be beside the point. Eastern culture shows us how Pagan mystery practices would have developed if they were still around today; they put the spirituality (the experience) above the ritual and practice (the form) in importance. What we see is Wicca slowly moving in this direction where experience and belief becomes more important than form, particularly when it comes to working with the gods and goddesses that are a central part of the belief structure. Witchcraft is now becoming deity-centered as opposed to magic-centred.

Endnotes

1. Personal communication between ourselves and Brendan Myers. Brendan Myers is inspired by the works of eminent philosopher Paul Ricoeur.
2. Gnosis is not strictly a Christian term. According to the Oxford Dictionary it means "Knowledge of Spiritual Mysteries" and can just as readily be applied to the Wiccan Mysteries.
3. Chapter 12, page 157 (*see* Bibliography).
4. Jung was heavily influenced by his study of Gnosticism, particularly the Gnostic Gospels. They became a cornerstone for his psychological theories, particularly those related to Valentinus, according to Elaine Pagels in *The Gnostic Gospels* (*see* Bibliography).
5. Many of the Grimm brother's fairy tales are actually retellings of mystery stories originating in Pagan mythology.
6. The Wheel of the Year in Wicca consists of the Eight festivals, what are referred to as the Celtic Fire festivals (Imbolg, Beltane, Lughnasda, and Samhain) and the Solar festivals: Spring Equinox (Ostara), Summer Solstice (Litha), Autumn Equinox (Mabon), and Winter Solstice (Yule).
7. The same myth is in fact found in many cultures, including that of the Assyro-Babylonians in the myths of Tammuz and Ishtar.
8. From R.E. Witt's *Isis in the Graeco-Roman World*. He recounts Lucius's journey through the Isiac mysteries. It is interesting to note that he takes also takes his third and becomes accepted into the Priesthood.
9. According to R.E Witt (pages 153–154 of *Isis in the Graeco-Roman World*) the Cabiri were "originally demi-gods, sons of Hephaestus, who could themselves share in the chthonic rites of Demeter and Kore." Herodotus wrote about the rites of the Cabiri being a combination of both Egyptian and Greek mysteries and the originators of the word *mysterion* from where our word *mystery* derives.

Chapter 4

The Gods and Goddesses: Deity-Centered Witchcraft

God(dess) must become an activity in our consciousness.

—Joel S. Goldsmith, *The Infinite Way[1]*

Janet lovingly calls our home the "house of a hundred deities." The reason is obvious if you have ever visited us. Statues and pictures of deities can be found in every room of the house. One room is given over completely to Far Eastern and Buddhist statuary. In the passageway are Native American representations. The kitchen has plates from Crete representing the Greek myths. But the majority are in the living room. These range from traditional bronze and brass Hindu deities—including Shiva, Krishna, and of course Ganesha, foremost of the Indian gods[2]—to the common white plaster figures of the Greek gods and goddesses Zeus, Athena, Artemis, and Ceres. Modern Neo-Pagan representations also appear: a beautiful statue of Odin holding his spear, Gungnir, escorted by his two wolves and two ravens; Gaea clutching the world, decorated with the beasts of land, sea, and air; and a haughty Morrigan with her shield, her head up high with an air of disdain about her. We have lost count of the number that we have. They grow every time we enter an occult shop or go on a new odyssey abroad.

There is an old occult law that you don't mix traditions; maybe that should be that you don't mix gods! For, although they all get along, there is the occasional spat between them. We discovered very quickly that some of the Japanese deities don't get on with the Celtic, but it is just a difference of temperament more than anything. The standoffish Greek gods prefer to be higher than anyone else in the room; hence they are on a shelf above the library door. The Indian deities, by contrast, have the demeanour of an Indian shopkeeper, always chatty and willing to please. This has a habit of winding up the Greek gods to no end, much to Odin's and our amusement. We have been plagued with stray cats in recent years due to the increasing number of Bast statues on her shrine in one corner of the room. Additionally, we have a statue of the Hindu Mother Goddess Durga with her lion on the mantlepiece. This is just asking for an ever increasing cat food bill. Being Priest and Priestess of a cat goddess, we are obliged to find room and board for every one of them.

In the corner of the living room is Freya, the most important deity to both of us. She is a statue crafted by Paul Borda, which Gavin took part in designing. She sits permanently on a shrine in the corner of the room, surrounded by the amber and trinkets that she loves: a drinking horn, a rune circlet, and numerous precious stones. She is our principal deity. She guides our lives and our practice of witchcraft. She is also in our genes, as an ancestral deity of the Anglo-Saxons and the Norse. Some may think it odd that she sits in a house nestled in the wilds of Ireland, but both of us are English with strong magical connections to our roots. Over the years, Freya has guided what direction we should take. She is a loving, consoling, flirty guide, who sometimes likes us to be outrageous to get the message across! We've had our ups and downs with her, just as you do with any friend, but she's never let us down. She is a goddess of love, but more importantly, as the older pre Indo-European, pre-Asatru[3] goddess, she is the principal deity of magic and Shamanism for her peoples. We work with her for ourselves rather than for anyone else.

It would be insulting of us to ignore the spirits and deities of the land we live on. When working magically outside, we first find ourselves having to appease the spirits, the fairy folk.[4] Not to do this is to ask for trouble, for they will delight in upsetting your work by tipping things off the altar, and so on. We also respect the deities of the land of Ireland. They surround us, for the Irish gods and goddesses are in the landscape itself, in the rivers, the hills, and the mountains. Close to us is the River Boyne (the goddess Boann) and Slieve na Callaighe (the Hill of the Witch, named after the crone goddess of wisdom). Most important of them all locally is the Hill of Ward, the residence of the goddess Tlachta, the Irish goddess of witchcraft and Samhain. When we work, we pay respect to them all. Not to do so would not only be bad magical practice, but it would also be downright rude!

Of course, this was not the way either of us were taught to relate to the gods. Janet and Stewart were originally taught there were only two true deities of witchcraft, Aradia and Karnayna. Aradia is Italo-Etruscan in origin, and Karnayna, often thought by Stewart to be Alex Sanders' mispronunciation of Cernunnos, was in fact an egotistical joke: It was the name given to Alexander the Great by the Carthaginians on his reaching godhood.[5] After moving to Ireland, Janet and Stewart changed their god name to Cernunnos, a more generic term of Gallic/Latin origin meaning simply "horned god." The dogma of only two true names for the God and Goddess continues today among some hard-liners of Alexandrian and Gardnerian Wicca. On moving to Ireland, Janet and Stewart were faced with the realization that they were surrounded by a country full of its own mythology. Aradia began to take a back seat in their practices as the old Irish gods demanded recognition.

Gavin's experience was different. Right from the beginning he was encouraged to choose two deities at his initiation into Seax-Wicca, although this was not strictly a practice of this tradition. Gavin had little contact with the spiritual aspects of witchcraft at that time, so his choice was very much guided by more Ego than anything else. Later on, he received similar teachings, from Janet and Stewart, related to Aradia from an orthodox Wiccan coven. Like them, he was also taught the dogma that Aradia was the only true goddess of Wicca.

Deity and Religion

The basic deity-teachings within Wicca centred on the triple goddess and dual god, although the origins of this teaching are far from ancient. It originated in Robert Graves's work, *The White Goddess.*[6] This book was standard reading for anyone coming into a coven at that time. There was little theological instruction similar to what would be found in other contemporary religions. Students of witchcraft were pretty much left to develop their own belief structures and ideas about the nature of the Divine, particularly when it came to connecting with a deity. Of course, when there is a vacuum in such circumstances, something has to fill it, and by the late 1970s, Cabala filled that gap. Cabala, being of Judeo-Christian monotheistic origin, is not a good example of what our Pagan ancestors believed about their deities. But it was easy for the witches of that period to accept, as its teachings did not contradict the religious norms and values that they had been taught in a predominantly Christian culture.

The original founders of modern witchcraft, Gerald Gardner and Doreen Valiente, referred to it as "the Old Religion," but it is neither old nor strictly a religion. The religious beliefs of witchcraft have always been that of Paganism. There are, of course, those who would argue with this statement, particularly those of a Judeo-Christian Cabalistic bent, but we have presented the evidence for such clearly in the first chapter of this work. It was called "the Old Religion" because Gardner and Valiente believed at the time (the 1950s) that it was the only survival of ancient Paganism. Arguably, there was also Druidism, but Druidism at that time was heavily Christian and also influenced by Freemasonry. Thus it was possible for the current Archbishop of Canterbury, Dr. Owen Williams, to be ordained a Druid. [7] As we have shown, witchcraft isn't a religion per se, but the survival of the Priesthood of the Pagan religion.

It is important to understand what the word *religion* actually means and where it comes from. The etymology of the word is from the Latin *ligare*, which means to join. Such words as *ligature*, an item that binds or ties, have their origins in this root word. Religion therefore means to rejoin, or reconnect to the Divine. According to Webster's Dictionary, in modern usage, "religion" has come to mean several things:

1. The service and worship of God or the supernatural.

2. Devotion to a religious faith.

3. A personal set or institutionalized system of religious beliefs, attitudes, and practices.

4. A cause, principle, or belief held to with faith and ardor.

Only the first meaning seems to link directly to the original etymology of the word *religion*. This is important because when witches talk about "the Old Religion," they are most definitely talking about it in this respect, as witchcraft has always been non-doctrinal. For witches, the religious aspects of their practices are about reconnecting with the Divine by using one of it's many faces, which manifest within the myriad of gods and goddesses that exist for the witch.

The word *Pagan* (from the Latin word *paganus,* meaning "country dweller") designates a series of ancient beliefs related to the natural environment. For a Pagan (and therefore the witch), the Divine is immanent in nature. The Divine is seen to be in the animate—the plants, the trees, and the wildlife—and in the inanimate—in the wind, in the rivers, in the rocks—and most importantly, it is believed to be within us. Animistic beliefs still thrive today in the practices of the Sami-Lappish tribes of Finland, the Native American tribes, and the Aboriginal peoples of Australia. They are the original beliefs of humanity before the coming of organized religion. We are not separate from the Divine, nor the dynamic ongoing process of creation. The phrase "thou art God/Goddess"[8] is often used by Neo-Pagans. This is not to say that we are all deities in our own right (we find this a very egotistical concept). It means the Divine is in us just as it is in every aspect and part of creation. Everything we see around us is sacred and should therefore be treated as such. Thus, it is not surprising to find witches actively involved in protest and direct action to protect the environment.

These concepts within Paganism are very different from the teachings of monotheistic religions that base their belief structures on the idea of faith in a single invisible entity, which has created us separate from itself and has created the world for our personal use. A witch does not require this concept of faith (although they may have faith in an individual deity with whom they have connected). They just have to smell a flower, listen to the call of a bird, or watch the waves roll onto a beach to see the Divine and realize that they are an active part of what monotheism calls *God.* Although faith is not required, belief in the spiritual concept of immanence is. This is also more commonly referred to as pantheism. This is a particularly important concept when it comes to magical work, especially when it comes to working with the four elements and other areas of magical practice.

An example of this is when a witch calls a quarter to protect the circle that they are casting. In this act they call the spirit or "Lord" of the element. Here we see the concept of divine immanence practically applied in a magical rite.

Witchcraft and Our Relationship With Deity

So where does deity, the individual personalities which are the gods and goddesses, come in? Is deity part of witchcraft? Yes. From the historical evidence, there is plenty to prove that gods (and more importantly, goddesses) were central to witchcraft practice. Even the bard himself, William Shakespeare, refers to "pale faced Hekate" in reference to the "three weird sisters," the soothsaying witches who meet Macbeth on the road. He does not have the witches commanded by a Christian Satan, but by a classical Pagan goddess, in what can be see as an act of Drawing Down the Moon (see page 200).

One of the biggest problems that modern witches have had to face is the fact that there are few written records of what the actual philosophical beliefs of our ancestors were concerning divinity. We can surmise some ideas from the writings of the ancient Greeks. But the Christian monks who wrote down the mythologies of ancient peoples have influenced the histories of the Celts and the Norse. This can be seen in the major Norse-Icelandic work, the Poetic Edda, where Snorri Sturluson tried to align Odin with the Christian God. This is done by referring to Odin as "the All-Father." We have no real idea of how Odin was seen by his peoples and what their belief perceived him. Modern witches have had to draw on these works with their presupposition of the monotheistic and patriarchal Christian idea of God,[9] resulting in a concept of the Divine with strong Christian philosophical overtones. We can see this in the concept of duotheism: "All gods, one god; all goddesses, one goddess," which became a major doctrine of Wiccan thinking (see page 51).

Over the years, many witches have begun to question the ideas of what a god is. They have begun to look away from Cabala for what the true belief structure of Paganism really was, or for that matter, still is. We have come across many who have started to look into the contemporary Pagan religions of the present, including ourselves. Polytheistic belief systems can be found in Africa, India, and the Far East, which are untainted by monotheistic thought. During the 1990s, we began to look to these religions for understanding regarding the nature of the Divine. We are sure we are not the only ones. In Shinto, Hinduism, and the practices of the African Diaspora religions (Voudon, Santeria etc.) we can see ancient worship of deity both preserved and evolved just as we would have seen in Europe if Pagan practice had developed unhindered. The biggest problems many modern witches have when examining these contemporary religions is that the cultural symbolism is so alien to them. As evidence, it may be seen that many Western Pagans have great problems understanding the Voudon deities (loa) or those of Santeria (orishas), as they fit neither into their concept of a Spirit or that of a god. Yet the Voudon concept of deity is probably closer to our ancestors' idea of the way gods and goddesses worked than what was originally taught within Wicca. The major stumbling block in the development of Wiccan spirituality has been the monotheistic idea of *God* that most of us were brought up with in Western culture.

In Voudon, the practices of the African communities of the Caribbean, and the relationship between the follower and the deity is a very personal one. Trance and ecstatic vision are important parts of the practice, just as they would have been in ancient witchcraft. There are strong similarities between the practice of being possessed or *ridden* by a loa and the central witchcraft rite of Drawing Down the Moon, where the Priestess becomes the vessel through which a goddess communicates. The major difference is the nature of the ritual. The fact is, witchcraft has become less spontaneous and more *Apollonian* (logical and systemized) in its approach, whereas Voudon is more Shamanic, ecstatic, and *Dionysian*[10] (spontaneous and emotionally oriented). During a Voudon ceremony, anyone who is present has accepted that they may be *ridden* by a loa and become a vessel for that deity. Connection with the Divine in Voudon is therefore an integral part of the religion, enabling the practitioners to talk directly with their deity during the rite. It is the ultimate example of immanent divinity. The Voudon or Santeria belief in god-spirits would probably have been no different than ancient witchcraft belief, and certainly ancient witchcraft would have been more spontaneous and Dionysian in its approach. More importantly, it is an initiatory Mystery Tradition, like modern witchcraft, but unlike Wicca, the initiations are related to specific loa or orishas. A Voudon Priest (houngan) or Priestess (mambo) is therefore a servant of a specific deity.

Voudon also uses a system of offerings related to each loa, similar to the Western magical system of correspondences. Specific offerings are ritually made to the loa by their followers on particular days of the week. There are also specific taboos. Followers may not eat certain foods or have certain things in their homes that may offend the loa. Similar practices exist in Santeria, the kin path of Voudon, which evolved in Spanish America. In Santeria, followers place a clay or cement head to represent Eleggúa (Legba) with cowrie shells for features next to a door. They regularly "feed" him with toys, candy, and even cigars to bring good fortune to their home, as he is the Guardian of the crossroads, the gate Guardian to the other world. He is always the first to be recognized or worshipped in any ritual. In this respect, he has strong similarities with the Hindu Ganesha.

Most people would be quite shocked to know that the most worshipped male deity form in the world is none other than the elephant headed Hindu god Ganesha; the most worshipped deity overall is the Buddhist goddess Kwan Yin. For the Indian religion, Ganesha is "the foremost of the gods," the first to receive offerings, to ensure that the way is open for the devotees to send their messages to the gods of their choice. Unlike Voudon, Hinduism has been developing since pre-Christian times and gives us a strong idea of how Paganism would have developed in Europe had Christianity not put in an appearance. Within the religions of the Indian sub-continent, there are many similarities to Western and Northern European Paganism, due to the strong link with the ancient migration of the Indo-European peoples. As in Wicca, there are triple goddesses, and central mother goddesses, such as the Durga who also incorporates Kali, Lakshmi, and Sarasvati. There are two principle male deities, Shiva and Vishnu[11]. There is a plethora of lesser-known local and tribal deities, with many being incorporated into the main gods and goddesses of the religion. There are also fairy folk (devas) and spirits of nature, so the Divine is seen to be immanent in nature just as in Neo-Paganism. In many Hindu festivals, called Pajas, we see similarities with the established eight festivals of Wicca. Diwali, the festival of Lights, is a good example.[12]

Primary to Hinduism is the idea of the unknowable Divine, Brahma. Brahma is often portrayed as a wheel, as found on the Indian national flag. Brahma is not directly worshipped, but approached through the other gods and goddesses of the religion, a concept not alien to modern Pagan thought but only now developing. We would recommend every witch to go at least once in their life to a Hindu temple to understand the nature of this concept. It has to be experienced, as it cannot be put into words. When we have entered Hindu temples, we have always been warmly welcomed. The first things that strike you are the shrines and the statues to each individual and sometimes groups of gods and goddesses. Hinduism is idolatrous. It is believed that deity is present within the statues themselves. We have actually felt this when entering these temples. The power of the deity shines from them. The statues of the gods are regularly washed and dressed as part of the rites while being talked to as if they are alive because to the Priesthood, they are. An established Priesthood does exist within Hinduism, but it is not centralized like that of Christianities. These small Priesthoods often operate from one temple devoted specifically to one deity, but all the other major deities of the religion are present.

Could this be what the old Priesthoods of Europe and therefore witch-craft would have developed into? We believe so.

In Voudon and Hinduism we see the idea of immanence and the idea of absolute belief in the deities being worshipped. They are not seen as any form of psychological principal, as has occurred in recent years within Wicca, but as real personalities in their own right. In both these traditions the belief in deity is at the center of their practice, be it magical or religious. Only now are we seeing the return to true belief in the old gods of Europe within the modern witchcraft revival. So what is a god or a goddess? Carl Gustav Jung, the great psychologist, refers to them as Archetypes. But this is an intellectual approach, which needs to be balanced with spiritual experience.

Archetypes, the Goddess, and the Pagan Philosophy of Creation

The Archetypes are elements of the Collective Unconscious, what occultists call *the Astral Plane*. It is part of the psyche, which is universal to all periods and cultures; hence Mother Goddesses appear in every culture in the world. We inherit the Collective Unconscious from the human race as a whole, not through the filter of our parents or the culture we are brought up in. Right from the beginning of the modern revival of witchcraft, there was the idea of the Goddess taking precedence over the God in Wiccan thinking. One of the primary reasons for this was the rejection of the patriarchal values of monotheistic religion. Intrinsic to this was the idea of creation. Philosophically, the Goddess as the center of the universe is incompatible with the mechanistic creation of the universe by a male god who creates or molds the cosmos as a craftsman. In the Goddess-centred belief structure, that idea is replaced with the more natural idea of the Universe being given birth to by the Divine itself. That act is not dependent on the egocentric symbolism of human activity. More importantly, the natural world replaces man as the central focus of the theology. This takes away the emphasis on science for an explanation of the cosmos as a mechanism. It makes us consider the possibility that our planet as well as the Universe is actually alive, and it supports the idea of immanence. In many cultures this divine figure has become symbolised as the cow: There is Hathor of the Egyptians, Audhumla of the Norse creation myth, and Boann of the Irish Celts. In contemporary Hinduism, cows are sacred for this same reason. They are considered "The Mothers of the Universe."[13]

The symbols by which we become aware of the Archetypes may be culturally or individually conditioned to a certain extent, but the Archetypes themselves are not. They "continue eternal and always after the same manner." As Jung says, the term Archetype, "is not meant to denote an inherited idea, but rather an inherited mode of psychic functioning, corresponding to that inborn way according to which the chick merges from the egg; the bird builds its nest; a certain kind of wasp stings the ganglion of a caterpillar; and eels find their way to the Bahamas. In other words, it is a pattern of behavior. This aspect of the Archetype is the biological one—it is the concern of psychology. But the picture changes at once when looked at from the inside; that is, from the realm of the subjective psyche. Here the Archetype presents itself as numinous; that is, it appears as an experience of fundamental importance. Whenever it clothes itself with adequate symbols, which is not always the case, it takes hold of the individual in a startling way, creating a condition of being 'deeply moved.' It is for this reason that the Archetype is so important for the psychology of religion."

We believe Jung's concepts are intellectually correct and show a deep understanding of the subjective psyche. But from a spiritual and occult perspective, something else is also happening. Quite simply put, we cannot experience the Ultimate Divine. We would be like ants trying to understand a computer. The Divine is unfathomable and beyond our comprehension. This idea is common in ancient religions. In Judaism it is believed that "you could not look upon the face of God and live." Hinduism reflects this idea as Brahma. Many religions have attempted to focus worship directly on the Unknowable Divine, but most fail. Judaism, Christianity, Islam, and Buddhism have all attempted to encourage worship of this faceless Divine, only to have human nature put a face on it. A good example of this is in Christianity, where God was personified as Jesus and, by the time of the Renaissance, had developed the visual perception of God along the same lines as the classical Greek Zeus, as can be seen in the Sistine Chapel. Islam regards images of Allah as blasphemous, which has resulted in his personification through the use of Arabic script and cult-like devotion to his prophets. Each time this personification happens, it produces a deity as we understand it in witchcraft and the occult sciences. It is also one of the reasons why the concept of duotheism, which existed in early Wiccan practice, will ultimately fail to fulfill the needs of the new generation of witches. It makes the same mistake as monotheism: It tries to make a faceless God and Goddess.

It is human nature to anthropomorphize the world around us. As children, when we paint and draw, we put smiley faces on flowers, the sun, and the moon. As we grow up we give inanimate objects, such as cars, names, and personalities. This is the *inherited mode of psychic functioning* at its most basic level. What Jung doesn't cover is the result of this personification, the creation of super-charged thought forms that we call Gods and Goddesses, which have developed personalities as real as our own.

One big problem for modern Pagans is that the old Gods and Goddesses have been asleep. Devoid of worship and recognition for so long, they have become psychically dormant. In other religions, this is of course, not the case. Both in Hinduism and Voudon the deities are wide awake and kicking, so to speak. We have found almost direct evidence from working with the Hindu god Ganesha because he is so extensively worshipped around the world, and we know of practitioners of Santeria and Voudon who talk about similar experiences. This is because there is an unbroken level of devotion to them, which has kept them charged psychically over the years. It is not surprising that many Pagans become drawn to these religions. We see it is as the role of modern witches and Pagans to "wake the gods" just as Tim Robbins' character Eric did in the film *Eric the Viking*.[14]

The Gods and Goddesses Are Alive

The Unknowable Divine is the source of power for the numerous gods and goddesses that exist around the world. But it is humanity and its culture that gives them their personality and attributes. Stewart Farrar often quoted a well know Greek philosopher Xenophon[15] saying, "If I was a horse, my god would be a horse." Like us, they have developed personalities no different from our own. We mold the Divine Power like clay through worship and belief over periods of time, just as it takes each of us 20 years or more to finalize our personalities. They differ in that they have no bodies, and their Spirits remain directly connected to the Unknowable Divine. Gods and goddesses also have personas, but theirs may have taken much longer to develop than ours, and their connection with the Unknowable Divine is more direct.

From our personal experiences, we can say without doubt that the gods and goddesses of the ancient world are real. Like human personalities, they can have strange nuances and flaws. For this reason, the faces of

Divine should always be accepted as individuals. You must believe in them as persons in their own right if you are going to connect and work with them. It is not recommended that you work with them as Jungian concepts alone. It simply won't work. It is necessary to believe in them.

The principle deities of witchcraft have always been goddesses. Witchcraft has always been a feminine art, regardless of which sex practiced it. In European culture—Northern (Germanic), Western (Celtic), and Southern (Graeco-Roman)—our ancestors had deity forms that related to specific crafts. There were also therefore specific goddesses related to "the dark arts," the occult crafts of dealing with Spirits, for the purposes of healing or oracular work. Nearly all of these goddesses have associations with the cat, and the moon and water as common symbolism related to them. One of the reasons for this is that they all stem from the same Archetype and, in some cases, have the same historical roots. But even then you can see an initial separation between them into the young sexual sorceress, such as Freya and Diana, and the crone of magical wisdom, normally an Underworld goddess, such as Cerridwen or Hecate. This can also be seen in the White Isis and Black Isis used by the Egyptians. But this division quickly came to include the middle concept of the mother in modern Wiccan thinking. Regardless of the attempt to relegate her to a side role in Western religion, it was impossible to ignore her for both psychological and historical reasons.

It is impossible to remove the idea of the Mother from any goddess Archetype. She is simply too strong a force. Even the Church had to bow to the pressure of this Archetype in the human psyche and incorporate Mary as a major part of the Church's theology. Mary was a reflection of Isis/Artemis whose symbolism she incorporated. We are all born from mothers, so it is the first Archetype within our subconscious minds to surface after birth. It is therefore not surprising that this Archetype quickly bridged the gap between the psychological and the spiritual in human consciousness and culture.

The Triple Goddess is the most common deity form taught within Wicca. Always lunar, she represents the three stages of the moon. The waxing, full, and waning moon echo the three stages of womanhood: maiden, mother, and crone. The moon has always been associated with magic and witchcraft because of its psychological and psychic effect on the individual and because of its associations with the woman's menstrual cycle, which was considered by the ancients to have magical properties.

But the concept of the Triple Goddess in this form may be quite modern. When we look at more ancient forms, such as those found among the Greek and Norse, we find triple goddesses that all are bracketed into the same age groups, for example the three maidens of the Greek muses or Macbeth's crones surrounding a bubbling cauldron. The modern Wiccan concept of the Triple Goddess is probably a synthesis of three times three goddesses. The concept has nine specific Archetypes,[16] not necessarily associated with witchcraft or the magical arts themselves. In traditional occult correspondences, nine is associated with the planet and the goddess Venus. This synthesis from nine to three can be attributed to Robert Graves's work *The White Goddess,* a major source of inspiration for the early founders of Wiccan theology.

The God of witchcraft has always been problematic from a theological viewpoint. Basically, he is the Horned God of Nature, commonly known within the orthodox Wiccan traditions as Herne or Cernunnos. He is divided into two: the god of fertility and life and the god of death, the Underworld, and resurrection. He is an essential part of modern witchcraft belief as he plays an important part in the mysteries of Wicca. Unlike most of the goddesses, there is little history about him or his Archetype. The name *Cernunnos* was found on a stone in Notre Dame. It was a Latinized Gaelic inscription simply meaning "horned one." That is the actual historical limit of our knowledge of Cernunnos. Herne, whom he has come to be strongly associated with, is a different matter. He is of Anglo-Saxon origin, with a central myth related to the Tudor period and a woodsman of Great Windsor Forest named John Herne. This historically recorded figure was convicted of poaching the King's deer and hung on the Great Oak in the forest. Many of the attributes associated with him were adopted from myths of other gods. He is said to haunt the forest leading the Wild Hunt, also associated both with the Northern Odin and the Welsh Gwynn Ap Nudd—both Underworld deities. The perception of Herne by modern Paganism also has to do with a British television series from the 1980s, *Robin of Sherwood.*[17] Here we see both aspects of the horned god coming together. Like the Triple Goddess, the modern Wiccan movement has filled in the historical facts with archetypal understanding. Does this invalidate him or the triple goddess? We would say no, as what has occurred is the natural understanding of these deities by those who have connected with them on a psychic and spiritual level. At the end of the day, we believe you can learn more about the gods and goddesses from meeting and connecting with them than you ever can from reading about them in a book, and we believe this is what has occurred on a collective level with modern witchcraft.

Our experiences of meeting deities have been interesting. In many cases, we have found that they have updated their appearance. Janet once had a vivid dream that she was at the "club at the end of the universe." There was a host of many different gods and goddesses there, but they were not dressed traditionally. Frey, the Norse of god of abundance, peace, and prosperity was in an Armani suit with a wad of credit cards in his wallet. He was chatting up Aphrodite, who was standing at the bar in a "small black number" with high heels and bright red lipstick. Anubis was the bouncer on the door. No jackal-headed mask, but instead a black suit and tie and a Doberman by his side. Then there was poor old Yahweh in the corner. Everyone was ignoring him. He wasn't having a good time standing there, propping up the bar, dressed in a white night shirt. Why shouldn't the gods and goddesses change their appearance, particularly as many of them are traditionally shape shifters? Gavin has such an experience with one shape shifter after some magical work.

Gavin had been working with runes at the time. He had finished learning the Anglo-Saxon Futhark (33 rune system) and was creating his rune staff. He had done it traditionally with a process known as blatting where you paint the runes down the staff while doing the appropriate invocation. He was not doing this at home, but at a friend's house, where he had to leave the staff, as it was too big to carry on his motorcycle. A few days later, his friends telephoned him and sounded very upset. A figure had started to appear on the landing at the top of the stairs. They described him as wearing a long leather coat and a wide brimmed hat pulled down over his face, which they could not see. As they were also witches, they realized some sort of manifestation was occurring and that it was related to Gavin's staff. They wrapped the staff up, put a magical binding around it, and put it in the basement for Gavin to collect later.

So what had happened? Without realising it, Gavin had used a traditional invocation for the god Woden (Odin). He had come looking for the owner of the staff. But he had appeared in modern dress appropriate for his personality and magical nature. Woden is, of course, traditionally a shape shifter in Northern European myth. There is an important point here. Be aware that many magical invocations and charms are specifically aimed at manifesting deity, so you must research them fully before using them.

Endnotes

1. Joel S. Goldsmith lived from 1892 to 1964. He was a great mystical teacher, author, and healer. In 1947, he gained national recognition with the publication of his book, *The Infinite Way*. This book came about as a result of Joel's many years of study and meditation, his healing work, and the spiritual revelations that came to him during the course of his lifetime. He went on to write numerous books on mysticism and mystical living.
2. Ganesha (also spelled Ganesh) is the first god to be worshipped in the Hindu pantheon by decree of Shiva, as an act of recompense for the loss of his human head and its replacement with that of an elephant. He is the most worshipped god form in the world.
3. Asatru is the practice related to Odinism as "All-father." Freya and her brother Frey belong to an older group of gods and goddesses called the Vanir, who are agricultural and magical in nature.
4. The fairy or faery are a folk memory of the Tuatha De Danann, the older gods of Ireland who are similar to the aforementioned Vanir. In fact, there are strong similarities and evidence that, in many cases, they are the same gods and goddesses with different cultural overlays.
5. The name can be found with reference to Alexander in the Koran, the holy book of Islam.
6. Graves's *The White Goddess* was compulsory reading material for most witches, although very few ever managed to read it from cover to cover due Grave's style of writing.
7. This took place On Monday, August 5th, 2002 at the National Eisteddfod in Wales. According to the Welsh Gorsedd this was acceptable as "The Welsh Gorsedd of Bards, into which the Archbishop was initiated, is not now, and never has been, a Pagan institution. It was founded in 1792 by Iolo Morganwg, a stonemason, failed farmer and shipping magnate, revolutionary, sometime jailbird, laudanum addict, collector of medieval manuscripts, forger of same, poet and antiquarian. He was also a minister of the Christian Unitarian church and composer of a number of hymns still popular in Wales today."
8. A phrase most commonly used by the U.S.-based Church of All Worlds.
9. The doctrine of monotheism found in the Middle East is believed to have derived from the Akhanaten heresy of Egypt of the 18th Dynasty (1567-1320). The Priesthood of Amun-Ra crushed the heresy, but not before it had gained root in the foreign workers within the Northern Kingdom. Judaism and Islam are believed to have derived their doctrinal origins from these Semitic peoples who continued in their cult of the only god, the Aten.
10. The terms Apollonian and Dionysian derive from the philosopher Frederich Nietzsche and his work *The Birth of Tragedy*.
11. Which of the male gods takes precedence depends on the Hindu temple and the area of India it originates from. It should also be remembered that Krishna is an incarnation of Vishnu.
12. Diwali is the major festival of truth and light. It is celebrated on Amavasya—the 15th day of the dark fortnight of the Hindu month of Ashwin (Aasho) (October/November) every year.

13. This statement comes from Bhishma, in the Mahabharata, Anusasana Parva, Sections LXXXIII–LXXVII–LXXVI. In Vedic script there are seven mothers: the birth mother, the nurse, the wife of the father (if she is not the birth mother), the wife of the king, the wife of the spiritual master, the Earth, and the cow.

14. *Eric the Viking* was produced by Handmade Films in 1989. In the story Tim Robbins as Eric, a sensitive Norseman, goes in search of the Horn Resounding to wake the gods and end the bloody world of Ragnarok. The Gods turn out to be children, and clearly not in control of the fate of man.

15. An Athenian, the son of Gryllus, Xenophon was born about 444 B.C.E. In his early life he was a pupil of Socrates.

16. Cherry Gilchrist in *The Circle of Nine: The Feminine Psyche Revealed Through Nine Contemporary Archetypes* (see Bibliography), pages 4–13, points to this importance in mythology and its continued relevance today.

17. A highly successful series from Harlech TV. It prominently brought mysticism and magic into the Robin Hood legend. Herne was portrayed by John Alberini as a real man who played the part of a Shaman figure for the local village, Wickham. At different times, the series explored Cabala, Luciferian Satanism, witchcraft (positively), and Anglo-Saxon, Norse, and Celtic myth.

Chapter 5

The Progressive Coven: The Witch's "Family"

Call it a clan, call it a network, call it a tribe, call it a family. Whatever you call it, whoever you are, you need one.

—Jane Howard, *Families*[1]

The origins of the word *coven* do not seem to go any further back than the Middle Ages. It is doubtful that any form of village Priesthood would have even have used it. Etymologically, its origins are in the word *covenant*, which means "to make an agreement" or "to take an oath together." So a coven would consist of a group of witches who have taken an oath together, which relates directly to the oath taken on initiation. Traditionally, this is said to have been 13 witches or less. Any larger, and the intimacy required for magical working would be lost. Doreen Valiente in *An ABC of Witchcraft Past and Present*[2] also points out that there were also covens of eight[3] more experienced witches that came together for purely magical work. Nearly the majority of all covens nowadays are training covens, so we feel that the original meaning of the word *coven* related to oath-taking remains the most workable definition that you can come across, and is still appropriate to the way modern covens work, particularly those that fall under the category of *progressive witchcraft*.

The coven as the primary social unit for witches is important for another reason. In the last few decades of the 20th century, the extended family has almost completely broken down and been replaced with what sociologist refer to as the nuclear family. Before then, families consisted of several generations, including grandparents, and even aunts and uncles, not only in close contact, but also in many cases living in the same home together. They shared their wisdom and knowledge with the younger generation that grew up around them. From the 1970s onwards, the nuclear family developed, consisting of just parents and children living under the same roof. The wisdom of the older generation ceased to be passed down.[4] You may think this has little to do with witchcraft and the coven, but many who come into witchcraft are in fact looking for the extended family. The coven provides this, as the average coven consists of a mix of age groups.[5] Those interested in Wicca are often drawn to the closeness and intimacy within the coven, as well as the knowledge that it can provide on both the mundane and magical level. For some, the coven becomes a surrogate family with parental figures (the High Priestess and High Priest) and older brothers and sisters (the senior members of the coven). Some might query whether this is a valid way to view the coven, but it should be remembered that the original hereditary coven prior to the Middle Ages was an extended family in the true sense of the word. The coven has now really become a family affair. Members bring their children along to the more open festivals and coven members become adopted "aunts and uncles" to the children of the other witches. We have attended several such coven meetings both in Europe and the United States. This style of coven would have been unheard of during the time of Gerald Gardner and Alex Sanders.

Coven Structure

There are many different ways of running a coven, all of which can be successful. Janet and Stewart were taught in the more formalized Alexandrian tradition, which had a fixed method handed down during training. In this tradition, as well as the Gardnerian, it is a benign dictatorship in which the High Priestess of the coven rules jointly with the High Priest and traditionally always gets the last word. She is expected to follow the craft laws in her rulership. In the Alexandrian tradition there are 161 of these[6] (some have been added and removed by some covens) and in the Gardnerian tradition, there are approximately 50 laws.

In Seax-Wicca, Raymond Buckland created a democratic system. The High Priest and Priestess are elected yearly by the coven. Seax-Wicca covens still survive using the same system, proving that this system works. This was the system that Gavin was first introduced to. Buckland's reasons for introducing this system, from a letter he recently wrote to us on the subject:

> "One of the problems that led to the ego-trips in Gardnerian was the degree system. It had always worked fine in the past, due to the very slow growth, with accompanying careful selection of leaders. But with the then new desire to expand and embrace everyone, it inevitably led to poor quality leaders (not all of them, obviously. There were and still are some excellent ones.) Anyway, to counteract this possibility I gave Seax-Wica a more democratic form; no degrees, leaders chosen by the group, to lead for a year and a day."
>
> —Ray Buckland,
> 28th November 2002

Ray Buckland's points are quite valid. The degree system is not at the center of witchcraft practice, and there is no reason why a coven cannot run without it. The same applies with the idea of a democratic leadership, which is particularly effective in newly formed, self-initiate based groups, which the Seax-Wicca system appeals to.

Over the years, we have come across other ways of structuring a coven. There are no right or wrong ways, just different ways suitable for different situations. Many covens that are newly formed may experiment with several ways until they are happy with one that works for them. This is to be expected, particularly in a coven that is progressive in nature. We have done this ourselves: We have amended the way we work over the years so that our method of working is now very different from the way it was when we formed our first working magical group. Our experiences show that most good covens develop a family atmosphere regardless of how they work, and tend to develop their own unique ways of doing things over time.

We give here an outline of the most common systems we have come across in use. Many of these systems may fuse ideas from each other. We also try to show the basic underlying principles of each.

High Priestess-oriented

This is the system used in traditional Gardnerian and Alexandrian covens. It is based on the idea that the High Priestess acts as the voice for deity in circle, and therefore, the Goddess directs the coven's activities through her. This does, of course, require a trance component to ritual within the magical practices of the coven. The High Priestess must therefore be able to successfully channel the divine wishes of the Goddess rather than her own ego. She must also possess excellent leadership skills. This system only really works when there are differences in the levels of training and experience amongst the members; the most experienced individuals being the High Priestess and Priest. By nature, these are ideal training covens.

Elected Priesthood

The leaders of the coven are elected on a regular basis—monthly, annually, or whenever the coven decides. Seax-Wicca works on a yearly basis, and this seems to be the most effective timespan. This system works best when a group of witches is forming a coven for the first time as equals, regardless of whether they all have had experience or not. It is common to find such covens formed by those who have been witches for many years and want to come together in a group for magical work rather than for training. This is the system we recommend to those with little experience who are getting together with others to form a coven for the first time and wish to train together on an equal basis.

Democratic

All members of the coven have equal say in decisions made within the coven, either by vote or consensus of opinion. Compromises are made to accommodate everyone's view. In practice, we have found that it normally needs someone to act as a chairperson to make it work. You may get combinations of this kind of coven with the other ways of working, such as within a High Priestess-oriented coven where she refers decisions to those higher than second degree. It suits covens that are likely to be short term, such as for purely magical work within a time frame.

Rotational Priesthood

When the coven is formed, the existing members take turns to take on the roles of High Priestess and Priest of the coven over allotted periods of time (from circle to circle, month to month, or even year to year). If the period of time is short, decisions affecting the whole coven will need to be made on a democratic basis.

Constitutional Priesthood

The High Priest and Priestess rule with the consent of the coven. This is confirmed on a yearly basis, sometimes by symbolic ritual. This is very similar to the High Priestess-oriented coven. The major difference is that the Priestess and Priest refer decisions back to the whole coven on a regular basis on matters such as acceptance of new members. They both retain the right of veto on decisions if they feel it threatens the cohesion or security of the coven, but such vetoes are only used if it is really necessary, as the members of the coven might not reconfirm their position if the veto has been used unwisely. In our view, this coven structure has the best elements of all. We feel it is a truly progressive way of working, which retains flexibility while allowing the leaders of the coven to express their leadership skills.

This is, in fact, our current way of working. We introduced it for several reasons. The most important has to do with the group mind and the effect new members can have on it (see page 104). The sword as a magical tool has taken on a new significance for us as it now represents the sovereignty of the group (as opposed to being the coven leadership's symbol of power), and it belongs to the whole coven. We now have a ritual related to this concept that involves the whole coven handing power to us for a year and a day. This system is written into our coven's rules, which, in our group override the old craft laws that were received from our Alexandrian heritage. The coven rules form the basis for the coven and the level of power given to the Priesthood.

Laws and rules

The original Gardnerian laws were drafted by Gerald Gardner after Doreen Valiente and members of their coven at the time presented to him *The Provisional Rules of the Craft.*[7] These rules came about because Gardner had a habit of breaking his own oath of secrecy every time the press appeared on his doorstep! It was apparent to the coven members that a written set of rules was necessary to keep old Gerald under control. The history aside, it is our experience that any group of people working together for a period of time needs some set of rules. This is reflected in the rules you find in the workplace, and even the unwritten rules you find in the family home. The rules within witchcraft should be no different. Yet they need to be practical and appropriate to the present.

Over the years, we have found that the laws of the craft, as they were handed down to us, are unworkable anachronisms. Gerald Gardner created them as a direct response to Valiente's *Provisional Rules.* To give them weight, he attempted to make them look old rather than practical. Stewart, Janet's late husband and co-author, was particularly critical of them, as the language in them wasn't even consistent with old English, the pronunciation of which he was an expert on. Most working covens of Gardnerian or Alexandrian origin that we have talked to have had to create their own coven rules to supplement the craft laws they first received.

The first thing that any set of rules has to do is lay down how the coven system works. They must describe the degree system or system of levels (if there is one) and the individual rules of behavior for the individual members, such as the level of secrecy, preparation for circle, etc. Here is an example of a set of rules, which is loosely based on what we use today. Please note that we have included reference to the level system we have incorporated in this book (see page 116). This set of rules can easily be amended to suit any coven and the structures they use:

1. All members of the coven are governed by these rules regardless of initiatory status.

2. These rules may be changed only by a majority decision of the coven.

3. The Coven Priest and Priestess rule by consent of the coven. A yearly ritual will be performed to confirm that sovereignty is granted to them by the will of the coven.

4. The level system within the coven is that of the four elements: dedication—Path of Earth; first initiation—Path of Water; second initiation—Path of Fire; third initiation—Path of Air. The decision to initiate a member to a specific level is based on completion of work during a year and at the discretion of the Coven Priest and Priestess.

5. The basic ritual frame is the system of ritual that is laid down in the coven's *Book of Shadows.*

6. All members of the coven are oath-bound to maintain the anonymity of the other members of the coven.

7. All members of the coven are oath-bound not to reveal the secrets entrusted to them in circle, and not to reveal the activities of the coven.

8. All members of the coven are to attend circles "properly prepared." This means to be ready with appropriate robes and working tools as needed. They are also expected to maintain a high standard of personal cleanliness before circle.

9. Potential members must be introduced to the other members of the coven. A unanimous decision must be made if they are to be asked to join, and even after this, they must attend three circles before the Coven Priest and Priestess confirm this decision.

10. It is intended that the coven will hold 21 or more meetings in a year. These will consist of the eight Sabbats (festivals) and 13 Esbats (full moons). There may also be supplementary training Esbats, workshops, and seminars. All members are expected to try to attend. If they are unable, they must inform the coven.

11. All problems within the coven should be brought to the attention of the Coven Priest or Priestess or brought up at coven business. It should not be discussed inappropriately with other coven members outside of circle.

12. Coven business is carried out after the Blessing of the Cakes and Ale at the end of the ritual. Every member has the right to speak freely about anything related to the coven and its running. It is also a time when disputes, if present, should be settled between coven members, adjudicated by the Coven Priest or Priestess or someone appointed by the other members.

13. A member may leave at any time, but must give notice of their leaving and their reasons why in a letter to be read out at coven business. This allows appropriate action to be taken to remove any psychic link they have with the coven.

Roles within the coven

- **Coven Priestess and Priest:** Traditionally known as the High Priestess and High Priest. It is the Coven Priestess who, in matriarchal traditional witchcraft, is considered to be the head of the coven and the representative of the Goddess. Likewise, the Coven Priest is considered to be representative of the God. In most covens we have found, including our own, they tend to be an equal partnership. In the past, it was necessary to have the Priestess as the principle leader, as society was so male-oriented. This ensured that she received an equal say and that there was a true balance of male and female energy within the coven. They are the leaders of the coven, directing ritual, training, and enforcing the rules and the laws by which the coven runs. In ritual, the Priestess takes on another role, directing any psychic energy raised by the coven. In this respect, she is not unlike the conductor of an orchestra, allowing the orchestra (the coven) to concentrate on the music (the raising of energy).

  Good leadership skills are essential in this role. Good Coven Priestesses and Priests consider themselves servants of the coven rather than leaders. They tend not to rule so much as assist the coven in the direction its members want it to go in. Like all good leaders, they listen carefully to what the coven members want before making any unilateral decisions. A good sense of humor and humility are essential.

  Good High Priestesses or Priests look for the inherent skills in each member of the coven and encourage them in these directions. They give out unconditional love to its members equally, and act as mediators if problems occur between members. They are not judgmental regarding the individual members' personal or private lives, and do not interfere in them, although they are willing to give unbiased advice on such matters if it is requested.

  Like all good leaders, they stand by what they believe in, particularly when it comes to the ethical principles that they follow. But it must be remembered that, like all humans, they can make mistakes. They are well aware that they are not infallible; they are aware of the dangers of ego. They know when they have made a mistake and will admit openly when they have been wrong. They do not necessarily have to have a lot of knowledge, but they must have the willingness to learn and a good dose of common sense.

- **Assistants to the Priestess and Priest:** The female assistant to the Coven Priestess is traditionally known as the Maiden, whose role is to assist the Priestess during ritual. Her opposite is the Assistant Coven Priest. They act as support to the Priestess and Priest; they hold the circles when the Priest and Priestess are not present and assist in training. Traditionally, there is also a figure known as the Man in Black, or Coven Summoner. We have even heard the name "Black Rod" used. He is responsible for calling the coven together, hence the traditional name of Summoner used by some covens. Sometimes his role is combined with that of the Assistant Coven Priest. He may also move between covens, acting as a messenger between different groups, so he needs to be someone that people trust. He can be likened to being the coven's "intelligence officer."

Another role is the Scribe. His or her job is to take and keep notes on the ritual workings performed by the group. This can also include updating the *Book of Shadows* both in its hand-written and computerized forms. In today's modern world, the Scribe has to have computer skills to do this, as the days of keeping purely hand-written notes for the coven are now pretty much over.

These roles are given normally, but not necessarily, to those who have reached second degree (our Path of Fire) in covens with a system of degrees. In a new coven, it may be necessary for first-degree initiates to take on these roles. Second degree is normally a preparation for them to hive off and run their own coven in the future.

Types of meetings

- ✣ **Festival Circle:** These are the traditional Witches Sabbats held eight times a year, on the Celtic Fire festivals and the Solar festivals (Equinoxes and Solstices). These tend to be celebrations rather than working circles. The Wheel of the Year is a standard teaching in Wicca, particularly regarding what is referred to as *the power tides*, the ebb and flow of fertility energy during the year (see page 187). Any magical work carried out during a Sabbat will be related to this flow, particularly on the naturally occurring Solar festivals.

- ✣ **Moon Circle:** These are the traditional Esbats, held every full moon or as close as possible to it, although they may also be held on the new moon or waning moon. The moon is considered to have a psychic effect on the individual in occult teaching, and therefore its phases have particular magical influences.

❧ **Training Circle:** Most covens have additional meetings or Esbats for the purposes of training. They may be less formal than the other circles, with everyday clothing and possibly even no circle cast if there is purely going to be a teaching session. Most covens try to keep them within the moon cycle and try to avoid the dark of the moon.

The Coven Mind and Its Creation

Understanding that a coven is more than just a group of people worshipping together is vitally important if it is going to run successfully. The use of magic, psychic skills, and spiritual experiences within the coven develops a group mind; it becomes an entity in its own right, developing its own personality and ways of expressing itself. The words "perfect love and perfect trust," the passwords used at traditional Wiccan initiation, are the expression of the bonding of the individual into the coven. This has become an important ideal within modern witchcraft: that coven members have unconditional love for one another resulting from the formation of the Coven Mind. An understanding of some aspects of psychology, including Carl Gustav Jung's theories regarding the Collective Unconscious and Max Wertheimer's Gestalt Theory, are therefore essential.

According to Jung, we are all psychologically connected on a level known as the Collective Unconscious. In occult practice this is believed to directly interface with the different levels of reality that make up spiritual and magical cosmology, such as the elemental, Underworld, Astral Realm, and so on (see page 137). We are unaware of the Collective Unconscious in everyday waking consciousness, although we may enter it to a certain degree during dream or rapid eye movement (REM) sleep (see page 205). Those adept at visualization and trance techniques can also achieve this, hence their importance in magical practice. Many animals work on this level all the time, as evidenced in herd behavior and the collective instincts that some animals seem to manifest. In humans, it sometimes manifests as psychic experiences in which someone is aware of something traumatic happening to a loved one, or a feeling that something isn't right in the world when something disastrous has just happened, but such genuine experiences are uncommon. Therefore, every time a circle or a magical item is consecrated, an Astral double, a magical reflection (see page 169) is created on Jung's Collective Unconscious (see Figure 2 on page 103). A coven, therefore, works principally within this area of consciousness when it performs any form of magic.

The Coven Mind

Figure 2

Max Wertheimer explained Gestalt theory in the following way:

> "The fundamental 'formula' of Gestalt theory might be expressed in this way. There are wholes, the behaviour of which is not determined by that of their individual elements, but where the part-processes are themselves determined by the intrinsic nature of the whole."
>
> —Lecture for the Kant Society,
> Berlin, 7th December, 1924

This can be summed up quite simply as "the whole is more than the sum of its parts." Gestalt theorists use this process in education as well as in therapies for cognitive disorders. It is also applied to groups that develop their own identities within society.

When these two theories are applied to a group, such as a coven, it comes to light that any group working closely together on a Collective Unconscious, or astral level will develop its own personality separate from those of the individuals in it; it creates a permanent astral imprint similar to the consecration of a magical item. This of course, can have both positive and negative effects, which anyone running a coven should be aware of.

First of all, anyone joining a coven that has been running fora long time needs to be allowed to enter the Coven Mind slowly. If they enter it too fast, it can be like a body rejecting a transplanted organ. This is one of the many reasons why we have incorporated a Dedication ritual (Earth initiation) into our practice; it allows the newly accepted witch to enter the Gestalt mind of the coven slowly (see page 117). As most coven leaders know, the moment you form a coven successfully, you set up a flashing beacon on the astral level, so to speak, which will attract those who are suited to the coven. This is one of the reasons there is no need to actively recruit. Proselytising will very likely create members who do not naturally adjust to the Coven Mind.

One of the biggest dangers is the Gestalt being manipulated by those who run cults. Leaders of such religious groups manipulate the Gestalt created by the group of people they are trying to control so that they act as the group's nervous system. If this occurs within a coven, it will be noticeable that the leader not only becomes the dominant personality, but will also attempt to control its members. One may even try to prevent members from leaving or even try to interfere in their everyday lives. If the leader is successful, the members of such a group loose their personal identify outside of the coven. This is avoided by ensuring that everyone has equal rights within the coven's system of rules and laws, with adequate checks and balances to prevent this from happening. Hence, we have incorporated the idea of a constitutional Coven Priestess and Priest within our current coven rules and encourage individuals to follow their own spiritual paths. This is what separates Wicca from the many religious cults that are out there: free expression, creativity, and the encouragement of individual identity within the group mind.

The positive aspects more than compensate for the awareness needed to counter the negative ones. The first noticeable effect is from a magical perspective: The coven raises more energy than "the sum of its parts." A coven with a good group mind finds that they are strongly linked like a family, and have caring and loving feelings towards each other. Strong psychic connections naturally exist, and we have experienced psychic occurrences between members where they have known a member of the coven is in trouble. Magic in such an environment becomes natural, and it is common for spontaneously flowing rituals to occur without pre-planning, or any specific individual directing the group. It does, literally, take on a mind of its own and begin to run itself.

There are several ways we have learned to encourage the development of a Coven Mind, and most of these revolve around creating a specific identity. We have listed these below.

- **A name that identifies the coven's personality:** Just as a name comes to represent you to other people, a coven name does the same thing. We have come across several different types of names for coven: ones related to deities; totemic ones, using the names of animals or mythical beasts; ones related to myth; and ones related to places, such as sacred sites. Sometimes names can be a combination of all of these. Our current coven's name incorporates a goddess, a sacred site, and a myth, and for this reason, is quite powerful. Whatever name is chosen, it should reflect the aspirations, personality, and feel that the members want for the coven.

- **Coven deities:** When Gavin joined his first coven, there was nothing but arguments over the names for the deities for the coven. Everyone wanted his or her own deities, so in the end they just used Lord and Lady as titles and let the gods decide who was going to turn up! Within the more rigid traditions, these are fixed, such as Aradia and Cernunnos in the Gardnerian tradition, as well as hidden names. More progressive covens are likely to have a more flexible approach. We certainly see no point in having an Etruscan goddess, such as Aradia, for a coven in central Ireland. Whatever is decided, the deities chosen should be the coven's deities, not those of the individual members. They should, like the name, reflect the innate nature of the group. If the coven is oriented towards healing, it should be a healing deity; if a coven is naturally oriented towards environmental work, it should be a deity of nature, etc.

- **Symbols that are specific to the coven:** Symbols are powerful things, and there is nothing more effective in uniting a group of people than the use of a flag or emblem that represents the group identity. Symbols have always been used in Wicca in this way. They can be found on the handles of athames, on the pentacle, and on the wand. There is no reason why a coven cannot have its own separate symbols to represent itself, without excluding the more traditional symbols. We know members of one tradition that actually have a tattoo put on their wrist after initiation as a memory of the witches' mark of the Middle Ages. Some may consider this extreme, but they are certainly not alone in this level of committed practice.

- **Magical items given at initiation:** The first item we give to our initiates at dedication is a platted cord of three colors. It has actually replaced the measure during the taking of the coven oath (see "Secrecy and the Measure" on page 107). These colors were chosen carefully, as they are connected to the deity and name of our coven. Every time members of our coven put on their cords, they are reaffirming the coven's collective mind; every time they take them off, they are disconnecting from it on a lower level. We must point out that these are not the traditional cords given at first degree. They do not make someone a witch, but a coven member. Within the mainstream forms of Wicca, it was traditional to give a chalice and the magical cords at first-degree initiation;[8] we still do this as well as giving other items related to the system of levels or degrees that we work. These are unique to our current coven. There are other items that can be given; for example, jewelery or combinations of jewelery that identify the coven members in a subtle way. Some covens also have embroidered patches made up for robes and cloaks.

- **Robes and cloaks:** Some covens insist on specific colors for their initiates. This is not uncommon, and some go as far as to have both robes and cloaks made especially for them. White and black are the most common colors used, and most common after those are greens, browns, and natural colors. The use of robes in one color actually performs the same role as going skyclad. They merge the initiate into the group identity by removing clothes, which are expressions of individual identity. Our preference is for our coven members to choose robes for themselves, so they maintain their own individuality rather than being uniformed.

- **Creation of the coven's own rituals:** The use of unique rituals that belong only to that coven are incredibly strong for creating a Coven Mind, particularly if they are created by the whole coven rather than passed down from a previous one. This allows the magical creativity of the coven to flow rather than be stifled by dogma. By doing so, the coven also creates its own non-dogmatic *Book of Shadows*. In our current BOS we have no written rituals as such, but only directions on how to perform them.

- **Use of energy work:** Using energy, or *prana* (to use the Hindu term), is essential for the creation of a Coven Mind. Yet we have found so few covens that consciously work with energy. Moving energy around the circle in visualizations helps to build the Gestalt on an astral level, just as ritual does. Understanding the chakra system and the levels of the aura is therefore essential learning for anyone involved in running a coven, as well as the individual members of the coven (see page 155). Therefore, we now use chakras as the basis for our magical teaching.

- **Secrecy and the measure:** We have put these together as they are both connected and represent the old method of creating a Coven Mind (we have already discussed the pros and cons related to secrecy in Chapter 2). There are advantages to a newly formed coven keeping its existence secret for a period of time after formation, as it helps to form the start of the Coven Mind. Normally, a year is adequate. Secrecy prevents energy from being dissipated psychically by people talking about its existence. The measure was traditionally taken at initiation in the Gardnerian and Alexandrian traditions of Wicca. It was originally a method for maintaining the secrecy of the coven's existence and preventing the coven oath from being broken. At initiation, the witch was measured with a piece of string from feet to crown and cut to that length. It was then measured around the forehead, the heart, and the hips, and marked off with a knot each time. A threat was then made that if the secrets were revealed they would be "damned to hell of the Christians," and the measure would be thrown into a bog or marsh so that the perpetrator themselves would rot. To this day, many covens keep the measure, but we quickly changed this, and as an act of love and trust ritually returned it to our initiates. Today, we have done away with it completely, feeling it is an anachronism. In fact, we have discovered enough evidence that indicates that its origins were with a Middle Eastern system of divination rather than with genuine witchcraft (see page 40). We have replaced it with the coven cord and Dedication ritual, which involves the taking of the oath.

A specific problem may occur when a member leaves. It can leave a gaping hole in the group mind, which needs to be filled to prevent problems. By nature this gap is a vacuum, which could easily fill with paranoia, mistrust, and even hate towards the person, particularly if they left on bad terms. Ideally, a leaving ritual should be performed with the person present, but this may not be possible if there is acrimony involved. The members of the coven should be encouraged to express their feelings about the situation. Afterwards, they should aim towards a resolution and wish the person leaving well on their new path. This reveals another reason why we have coven cords given at Dedication: These have to be returned to break the psychic bond between the coven and the person leaving.

Grounding your coven

This is an aspect of covencraft that we have rarely come across in published books. Grounding the coven is the process of linking the coven to the area it works in. It is no different to the grounding process an individual goes through when they work magically (see page 173). With a coven, though, this is more complex, as we are talking about a Gestalt entity. The grounding process is ongoing. It is necessary, as it prevents the coven from becoming spiritually and psychically unbalanced. The rule "As above, so below" applies as much to a coven as it does to an individual. An ungrounded coven is likely to be overly concerned with psychic matters, while ignoring everyday concerns.

In Ireland, grounding a coven is a very simple thing to do, as there are plenty of ancient sites for a coven to link to. Our current coven is linked to a series of megalithic tombs not far from our home, as well as a set of holy wells of ancient origin. This is common practice among the few covens there are in Ireland, and this is also common practice if you live in England or in Europe, as there are plenty of such sites. Of course, if you live elsewhere, this may not be so easy, particularly in parts of the United States, or if you are "town bound" so to speak. We do know of covens in the United States that link to local sites, sometimes of Native American origin, and they do so with great reverence and respect.[9] But there is no reason why you can't create your own sacred site. To a witch, the whole Earth is sacred, not just a series of sites that emanate power.

Sacred sites actually come about because of long periods of continual worship at them, so any outdoor site where rituals take place over a period of time become powerful due to the magical residue and astral imprint that is left there. After a while, such places are even detectable by dowsing; the only difference between them and the ancient megalithic sites is that they are just a bit more modern. This is particularly useful to know if you live in a town. We have heard of such a site developing within Central Park in New York City.

There are several methods to link a coven to a specific physical place. The first obvious one is regular ritual at the site. This is fine in secluded places, but not always possible in the middle of town. The next way is to leave a physical link. We have done this in Ireland by leaving ribbons tied to nearby trees; this is a common folk practice in Ireland. A physical link is very effective. We know some people who buy two identical crystals, burying one at one site and keeping the other at their altar. But you should be aware that by doing this, you are likely to pick up on any activity at the place, so you should be quite knowledgeable about activities that go on there. You can, of course, use this to your advantage. One of our local sites is used by the Catholic Church, who unknowingly donates prayer energy to us on a regular basis. We don't feel there is anything unethical in using this energy for the purposes of healing; otherwise it would just be going to waste, and that would be a sin from a Pagan viewpoint.

Endnotes

1. Jane Temple Howard (1935–1996), journalist and author, was born in Springfield, Illinois, U.S.A. Howard's first book, *Please Touch A Guided Tour of the Human Potential Movement* was published in 1970. *A Different Woman* appeared in 1973, *Families* in 1978, and the biography *Margaret Mead: A Life* in 1989.
2. Pages 69–73 (*see* Bibliography).
3. Reference to this can be found in Doreen Valiente's *ABC of Witchcraft,* page 69 (*see* Bibliography).
4. This is basic sociological theory, which also recognizes that alternatives (for example, the coven) will form to replace the extended family. From *Sociology: Themes And Perspectives,* pages 344–346, and 400–401 (*see* Bibliography).
5. During our time as coven leaders our age range of members has been from 18 to 74.
6. These can be found in their most complete form in June Johns' *King of the Witches: The World of Alex Sanders,* in 1969, pages 130–14, and they were published again two years later in Lady Sheba's *Book of Shadows* (*see* Bibliography).
7. These rules can be found in *Crafting the Art of Magic, Book I: A History of Modern Witchcraft, 1939–1964* by Aidan Kelly on pages 103–105 (*see* Bibliography). According to Kelly, this story originates from Fred Lamond who claimed it was Doreen Valiente's High Priest who drew the rules up.
8. Gavin was taught that these were a red, white, and blue set of cords, known as the "Cabletow," "Warwick," and "Warlock," respectively.
9. We'd like to point out the incredible importance of gaining permission from the local magical tradition when using such sites, as well as the importance of using rites appropriate to that tradition.

Chapter 6

Making the Witch:
Training Within Witchcraft

You can tell whether a man is clever by his answers. You tell whether a man is wise by his questions.

—Mahfouz Naguib[1]

So what was the traditional form of training that the village witch of the Middle Ages would have received? It was in fact what we shall call *generational training*. Children would have been taught the family trade from an early age. Their mothers would have taken them into the fields to collect herbs, and then they would have assisted in making the healing potions and balms. For the community rituals, all the family would have assisted, and the younger members of the family would have prepared the ritual space, decorating it, setting up the altar as they been taught, and so on. They would have then watched their parents at work, later asking questions and receiving answers. Most training would have been one on one—the origins of the sorcerer's apprentice image so loved by fantasy movies. There would have been no large group of people sitting down, learning by rote, researching, or reading—there were no books, and no one could read for that matter. These methods of training are very much a modern creation. This system was slow, but it worked, quite simply because the length of training was from birth to death. By the time a child reached his or her teenage years, the breadth of that child's knowledge would have been quite astounding, particularly as there were no other forms of education available. But times have changed, and now most witches start learning from the age when most traditional village witches from the past would have already been working with their parents in ritual for at least five years.

There is in fact an ethical imperative at work to take training seriously within Wicca. Not to train or gain knowledge is to break the Wiccan Rede itself, the very core ethic of Wicca. Similar ethics can be found in modern medical professions where there is an obligation for doctors and nurses to continually educate themselves in the latest healing techniques. You may wonder what this has to do with Wicca, but it should be remembered that the origins of modern witchcraft are in the village healers and Shamans of the past.

In Gardnerian/Alexandrian Wicca, training was not aimed at solitary witches or self-initiates. You had to join a coven or formal group of some sort to receive instruction. When both Janet and Gavin first came into Wicca, one was not expected to learn anything prior to initiation. In fact, you couldn't be taught anything by the coven until you were actually initiated, due to the oath that none of the "secrets of the craft" could be passed on until the person receiving them was "properly prepared" by being initiated in circle. The result was that there were a lot of initiated first-degree witches who knew next to nothing. There were a few books around, so it wasn't unusual for the initiate to have read only one book prior to being brought into the craft. This was, to say the least, a rather unsatisfactory situation, which continued in some covens right up until the 1980s.

There was in fact no system of training within witchcraft up until then. It was a conversation with Doreen Valiente that made us realize this. Gavin asked her what she thought about covens setting essays for their student initiates. She was visibly shocked by the idea and said, "In my day, it was on-the-job training!" She meant that once you were initiated, you were left to learn by watching the coven at work. There was no formal system of teaching sessions, and any one-on-one training would have been an informal affair. The only thing the new initiate was expected to do was faithfully copy out the *Book of Shadows*, spelling mistakes and all! Initiates were left to teach themselves. They were generally guided in what to read and left to watch what happened in ritual. In the 1970s, this changed.

Alex Sanders heavily influenced the incorporation of ceremonial ritual magic and Cabalistic teachings into Wicca in the United Kingdom. There had been influences prior to this, but not to the same degree of intensity. He changed Wicca from being Low Church Folk Magic to High Church Ceremonial Magic oriented. It was, again, one book that seemed to be the major influence on him to cause this change: W.E. Butler's *The Magician: His Training and Work*. Part Two of this work looks at the information that was conveyed to the postulant during training. Janet's late husband, Stewart, was quick to notice this influence in the notes he and Janet took from Alex while training with him. He went about researching and listing Alex's sources in a work Stewart labeled *Wicca Transcriptions*. Stewart noticed that Alex also scavenged information from several other works, passing them off as his own teachings, including Franz Bardon's *Initiation Into Hermetics*. But to be fair, much of it derived from his own philosophy and beliefs. Alex created several training books of out this information, including *The Book of Planets,* which remains unpublished and only passed on to recognized initiates of the Alexandrian tradition. He added and changed the information over periods of time, so there are several different versions of each book in circulation.

Of course, what Alex was doing was turning the traditional coven structure into a magical lodge. By doing so, he put the emphasis on ritual magic as the main magical practice within Wicca. His way of teaching was to sit his pupils down and to dictate to them, as a schoolmaster does to a group of 12-year-olds. On some occasions, he even went so far as to make student witches write out lines because they had misbehaved! His usual method of teaching consisted of demonstrations instead of practical workshops or one-on-one instruction. Janet recounts one demonstration that consisted of Alex running round in a loincloth with a feathered headdress, summoning an Aztec Spirit. At the climax of this bizarre ritual, Alex put a hot poker in his mouth.[2] After Janet and Stewart left to form their own coven, Alex's system of training continued to develop. Meanwhile, in the United States, things were progressing somewhat quicker than in the United Kingdom.

In the United States, The Pagan Way had been formed and was beginning to put forward a viable system of training accessible to all. According to Ed Fitch, *The Pagan Way*:

> "...came out of a general round-robin correspondence in 1969-70 which involved Joe Wilson, Tony Kelly, John Score, and several others in the U.K., plus John Hansen,

Fred and Martha Adler, and myself in the US. There was also some consulting with the late Susan Roberts, who had just written *Witches, USA*."

—From correspondence with authors,
September 2003

Ed Fitch, a practicing Gardnerian High Priest, although he has also written books on Asatru, was responsible for the creation of the group ritual and teaching structure of The Pagan Way, which was later published anonymously as *A Book of Pagan Rituals* (published by Herman Slater, Llewellyn Publications, and later by Samuel Weiser). The original idea was that it should be published anonymously because it was felt that such material needed to be freely available to the public. The original cooperative of writers, including Ed Fitch, never actually made a penny from it.

He later went on to publish the book *Magical Rites from the Crystal Well* in 1984. This was in fact a compilation of material published in *The Pagan Way* magazine, *Rites from the Cyrstal Well*, which he had been involved in publishing with John Hansen.[3] This material confirms that there was a system at work, although the introduction claims there was no consistent method. The second section of the first chapter, "Forming a Pagan Training Group," goes through eight ways to form a magical training group, suggesting ESP exercises, research and reading assignments, and meditative exercises.

Training and Level Systems

Witches' training goes through several specific phases, from accumulation of knowledge and skills to their final implementation in a practical environment. In our current way of training, we try to break these phases up by the elements and the system of degrees. We have found that a system of levels is necessary, for over a period of time, a training coven will have individuals with different levels of knowledge and skills. This can be a problem as you may find yourself repeating the learning process with the same students time and again as new members join. Of course, repetition itself is part of the learning process, but students who have been through the same seminar for the third time running are likely to get bored, and their time would be better spent learning something else. A system of levels (degrees or otherwise) helps to split the coven into useful levels of ability and avoids this problem as you can have separate training sessions with each level.

Some have rejected the degree system on the grounds that it is too hierarchical (see page 50). We rejected it for a short period for this reason but found it necessary to reinstate it. It made us examine the reasons why people found security in it, particularly in a training environment. We believe that degrees are not supposed to be a reflection of status, but of the individual's ability. We discovered that levels of attainment exist in all successful educational systems. The eminent psychologist Abraham Maslow in his *Hierarchy of Needs*[4] summarized the reason for this in his positive theory of human motivations. This was a theory Gavin had been taught while training as a nurse, and although he had always been a critic of the degree system in Wicca, he realized the necessity for a system of levels.

Maslow's theory is often portrayed as a triangular diagram divided horizontally into five levels (see Figure 3 on page 116). He described a hierarchy of needs as follows, from the bottom of the diagram to the top:

- **Physiological:** air, food, water, warmth, and rest.

- **Safety:** security, stability, protection, and order.

- **Love and Belonging:** affection and friendship.

- **Esteem:** recognition, dignity, and worth.

- **Self-Actualization:** the development and fulfilment of potential.

The final two are important here, as they motivate individuals to achieve. Maslow believed that if people did not have goals, then they would create them to assist in their motivation. This answered our question of why it was so hard to reject the degree system. In its purest form, it is no more than a system of attainable levels for the student to work toward. Degrees may actually mean nothing (as we shall show), but as most occultists know, it is the quest that gives meaning to the Grail, not the other way around. The quest is therefore more important than the actual Grail itself, which is nothing more than a symbol.[5] It is for this reason that initiations become triggers for spiritual change in the seeker in Wiccan and other occult practices. It is also important to point out that the serious quest for spiritual experience can only really take place when self-actualization has occurred—when the seeker has achieved the first four needs to some extent and has grounded him or herself in the process. Here we see the importance of the coven in this process, particularly in giving the seeker the sense of love, belonging, and esteem noted by Maslow.

Maslow's Triangle

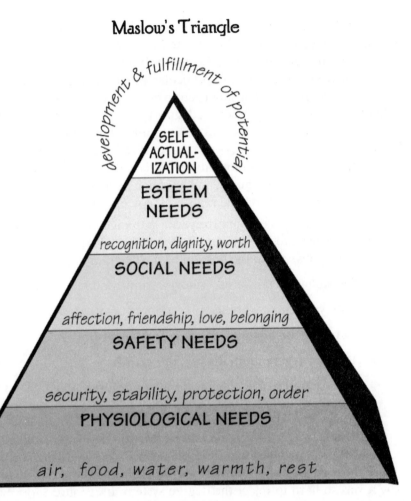

The Elemental System

We have related our current system into the four Elements: Earth, Water, Fire, and Air. These are the four basic correspondences that most witches learn early on in their training. Gavin belonged to a clan that did similar work, and we are sure there are others who have done likewise as it is such an obvious way of doing things from an occult perspective. They are often referred to as the Platonic Elements, from the philosopher Plato, but it was one of his contemporaries, Empedocles, who theorized that they were the building blocks of creation.[6] The accepted symbol of witchcraft—the pentagram worn around the necks of many witches—is representative of Spirit in control of the four elements. It is also safe to say that most witches, being polytheistic and believing in many truths, also believe that Spirit is attained by the fusion of the four to create ether, as represented by the Celtic cross.

It is within the elements that the witch can find keys to understanding the Mystery Tradition within Wiccan practice. This is organized by the use of the degree system into a system of goals to aim towards. There are four passage rites related directly to the elements:

- **Dedication:** The initiation and commencement of the Path of Earth.

- **The first degree:** The initiation and commencement of the Path of Water.

- **The second degree:** The initiation and commencement of the Path of Fire.

- **The third degree:** The initiation and commencement of the Path of Air.

Our use of an extra initiation, the Dedication, came about for several reasons. First of all, there was an inherent problem in the old system of secrecy. When Janet and Stewart came into the craft, they were not allowed to learn anything until they were initiated because of the oath that witches took at that time. This was very unsatisfactory, as it meant that you had a lot of initiated witches with very little knowledge. Many left covens because they didn't know what they were getting involved in nor the nature of the coven until after they had been initiated into it. This was not necessarily a fault with either side, but due to the fact, there was no waiting period in operation where the coven members and the potential new initiate could get to know each other. We therefore introduced the Dedication ritual to try to remedy this situation. Again, this is not new and has become common amongst many covens for reasons similar to ours. Another reason is that, unlike in the past, there is now a wealth of information available for the student witch. Most pre-initiates who approach a coven for initiation and solitary witches already know so much about Wicca that it is necessary to have some sort of buffer to discover the knowledge an individual has before serious training can commence, while still allowing them a sense of belonging to a working group. After Dedication, the potential initiate tends to show their real personality, which helps the members decide if the individual is suitable for joining a coven that has already formed a Coven Mind.

- **Path of Earth:** This commences after Dedication. The Element of Earth is one of stability and foundation. It is the first element that needs to be addressed by anyone commencing training as a witch. It lays the foundation of values that they will need as a witch and a Priest or Priestess. Training during this stage is therefore initially centered on basic knowledge: The Rede, the ethical code of witchcraft; history of witchcraft, ancient and modern; the structure of Wicca and what a coven actually is; the nature of Deity; the Wheel of the Year; and basic magical principles and laws. Practical knowledge is also important and relates to the techniques that they need for the learning process after their next initiation (such as visualization and meditative techniques).

- **Path of Water:** This commences after first-degree initiation. This element relates to emotion, connection, and flow. This path starts with the traditional first-degree initiation found in both Gardnerian and Alexandrian traditions. This is where the real training starts as far as we are concerned because Water is the first element of the mystery of connection with Spirit. It is during this time that the initiate is encouraged to find their god or goddess. Water is also the element of connection with the Arwen, or Anima/Animus, to use the Jungian term. This is an experiential process, not an intellectual one. We actually encourage our students to build a shrine and altar if they believe they have found the deity that they can relate to. At this stage, the initiate also starts to learn the more practical side of witchcraft: circle casting, working with energy, and commencement of psychic and astral training.

- **Path of Fire:** Commencing after second-degree initiation. We were taught that the old second-degree ritual was about facing your fears and understanding where they came from. Fire is about the use of will to do this, as the will is governed by the Element of Fire. The witch on this path faces his or her own "inner demons." He or she learns, in terms of Jungian psychology, to recognize and to come to terms with his or her own primal nature: the Id, the Shadow, and Ego. This can be a difficult process for them, for it is as much about personal growth as spiritual. The traditional symbol of second degree was the reversed pentagram; it represents the horned god of nature, the god who not only rules our own natural instincts, but also of course the psychopompous, the Guide to the Mysteries.

- **Path of Air:** Commencing after third-degree initiation. The Element of Air relates to wisdom and knowledge. Traditionally in Wicca, the initiation of third degree is marked with the symbol of the pentagram surmounted by the triangle, point upright. This is, of course, the symbol of Fire, and is used to mark the completion of that path. There is no training for Air. The reason is that by the time witches meet this stage, they should be, to quote Maslow, self-actualising; they should be able to guide themselves or seek guidance from the higher forces. It does not mean that they have finished learning even though they have finished training. Life is a learning process; even after death this continues as you go through life after life. This is why the idea of reincarnation is an important part of Wiccan thought. Janet always makes the statement, "If I say I know everything, kick me! I'm still learning and the more I learn the more I realize how little that I know."

One thing you will notice is that within the paths, the other Elements seem to exist within one another: Knowledge is governed by air, but can be found in the Path of Earth. This is intentional, as all the elements exist within one another. You will see this pattern again and again in any magical working you do. It is reflected in the use of the Pentagram rituals of ceremonial magic where, on appropriate occasions, the ceremonial magician will invoke one Element through all the others at each quarter to bring that pure Element into the circle.

This system is the way we work. There are other systems of levels that are just as valid. We are not the first to come to this conclusion. As early as the late 1960s, a coven in New York was putting its initiates through the three-degree system twice, creating a six level system, and Alex Sanders in the early 1980s had instituted two more degrees, initiating witches up to fifth degree. There is no reason why witches should dogmatically follow the old three-degree system. Systems of levels could be related to the chakras in a seven-degree system, or the four Elements and Spirit creating a five-degree system, and so on. It is more important that any system of levels has a magical basis rooted in common sense principles to make it viable, which includes the passage through the Mysteries as an intrinsic part of its ethos.

In both Gardnerian and Alexandrian traditions, there was a general rule of "a year and a day" between initiations, although there was originally no time frame prior to first degree. Janet was initiated by Alex Sanders within weeks of meeting him. Now most sensible coven leaders have implemented some sort of rule regarding this, just as we have. The time frame for initiations was based on the premise that first degree made you a witch, second degree made you capable of running rituals and a coven under supervision, and third degree made you a High Priest or Priestess in your own right, capable of running a coven, initiating new witches, and all the rest. The normal practice was for third degrees to hive off after receiving this initiation. In theory, you were initiated into the third degree within three years. Anyone looking for a coven is going to find different rules regarding this. Some may still use the old time frame, others may have a flexible system, and others may have none at all.

There are several problems with implementing fixed time periods within training, of course. People tend to learn at different rates, as well as the fact that you are trying to judge a spiritual change within that time period. We have the rule that we should know someone personally for at least a year before dedicating him or her. Because of this we were once accused of "only initiating friends." We consider this a compliment rather than a criticism. It must mean that we initiate in "perfect love and perfect trust," which must surely define the existence of a friendship.

In the Elemental system we use, before Dedication (Path of Earth) we must personally know someone for a year, and in that time they must show a certain amount of knowledge about Wicca. If someone comes to us knowing nothing, we send him or her away to do some reading. In the past, there was little reading material available, so it was not unusual for people to be initiated with very little knowledge of what they were getting into. Today, this is not the case. We feel that anyone seriously interested in becoming a witch would have already read through several books before coming to us. First degree (Path of Water) is given after a "year and a day," or more if the individual hasn't covered the necessary knowledge for that path. The same applies to the next two initiations. We try to base our decision about when to initiate someone on his or her personal spiritual growth as well as his or her intellectual learning or practical ability. We believe all the elements must be appropriately in balance for that person.

One problem for anyone running a coven is what to do when someone originally initiated by another coven asks to join yours. We are quite happy to accept anyone previously initiated by another coven, as long as they have left the previous group and they understand that they may have to start again from the beginning. This may seem quite harsh, but within Wicca, there are no fixed levels of training or rules on initiation. Each coven sets its own guidelines. The traditions within Wicca pass down rules regarding training, but you cannot guarantee that these will be followed by covens that have descended from them. There are some organizations that have tried to solve this problem, such as The Covenant of the Goddess[7] and The Aquarian Tabernacle Church.[8] They have strict guidelines for their associate covens, which needed to be implemented if they are to remain members of their organizations, but generally, these are related more to ethics rather than training.

Training Methods

Here we have tried to list the different types of training methods that can be used by covens, other magical training groups, and solitaries. Most of these are tried and tested techniques used not just within the occult community, but also in educational establishments. Anyone who comes to us for training must show a commitment to learning. We do not wish to waste our time assisting someone who is not self-motivated. We feel it is important to create individuality in our students, particularly with regard to their individual gifts. We feel it is important for witches to be "masters of one" rather than "Jacks of all trades" so to speak, with a thorough grounding in Wicca but specializing in a particular occult area, be it spiritual healing, counseling and divination, and so on.

We strongly believe that we all teach ourselves, so we tend to act more as mentors in the way we train people, being supportive and giving individual tutelage when necessary. It is important to remember that not all methods of learning suit everyone. This is reflected in the methods we have listed below.

- The *Book of Shadows*: "Now copy out the *Book of Shadows*" was the first thing said to initiates after they were initiated into a coven and is the earliest known form of training known in modern witchcraft. It was traditional to write it out "in your own hand," but times have changed and the initiate is just as likely to receive it on a CD or a floppy disk, or even download it from the Internet. They will still, of course, have to copy it out. In our collection, we have more than a dozen different books and their variations. Once kept highly secret, they are now regularly published in books—some traditional, some freshly created. The *Book of Shadows* should not be regarded as the equivalent of the Christian Bible, but should be seen instead as an expanding magical diary being handed down from generation to generation, each adding their own material. We still make our students copy them, but we also get them to compare the different ones we have. They are encouraged to add their own material as they learn as part of the process.

- **Reading assignments:** This is the standard, basic method that has always been used since Gerald Gardner's first coven, although it wasn't so formalized as it is today. There is nothing wrong with learning from books as long as you realize the basic rules. One is that they aren't always correct in what they're saying. Another rule is that you can't learn everything from a book. We once came across someone who actually believed they had the right to be initiated third degree because they had read through our book, *A Witches Bible*. Books are objective ideas written by subjective people, and this should always be remembered. We actively encourage our students to question what they read, particularly as there are now so many books on witchcraft with few original ideas or that go to the original academic first sources for material. Reading assignments free up valuable time that can be used by the Wiccan teacher to show practical techniques, and also continue the learning process outside of the coven environment.

- **Research:** We feel this is one of the most useful tools at hand for the education of a would-be witch. This can include books, magazines, and Websites. Research has several advantages over just a reading assignment: It encourages students to use their own initiative, to think for themselves, and to develop their own ideas. One other result is that research sometimes unearths information we do not know ourselves. For this reason, we get students to feed what they have learned back to the whole group, so the other members learn from it as well.

- **Setting essays:** This is closely linked to the idea of research, but the person produces a paper on a given subject. One advantage is that the resultant essay can be used as part of the individual's *Book of Shadows*. The disadvantage is that the information in the essay is not really shared with the rest of the coven. We have used it in the past to assess those who have asked to be trained with us prior to or even during the Path of Earth.

- **Group demonstrations:** This is pretty much self-explanatory. Almost all the circles we have done with our covens have included demonstrations. It is, as Doreen Valiente described it, "on the job training." We also give more specific demonstrations on how techniques work, such as talking the coven through Pentagram ritual, Casting Circle, creation of thought forms, and so on. In group demonstrations, unlike one-on-one training, there is no participatory involvement for the student, so it is more suited to those who have just joined a training coven.

- 🕯 **Group practical training:** This is similar to group demonstrations but with involvement of the coven. We use this with magical techniques such as Pentragram rituals, meditation and chakra techniques, etc., where it's possible for our students to copy our actions while we talk through what is happening with energy, visualization, and all the rest. We prefer it to group demonstrations as the students get a feel for what they are doing. We use this whenever possible.

- 🕯 **One-on-one practical training:** This is the most effective method when it comes to magical technique. The drawback, of course, is that it takes time. We tend to use it when we are training someone to perform rituals. Each meeting, we choose the couple or individual who will do the next Esbat or Sabbat. We then talk them through the technique.

This actually helps to build the students' confidence, and they do not feel so self-conscious. This method is also essential when you move on to experiential techniques, particularly in the second-degree phase of the person's path.

- **Seminars and talks:** Sit-down talks are useful for relaying information on more academic subjects, such as the history of witchcraft, origins of The Wheel of the Year, and other topics. But we never use it on its own; we tend to follow it up with something practical to reinforce the information that has been relayed. The reason for this is most people's attention span is approximately 20 minutes. After this, their minds start to wander, so we tend to keep any talks short.

- **Games and quizzes:** We have learned over the years that the more enjoyable an experience is, the more is learned from it, particularly if there is some sort of competition involved. We have found that the use of games is really a benefit in psychic exercises, where people try to guess what the other person has drawn or guess what tarot card he or she is concentrating on. Quizzes, on the other hand, are useful for assessing the progression of students, while making them aware of what subjects they need to concentrate more on.

- **The Internet:** Cyber covens exist, to use a magical phrase, "in a place which is not a place," amongst the bytes and electrons of the World Wide Web. The Internet is an incredible teaching tool. Apart from the obvious ease of communication for teaching purposes, and the unlimited research potential, it can also be used to set up "floating" coven Websites where training material and the *Book of Shadows* can be stored and easily accessed by the student. Such a site can be password protected for coven members only and can also include a message board where subjects can be regularly discussed.

Magical Systems Used in Training

The magical systems that are taught in Wicca are generally taught after first-degree initiation. We tend to use the analogy of the car when it comes to the importance of learning magical systems. Most witches who practice magic know how to drive the car. They know what the controls—the magical tools, are for; and they know how to use them to drive the car, which is to perform ritual. They also know the highway code—the laws of magic (see Appendix III). The main problem we have found is that very few know how the car works and that, we'd like to point out, is very different from knowing how to drive. Here we are talking about ritual mechanics. This is why it is important to have an understandable magical system related to your work as a witch. It is also important if you are going to create your own rituals and magical practices successfully and safely.

The four systems we list below are the ones we have found most often in Wicca. There are, of course, others that we have not mentioned. Here we give a brief outline.

⚜ **Ceremonial High Magic and Cabala:** When Janet and Stewart came into the Craft, the magical system used by Alex Sanders was Cabalistic Ceremonial High Magic. This is Air- based, as opposed to Earth-based, which witchcraft is supposed to be. It is also of Judeo-Christian origin rather than being truly Pagan; therefore it carries with it many of the philosophies and values of that tradition. Witchcraft's evolutionary process has included the slow removal of these influences. This is not to say that an understanding of Cabala or Ceremonial High Magic is not important in a witch's training. There is much that can be gained from them. But their importance has been overly emphasized within Wicca over the years. We now use it just for the purpose of explaining philosophical principles (as we have done in this book) and rely more on the following three systems.

⚜ **Shamanism:** Gavin started in a self-initiatory Seax-Wicca group where there was only a basic structure with no central magical system. This led him into the natural direction of studying rune craft and then into Anglo-Saxon/Norse Shamanism. He discovered within this a natural system of magic, which seemed to have more to do with witchcraft than Cabala, as it was Earth- rather than Air-based. With Janet and Stewart, he examined the similarities with and created a root cosmology from the remnants of the Celtic system that they were working with in Ireland, which is less complete than the Anglo-Saxon/Norse. We still teach this system. Shamanism is also much more experiential than Cabala and seems to explain the Mystery Tradition within Wicca more fully, as Jungian psychology fits perfectly into the Shamanic cosmology of worlds (see Chapter 7). One could even argue that we have returned to the origins of witchcraft by doing this, as a simplified version of this would more than likely have been the system used by the original village Priesthood many centuries ago.

- **The chakra system:** This is a system of spiritual anatomy and physiology (see Chapter 8). One of the first books specifically on witchcraft to put forward the idea of using chakras was Starhawk's *The Spiral Dance*. The use of chakras in Western occult practice, though, goes back to the end of the 19th century when they were incorporated into Theosophy. The Theosophists were heavily influenced by material emerging from the British occupation of India—particularly the translations of the Vedas. The chakra system became an accepted model of the energy centers of the human body among both Theosophists and occultists (see page 155). The most common argument against using them is that they are not a part of the Western tradition and that you are mixing systems by using them. Our argument is that there is plenty of evidence to support that a proto-energy system was known in Western culture, and we have talked more about this in one of our previous works, *The Healing Craft*.[9] The chakras explain many of the techniques that witches use in their ritual and magical practice from the perspective of energy, including Drawing Down the Moon (see page 200). More importantly, for an Earth-based spirituality, they reflect the important occult law "As above, so below."

- **Jungian psychology:** You might ask what psychology has to do with witchcraft, as modern science seems to be at odds with the idea of magic. But from a polytheistic point of view, this is not the case. Jung's teachings are far from out of place. Jung developed and elaborated upon the teachings of his mentor, Sigmund Freud, by examining Archetypes. He even published a treatise on the god Wotan[10] (Odin) while examining what was happening in religious and occult practices. To this day, his teachings remain standard reading for anyone involved in magical practice and are highly relevant when it comes to understanding the processes involved in the mysteries (see Chapter 3). Jungian psychology can help us understand many of the practices within magic and witchcraft. For example, in Shamanism, the descent into the Underworld is the descent into the Jungian idea of the Shadow, the dark and repressed sides of our nature. This is the same process that is triggered after the second-degree initiation in Wicca, our Path of Fire. Jung also gives good explanations of how the Astral Levels work—the levels beyond our reality—as well as explaining the importance of symbolism in magical work.

Knowledge-based Ritual

In the past, ritual was taught by having students memorize the ritual frame of circle casting, calling the quarters, and all the rest. They were encouraged to read it directly from the coven's *Book of Shadows* or learn it, word for word, before ritual. Both of us have fond memories of stammering over words while trying to conduct rituals from scrunched up pieces of paper or ungainly folders. Most witches before the 1980s tried to conduct rituals "from their heads" rather than "from their hearts." This resulted in the repetition of the same ritual. There were, of course, advantages to this system of learning ritual. The students would quickly learn the words for casting the circle and calling the quarters or face embarrassment in front of other coven members. But in many cases, students didn't necessarily know the significance of the symbolism they were using, or even know the true significance of what they were invoking. Of course, the same applied to the rituals for the eight festivals of the year. Here we see the development of a dogma—ritual for ritual's sake—as students continued to practice what they had been taught. The system did not encourage spontaneous ritual.

The influence of Shamanism in the 1980s began to change things. Members of the Neo-Pagan community began to do rituals straight from the heart that "felt right at the time!" Unfortunately, there was very little thought put into such rituals beforehand, and those conducting the ritual often had little knowledge of how ritual or raised energy worked. Sometimes there were dire consequences, as the energy of the circle got out of control and members found themselves becoming emotionally uncomfortable.

In both cases, the cause of the problem is lack of knowledge. We still teach students to learn the ritual frame, but only initially as a discipline. Once they have learned the basic Gardnerian/Alexandrian method of circle casting, we start to encourage them to merge "head and heart" in ritual. We do this by encouraging our students to learn the background knowledge of any rite they are going to perform. For example, if they were going to conduct a festival, they would learn the origins of it, as well as the symbolism and its purpose. With this knowledge, they should be able to do a successful ritual "from the heart" that flows naturally. Such a ritual would be spontaneous. The only writing we have is a listing of proceedings: Cast Circle, Call Quarters, Invoke Deity, etc. When you do ritual in this fashion, it ceases to be dogmatic and becomes an art form in its own right. You start to feel the energy of the ritual at work in the magical act you are performing. As we mentioned previously, it is not enough for a witch to drive the car. The witch must also know how the engine works. We feel this method of ritual is more in keeping with the progressive tradition that witchcraft is becoming. The only exceptions to this are those that maintain a bit of continuity and "tradition." We still use the same words we always have for some parts of ritual, such as the consecration of Cakes and Wine, and certain initiatory oaths.

The Importance of Life Experience

For a witch to really understand the Mysteries of Life, Death, and Rebirth, one must experience them. Our ancestors, who learned and taught witchcraft in tribes and villages, were faced with the realities of life and death every day as they struggled to survive in a potentially hostile world. It is from these experiences that they saw what we call the Mysteries impacting every aspect of their lives. At a young age, everyone had experienced death firsthand in the death of a tribal member due to an animal, disease, or injury. Even in the preparation of food by hunting, killing, and skinning an animal, our ancestors came to understand the cycles of life and death within nature. Nowadays, most of us live in a world where we are separated from nature within our towns and cities, where we rarely get to stare death in the face. Our meat is conveniently pre-packed and sealed, so we do not have to deal with the spiritual implications of where it originated.

Witchcraft is a holistic spirituality believing in the balance of both the physical and the spiritual. It is therefore not enough for a student witch just to learn from books, in ritual, or in meditative exercise; they must seek out the experience of Life itself if they are to fully understand the Mysteries of Life, Death, and Rebirth. This is one of the reasons why there has always been a belief that a witch must be a certain age to join the craft, but even at the accepted minimum of 18 years old, we are only just beginning to gain life experience. Life itself is training for a witch. Any student of witchcraft needs to realize this and that the collection of degrees and titles that exist in Wicca are meaningless unless there is the accumulated wisdom that can only be gained over time. The student witch must therefore seek out the experiences of life to truly understand the Mysteries of witchcraft. This is the most important training a witch can have.

Endnotes

1. Born in 1911, Mahfouz Naguib is the grand old man of Arabic fiction, enjoying the affection and reverence of both critics and a vast readership.
2. This same rite was shown in the documentary film *The Occult Experience*, by Nevil Drury.
3. The magazine *Rites from the Crystal Well* was originally published as *The Waxing Moon*. They were give out free of charge through two mailboxes, one in North Dakota and one in Philadelphia. Donations were asked for just to cover mailing costs.
4. In 1954, Abraham Maslow formulated a positive theory of motivation derived from clinical experience, which by integrating earlier theories arrives at a dynamic-holistic theory. Taught to health care professionals, this theory easily applies to all situations to explain motivational imperatives.
5. A general reference to the Arthurian myths and the quest for the Holy Grail, by those in the Western tradition of magic. In the quest, Perceval discovers that his experiences were more important than the Grail in saving Arthur and restoring Logres, the wasteland.
6. Empedocles was a citizen of Agrigentum in Sicily, around 444 B.C.E. He unreservedly accepts the doctrine of Parmenides that *what is* is uncreated and indestructible, and he only escapes from the further conclusions of the Eleatic by introducing the theory of elements, or *roots*. Of these he assumed four—fire, air, earth, and water—and in some respects, this was a return to primitive views that the Milesians (Celts) had already left behind them.
7. Covenant of the Goddess was formed in 1975 by 13 covens and a number of solitaries in Berkley, California. By 1980 it had members in at least 15 states. Abridged from Rosemary Ellen Guilley's *Encyclopedia of Witches and Witchcraft* (*see* Bibliography).
8. Founded in 1979 by Peter Pathfinder Davies. The ATC was formed as a coven dedicated to providing religious services to the larger Wiccan community. Today it has congregations in the United States, Canada, Ireland (ourselves), Australia, and South Africa. Abridged from Raymond Buckland's *The Witch Book: The Encyclopedia of Witchcraft, Wicca, and Neo-Paganism* (*see* Bibliography).
9. *The Healing Craft,* Chapter 6, pages 91–100.
10. Can be found in: *Wotan,* published in the *Neue Schweitzer Rundschau*, March 1936 (later published in *Essays on Contemporary Events*, 1947, and in the *Collected Works of C.G. Jung, Civilisation in Transition, Vol. 10*).

Chapter 7

Spiritual Cosmology:
Walking Between the Worlds

*The whole drift of my education goes to persuade
me that the world of our present consciousness is
only one out of many worlds of consciousness that
exist, and that those other worlds must contain
experiences which have a meaning for our life also.*

—William James[1]

Wicca has never truly had its own cosmology. In Gardnerian and Alexandrian practice, Cabala and its Tree of Life were used as the major magical philosophy in the thinking of these traditions from the end of the 1960s onwards. With its 10 sephiroth, it mimics many of the earlier spiritual cosmologies of the peoples of Europe, but it does not give a true map of the many other worlds that exist. A true spiritual cosmology is a graphic interpretation of the magical levels of reality. Such a map must include a physical, psychological, energetic, and spiritual approach, creating a holistic view of the cosmos, and abide by the old magical law "As above, so below." In practice, this means that you should be able to stand in a witch's circle and see the worlds around you on all levels. Cabala, often described as a philosophical and magical filing cabinet, simply does not do this. You cannot use it to explain the levels of the other worlds or realms, or how to access them. It is odd that Wicca, with its claim to be

European in origin, ignored existing European cosmological systems, but this can be accounted for by the fact that it adopted a ritual magic approach to the cosmos rather than a truly Pagan one. Its creators used what was available at the time. Cabala, with its roots in Judeo-Christian doctrine, was in the most accessible literature of the period.

As time has gone on, witches have begun to question the practices they were originally taught. Cabalistic ritual magic was one of these, and it has slowly been abandoned. As a result, Wicca has had no useful cosmology to speak of. Not surprisingly, many witches have been drawn to both Celtic and Northern European (Norse, Anglo-Saxon, etc.) magical worldviews. Both Celtic and Norse have integrated spiritual cosmologies of Shamanic origin that allow travel between different levels of reality. What becomes obvious when studying both Celtic and Northern European magic is that there are strong similarities between both, which has led us to believe that there was once a common European system before the cultural divisions of later times.[2]

In early hunter-gatherer cultures, the first cosmology to appear was the Three Worlds: an upper world, the abode of the gods; a middle world, the home of man; and a chthonic Underworld, home of the ancestors. To early man, these worlds were around him. He saw them in everyday activities. The cave became the gateway to the Underworld, and the mountain, often hazardous to climb, became the abode of the gods. This basic cosmological belief structure can still be found in Shamanic cultures today and is still used by modern Shamans. Spiritual cosmologies, therefore, reflect the physical nature of the universe as well as the internal psychology of man.

These three worlds are reflected in Jungian psychology as aspects of the individual psyche. The upper world becomes the Personal Unconscious (Freud's Subconscious); the middle world becomes normal everyday Consciousness; and the Underworld becomes the Collective Unconscious (see page 64). In ancient Greek mythology, these three worlds are referred to as Olympus, Earth, and Hades. The Underworld, in all myths, is a place of darkness and fear. It is what Jung called "the Shadow," and it is the first level accessed when traveling between worlds. Hence ancient man associated it with caves due to his fear of darkness and the possibility that a ferocious animal lived in it. This fear of the Shadow Realm is the same as a modern child's fear of the dark or of a monster under the bed. Christianity perverted this concept into Hell, a place of retribution and terror.

In the Brythonic Celtic and Druidic traditions, which visualize the three worlds as concentric circles, one extra realm joins the three worlds. In the center is Annwn, the Underworld. In his poem "Preiddeu Annwn," Taliesin talks about having to cross the sea to reach Annwn. Crossing water to reach the realm of the dead is common in many myths. In Ireland this is reflected in megalithic sites such as Brú na Bóinne (Newgrange) in County Meath, where it is necessary to cross the River Boyne (a goddess, by the way) to get to the burial chamber.[3] Water can therefore be seen to represent the unconscious mind. The next realm from the center is Abred, the middle world of struggle and evolution, and the world in which we live. The upper world of Celtic/Druidic cosmology differs, for it is split into two distinct realms: Gwynfyd, the realm of purity and attainment, and Ceugant, which in the bardic tradition is the abode of God. This division is similar to the one that occurs in the Northern traditions; their upper realm is Asaheimr (the equivalent of Gwynfyd) with the addition of Odin's throne, Hlidskjalf[4] (this being Ceugant). In Jungian psychology, this is referred to as the Superconscious, the Unknowable Divine itself.

To the other three realms were added four Elemental realms, Earth (or in Norse/Icelandic, Ice), Air, Fire, and Water. Again, all these are visible in humanity's surroundings as the building blocks of physical reality and the four states of matter (solid, gas, energy or plasma, and liquid). They quickly became associated with the four cardinal points, due to the environment people lived in. In Northern Europe the South is associated with Fire because of the position of the sun at midday. Water was associated with the West in Europe because of the Atlantic Ocean. Similarly, the East is associated with Air because of the Eastern winds, and the North with Earth because the facing sun nourishes its fertility. Of course, in the far North, this does not apply; hence in Norse/Icelandic practice, Earth becomes Ice.

The act of casting a circle in Wicca mimics the sun, which is why casting starts in the East where it rises and continues clockwise to follow its direction. This of course does not apply in the Southern Hemisphere (Australia, New Zealand, etc.) and witches below the equator have adjusted their practices appropriately, showing the necessity for flexibility and lack of dogma in practice.

In Irish Celtic culture, these four elemental realms were referred to as the "Cities" of Falias (North), Gorias (East), Finias (West), and Murias (South). The Underworld was referred to as Tir Fo Thuinn (The Land

Under The Water) and the Realm of the Gods, and of course, the heroic figures of Irish myth became commonly known as Tir Na Nog (The Land Of Youth).[5]

The most complete example of these magical realms combined is the Norse Yggdrasil, the World Tree. The most complete description of this can be found in the Icelandic *Poetic Edda,* recorded by Snorri Sturluson. In the first chapter, the *Voluspa* (the song of the seeress) a practitioner of Seidr descends the tree in trance and describes the worlds that exist on its branches.[6] The tree is an ancient motif for the Axis-Mundi (central axis) of the world and is symbolically important in numerous cultures.[7] In Ireland, it was believed that a great oak stood in the center of the Island at Uisneach, County Westmeath, one of the five great Bíle Trees that brought luck to the provinces.[8] In Assyro-Babylonian culture there is the Moon Tree, and in Anglo-Saxon practice, a stone pillar was placed in the center of the temple to represent Irminsul, the axis of the world. Even in the Middle Ages the custom of perrons (stone pillars) in the center of a town or village was common practice. These represented the center of village life, and in the later Christian period, were replaced with the village or town cross.

Perron

The Norse World Tree, Yggdrasil, consists of the seven worlds we have already mentioned, plus a further two making nine. These two realms probably belonged to the pre-Indo-European faery culture.[9] The central axis consists of the uppermost realms: Asgardhr, the abode of the Gods and consciousness; Ljossalfheimr, the realms of the light elves and the intellect; Midgardhr, the abode of man; Svartalfheimr, the realm of the dwarves and emotion; and finally Helheimr, the Underworld, the abode of the Goddess Hel and the Unconscious. These five worlds make up the Axis of Consciousness, the Axis-Mundi mentioned earlier. Midgardhr has the four elemental realms revolving around it, making up the physical realms. These are Niflheimr, Ice and matter; Jotunheimr, Air and motion; Vanaheimr, Water and balance; and Muspellsheimr, Fire and energy. This system of worlds continues to be taught within Asatru, modern Norse magical practice.

From examining Celtic, Norse and other sources, it has become apparent to us that there is a common root source to both the cosmologies we have mentioned. Over the last few years, we have tried to reconstruct this, with quite successful results. It follows very much the same pattern as Yggdrasil and the worlds that exist on it. This is hardly surprising, as it is a reflection of magical reality. When you stand in the witches' magic circle, you stand within the first seven realms—you center yourself in the universe around you. This spiritual act of centering allows you to understand the universe and its levels of reality. It is the first act any magical practitioner does when creating sacred space.

Seven is an important number in magic. There are seven chakras, seven planetary correspondences, and seven days of the week. Although there can be said to be nine realms, only seven are fully accessible to the magical practitioner. In Anglo-Saxon magical practice, the most important magical symbol was the seven-pointed star, often called the fairy or more correctly the elven star (see Figure 4 on page 136). It can still be found in stained glassed windows in churches in the South of England, where it is called the Lady's Star. In the Middle East it is known as the Star of Ishtar, so its association with the Madonna and therefore the Goddess can hardly be a coincidence.

When standing in the magic circle, you stand in the first realm. It is from here that you experience the others. The four elemental realms of Earth, Air, Fire, and Water are on a horizontal axis, with the two central realms above and below you, on the vertical. The World Tree therefore represents a common magical symbolism. The benefits of this system are apparent, as no other system offers the same level of integration into practical magical and spiritual work. But there is something more important about it. From our experiences, we have discovered it maps psychological processes, the levels of reality, and the physical realities of magic. This is particularly important when exploring the Mysteries, as it grants the seeker a systematic process with which to experience them directly, given time and practice.

We have found a great deal of agreement among the experiences of people who use it. They often describe seeing the same symbolism and

The Seven-pointed Lady's Star

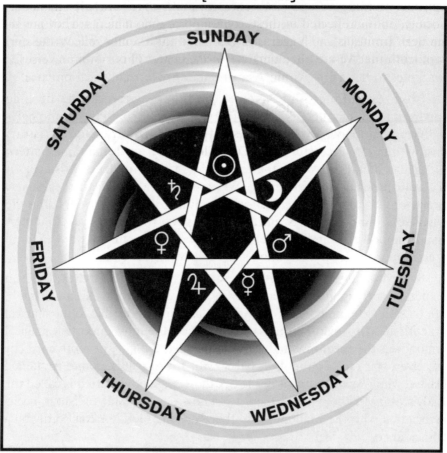

Figure 4

the same Guardians while meditating. This has prompted us to use it as our primary spiritual cosmology when we teach our students how to "walk between the worlds" along the spiral paths that connect each realm. Our experiences have shown that there is a spiritual truth in this system.

One might think that after the advent of the age of reason—the Renaissance—when it was discovered that the Earth circled the sun, that man would have gone past the point of centering himself in the universe as he did in Pagan times. The facts actually show the reverse: Man continues to create monuments in every major city to mark the center of his world. London has Nelson's Column, Paris has the Eiffel Tower, and Washington D.C. has the Washington Monument. While writing this book, a metal spire called the Millennium Spike was erected in the center of Dublin. The spiritual yearning for a physical center for our lives remains even in modern society, and is reflected in these contemporary monuments. They are the modern Irminsuls and Yggdrasils. Our need for a center reflects the spiritual truth that we are all, ultimately, at the center of our own universes.[10]

The Wiccan Cosmology

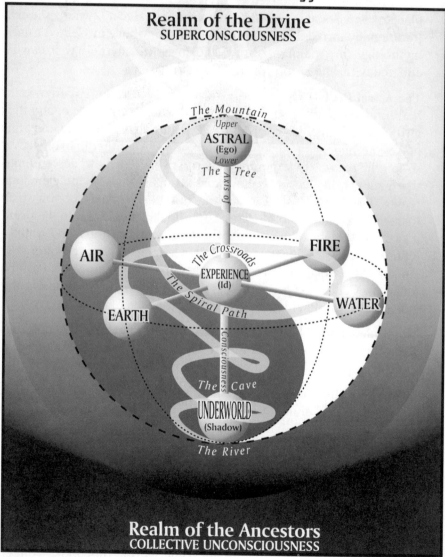

Figure 5

The Axis of Consciousness

⚜ **The Realm of Experience:** This is the central realm on the axis of the tree and corresponds with the Id, the element of our psyche that strives for the most basic needs: food, shelter, procreation, etc. The Id forces us into the world and causes us to experience it. It is satiated or repressed by the effect of the other five realms that intersect with it, such as the Realm of Water, which makes us feel emotion. This intersection of realms is symbolized by the crossroads, a traditional meeting place of witches and sacred to the Goddess Hecate, where she was traditionally invoked by Drawing Down the Moon. In Celtic/Druidic mythology this realm is Abred, and in Norse mythology it can be equated with Midgardhr, or Middle Earth.

⚜ **The Astral Realm:** This is above the central Realm of Experience. In both Freudian and Jungian terms, it is the abode of the Ego, and thus anything we perceive here is clothed by our Ego. Unfortunately, this makes our understanding of this realm subjective rather than objective, so to fully realize the experiences here, it is necessary to descend into the Underworld, Jung's Shadow, and also pass through the elemental realms. The Astral Realm is where one finds the World Tree, with which to travel between the worlds. The Astral Realm intersects with the world above it, the Realm of the Divine, where many of the entities and symbols found on the Astral Plane originate. It is here that one meets both your guide and Guardian, and also where the Shamanic totem animal can be found. In Celtic/Druidic mythology, it is world of Gwynfyd and in the Norse it is Ljossalfheimr, the Realm of the Light Elves.

⚜ **The Underworld:** This corresponds with Jung's Personal Unconscious where the Shadow dwells. It is here that the Ego sends the impulses it wants to repress. The Shadow is the Norse Svartalfheimr, the Realm of Dwarf and Dark Fairy, and the world of the Dark Elves. Deep within this realm are all the fears and negative aspects of the self rejected by the personality. Not surprisingly, many of the images are frightening, but to understand what you see here you must face yourself. Before exploring this realm, it is also necessary to find a guide, the psychopompous. In this realm, the seeker meets the dark Goddess of Wisdom, the Goddess of witchcraft, who travels up from the Ancestral Realm. It is she who holds the mirror up so you can see your true image. In this way you can find your "soul," or Anima/Animus, which also abides here. The Anima/Animus exists in an area the Neo-Jungians call the Bright Shadow, which is often symbolized as a pleasant, peaceful area hidden among the dark images of the Shadow.[11] The Underworld can be accessed several ways, and each method allows access to different areas and grants specific kinds of knowledge. One way is to descend down the roots of the World Tree, found on the Astral Realm, or to descend the Left-Hand Spiral Path into the traditional entrance to the Shadow, which is the cave. There are, of course, other traditional entrance symbols, such as the well, an entrance taken through the Realm of Water. Whatever way is chosen, dark areas are always barred by the Guardian of the Mysteries, unless the person is ready to proceed.

The Elemental Realms

- **The Realm of Earth:** This realm, on the material level of reality, gives us our experiences of solid matter, form, and substance. Intersecting with the Realm of Experience, it gives the sensation of touch. It is therefore the element that governs manifestation. But it also intersects with the lower area of the Astral Realm to give us intellectual stability, wisdom, and psychic grounding. The association with stability makes this realm a place of restriction and of preservation of the status quo. The symbols found here come up from the realm below, the Underworld, and relate directly to these two functions. Thus Earth, is also the element of death and the grave. The cave or dolmen entrance to the Underworld is found here, as well as the place of grounding symbolized as a stone circle or forest grove.

- **The Realm of Air:** This realm gives us the sensations of smell and taste, both associated with the air of breath. It gives us our intellectual capability when it intersects with the lower Astral Realm, allowing logical reasoning and thought, as well as the ability to communicate. Because of its mental correspondence, it is possible to access the Akashic records through the Realm of Air. The memory of past lives and events both personal and universal are contained here; hence its association with knowledge. This may be symbolically seen as a great building, a library, which can be accessed by the traveler when the time is right.

- **The Realm of Fire:** The Element of Fire is traditionally associated with sight. Our drive and our "spark" come to us from the Astral

Realm through Fire. It is the Element of energy, raw and uncontained, with potential for creation and destruction. The symbolism related to it reflects this. The magical sword or athame is forged by smithcraft, so it is not surprising that sometimes the traveler finds a forge with the smith hard at work. The smith can reshape you to travel to other realms, by destroying the old self and creating a new one within the fire of the forge.

- **The Realm of Water:** Physically, this realm gives us the sense of hearing and is responsible for the manifestation of all our senses in the other Elements. It is the Element of emotion. In the Astral Realm, these manifest positively, while negative emotions are repressed into the Underworld. Because of this, it is the most commonly used elemental realm with which to access the Underworld. The most commonly found symbolism here is the well, lake, river, etc. While wells and lakes may be used to descend into the Underworld, rivers are often used to mark the boundaries between the different realms, as they mark psychological crossing points.

The Outer Realms

- **The Realm of the Divine:** This is what is referred to by Jungian psychologists as the Superconscious, or by the occultist as the Higher Astral. It is found above the Astral Realm. It is the realm of the Divine, the unknowable force that is the intelligence of the Universe itself. In Druidic terms, it is Ceugant. To understand it, think of "Heaven" and "God" as the same thing. Cabalists would call this "Ain Soph Aur," the unknowable. It has no form as such until it descends into the realms below, where it takes on the forms that human consciousness has assigned to it. For example, in passing through the Astral Realm it becomes what we know as a god or goddess. It cannot manifest without this mediation first taking place. Hence, deities have associations with the elements, the Underworld, etc. It is an unattainable realm, which means we cannot enter it in our current state of consciousness, although a gifted traveler or psychic may catch a glimpse of this realm. This is the place our souls ultimately reach after death, before reincarnation. The Buddhists refer to this realm as Nirvana, and seek to rejoin it rather than reincarnating.

⚛ **The Realm of the Ancestors:** This is the Collective Unconscious, where the many images of Jung's numinous Archetypes are stored. It is positioned below the Underworld. This is the true realm of the dead and the ancestors, and in many myths can only be accessed by dying, crossing the River of Death itself. A good example is the Greek myth of the River Styx. It has been portrayed in many ways, as Helheim to the Norse and Annwn to the Druids. The Greeks saw it as Tartarus, the abode below Hades. It is important to recognize the culturally different ways to view it, as it is easy to confuse this realm with the Underworld. Like the Realm of the Divine, it cannot be accessed directly from the Realm of Experience. Its passage through the other realms shapes the images originating from it, just as with the Realm of the Divine. It is possible to stand at its gates and see some of the images within it, but it can be dangerous to attempt to enter. In the flood of imagery that would overcome your senses, you would literally risk loosing your mind. In all cultures, this is a realm of danger, death, and horrific images.

Guides and Guardians

⚛ **The Astral Guardian:** This Guardian is our Higher Self, the aspect of our being that exists on the Higher Astral level, the Realm of the Divine. It is the part of our soul that is permanently connected to the Unknowable Divine. It is linked strongly with the crown center, particularly when it has been opened. Its purpose is to protect us spiritually and psychically from intrusion. It tries to guide us through our lives by encouraging our spiritual and karmic development. In Cabalistic and traditional Western magic, it is often referred to as the *Holy Guardian Angel*. Practitioners attempted to spiritually unify with it, which is to unify with one's true spiritual self. This still applies in all true occult practices, including witchcraft. Its symbolism may take the form of a deity, when someone dedicates himself or herself to serve a specific god or goddess—a *primary life guide* (see page 195). It may even manifest through the Anima/Animus if the individual's spiritual potential has been repressed. Any exercise to find the Astral Guardian normally will involve exploring the higher areas of the Astral and calling the Guardian to descend to meet you there.

⚛ **The Astral Guide:** The role of the Astral Guide is to show us around the Astral Realms that are safe to access at any given stage of our spiritual development. It therefore tends to be encountered only in the Astral Realm and higher levels of the Elemental Realms. It can be seen as a lower aspect of the Astral Guardian, and can manifest in human form or as a totem animal. In Shamanic magical practices, one can ride totem animals to explore the worlds. It is important to realize that totem animals are not power animals: Totem animals have a completely different role, restricted to the Astral Realms. They generally take the form of the animal or mythological creature that a person's Ego aspires to be like, such as a dragon, unicorn, lion, eagle, etc.—usually winged creatures. It is important to realize that the Astral Guide will be clothed by your ego in this realm, and that you will be unable to see its true form until you have performed an Underworld descent.

- **The Guardian of the Mysteries:** The role of the Guardian of the Mysteries is to protect the Mysteries from those who are unready to experience them. It guards both the entrance to the Underworld and the gate to the Realm of the Ancestors. Its form will always be terrifying, to scare the seeker and thereby warn of the dangers beyond. It challenges the seeker with a question or a riddle. If not answered satisfactorily, the seeker will be turned back until they are ready to proceed. To continue anyway is to face its wrath! In the Greek mysteries, the Guardian was Cerberus the monster, sometimes seen as male (a three-headed dog), sometimes as female (a hybrid of lioness, lynx, and sow) that challenged everyone approaching the gates of Hades, the Underworld.

- **The Underworld Guide—the psychopompous and power animal:** This performs a similar role to the Astral Guide, but it helps the seeker explore the Shadow Realm, the Underworld. In modern Wicca, Cernunnos, the Horned God and Lord of Death and Resurrection performs this role. In Norse tradition, Odin (or Woden) fulfils the same role. In the mysteries of Greece and Ptolemaic Egypt it was Hermes, in the form of Hermes Trismegistus and Anubis.[12] All these images of the psychopompous have animal aspects about them: Hermes, the son of Pan, inherited his fathers' cloven hooves; Cernunnos is part stag; and Anubis has the head of a jackal. Odin (Woden) is the exception, but as he is escorted by two wolves and two ravens, the animal aspect is still there. In Shamanism, the psychopompous is traditionally the power animal. As mentioned earlier, it is important to understand that the power animal is very different from the totem animal. Generally, the power animal is a real mammal or bird, or very rarely, a reptile. Before any exploration of the Underworld, the psychopompous should be actively sought by descending to find it via the Id, the Realm of Experience. In seeking it, a bridge is made between the human and animal Collective Unconscious. The animal recognises the Id in the seeker as its own and comes to meet them; the same will apply to the psychopompous as a deity form. Thus when you seek the Underworld guide, the Underworld guide finds you. Once found, the Underworld guide needs to be connected with regularly. It is traditional in Shamanism to exercise your power animal, to dance with it. The same applies to the Underworld guide, whatever form it takes. It is able to act as a guide in the Underworld because of its association with the individual's Id, the Shadow, which is, of course, the area where many impulses from the Id are repressed.

The Four Elemental Guardians: Every witch who calls the quarters correctly has invoked the elemental Guardians. They are the same Lords of the Watchtowers[13] that are invoked in traditional Wiccan practice. These are the spirits, the higher forms, of the elements themselves whose role is to control the raw form of the element; hence the need to invoke them in ritual when using Element-based magic. What is rarely talked about is the fact that they can also act as guides to their own realms. They may manifest in several different guises. They may relate directly to their sexual association—a maiden for Water, a mother for Earth, a young male warrior for Fire, and an old wizard figure for Air. But they can be just as easily represented by other forms of mythological creatures, such as the Dragon for Fire, etc. It will depend very much on the individual, as most symbolism does. These Guardians can be met at the entrance to each elemental realm as you ascend the Spiral Path. If you try to enter their realms and are not ready, they will challenge you with a question before allowing you to pass.

The Spiral Path

The Spiral Path is a pathway that starts from the bottom realm, the Realm of the Ancestors, and ascends through each realm, spiralling clockwise as it goes. After leaving the Underworld, it then proceeds to spiral past the entrance to each of the Elements, starting with Earth and proceeding through Air, Fire, and finally Water. At the last Elemental Realm it becomes "the bridge" to the Astral Realm. After passing over the bridge, the path divides into two, the Left-Hand Path and the Right-Hand Path. Between these two paths exists the Tree of Life, with its roots passing down into the Realm of Experience and finally into the Underworld and Ancestral Realms. Its trunk goes upwards and branches into the higher Realm of the Divine. The Right-Hand Path takes you into the Astral Realm, while the left hand descends downwards, anti-clockwise through the elements again, and into the Realm of the Underworld. It is at this junction that the Astral Guide can be met.

Ascending the Spiral Path: This practical visualization exercise in exploring the cosmology of the other worlds can be done in a coven or group setting. It can be done individually, but one would need someone who can read out the following pathworking, or one would have to memorize the realms and the pathworking.

This exercise is designed to give you a taste of the realms. It lays the ground rules for the exploration of these worlds as you walk between them. Be aware that everything that you meet here is real, although clothed in imagery generated from your own unconscious mind and that of the Collective Unconscious. All entities should be treated with the reverence they deserve. If you treat them as real, they will act as real. Be aware that many of the symbols we have talked about may appear slightly different than you expect. Do not be put off by this. This is normal. We each clothe these experiences in the symbols that we understand. Just allow yourself to flow with the experience.

You first need to get yourself comfortable, in a quiet, warm room. Breathe rhythmically and deeply for several minutes before you start (you may want to use the same breathing technique used for opening the chakras). Try to block out all the memories and activities of the day that seem to intrude upon your thoughts. Visualize yourself in darkness, quiet and alone:

> You are in darkness. You are standing, your feet on a
> path of stones and pebbles. You can feel them beneath
> your feet and hear their crunching.
>
> Slowly you can make out points of light emerging
> above your line of vision, the stars twinkling in the heavens.

As you breathe in, you can feel the cold air of the night on your lungs and slowly you start to make out images in the darkness.

Ahead of you, you can slowly make out a path winding upwards and to the right, through a forest of dense trees.

Above this tree line, you can see a new sickle moon rising, lighting the path ahead of you that ascends, always to the right, into the darkness.

You breathe in and you can feel the cold air of the night on your lungs. Slowly you start to make your way up the path, heading towards the sickle moon set amongst the twinkling stars.

You can hear the crunch of pebbles beneath your feet, and hear the rustling and calls of the animals of the night as you commence your journey.

As you slowly round the first bend, you can make out two points of light in the distance, a shadowy figure between them.

You breathe in and you can feel the cold air of the night on your lungs. As you look up, the moon has grown fuller, and is now reaching almost a quarter, set amongst the twinkling stars.

As you continue your journey along the path, you can see more clearly the figure standing between what now appears to be two torches.

You come closer and closer, until finally you stand before the Guardian of Earth. The Guardian asks you a question. You reply, and then you continue on your journey up the path, always to the right.

You breathe in and you can feel the cold air of the night on your lungs. As you look up, the moon has grown, and is now reaching almost a half, set amongst the twinkling stars.

As you slowly round the first bend, you can make out two points of light in the distance, and a shadowy figure between them.

You can hear the crunch of pebbles beneath your feet, and hear the rustling and calls of the animals of the night as you commence your journey.

As you continue your journey along the path, you can see more clearly the figure standing between what now appears to be two torches.

You come closer and closer, until finally you stand before the Guardian of Air. The Guardian asks you a question. You reply, and then you continue on your journey up the path, always to the right.

You breathe in and you can feel the cold air of the night on your lungs. As you look up, the moon has grown, and is now almost three-quarters full, set amongst the twinkling stars.

As you slowly round the first bend, you can make out two points of light in the distance, and a shadowy figure between them.

You can hear the crunch of pebbles beneath your feet, and hear the rustling and calls of the animals of the night as you commence your journey.

As you continue your journey along the path, you can see more clearly the figure standing between what now appears to be two torches.

You come closer and closer, until finally you stand before the Guardian of Fire. The Guardian asks you a question. You reply, and then you continue on your journey up the path, always to the right.

You breathe in and you can feel the cold air of the night on your lungs. As you look up, the moon is now almost full, set amongst the twinkling stars, and in the distance you can hear the quiet trickling of water.

As you slowly round the first bend, you can make out two points of light in the distance, and a shadowy figure between them.

You can hear the crunch of pebbles beneath your feet, and the sound of water now seems to be louder. Its roar fills the forest.

As you continue your journey along the path, you can see more clearly the figure standing between what now appears to be two torches, and behind them you can make out a bridge crossing over the river that you have been hearing.

You come closer and closer, until finally you stand before the Guardian of Water. The Guardian asks you a question. You reply. The Guardian points to the bridge, beckoning you to cross into the next world.

With the sound of the roar of water in your ears, you cross the bridge, the torrent of water beneath you. You feel the bridge beneath your feet and make your way to the other side.

You breathe in and you can feel the cold air of the night on your lungs. As you look up, the moon is now full, set amongst the twinkling stars.

You can hear the crunch of pebbles beneath your feet, but otherwise, all is quiet as you continue the journey along the path.

The path seems to straighten, and very slowly you begin to make out something ahead that seems to block the path.

As you move closer you realize it is the Great Tree, the Tree of Life itself. It seems to grow larger and larger as you approach it.

You are finally standing in front of it. As you look up, you see the tree seemingly disappear into the heavens, its great trunk almost three times the width it would take for your arms to enfold it.

You can see that the path divides into two in front of the Great Tree. One path goes to the right carrying on to the right and up, the continuation of the path you are already on. One path goes to the left, always curving downwards in that direction into the darkness of the night.

Looking down you see the great buttressed roots disappear into the ground, and you notice a hole that is big enough to squeeze in if you dare—the entrance that would take you to the cave where your Underworld guide resides.

You become aware of a presence. As you step back from the tree, you become sure that you are not alone. You are not. From behind the tree, a figure appears. Under the light of the moon you can make out the figure's face and clothing.

The figure is your guide to this world. You ask its name. The guide replies explaining its purpose for being here at this time to meet you. The guide tells you that you can meet with it here again whenever you wish to explore this realm.

But, now it is time to return. Time to return to the world of illusion hidden in the normality of everyday living. Return. Return. Return, to the place where you started, the place where this all began.

Now open your eyes.

After completing this exercise, you may feel light-headed. If you do, this is an indication that you need to be grounded (see the grounding and chakra closing exercises found on pages 173). It is not unusual in such exercises for things to happen at a different pace from that of the person reading the pathworking out. If this happens, go at your own speed and allow things to happen in your own time. Unexpected things may also happen. One of the entities you meet, possibly one of the Elemental Guardians, or even your guide, may give you a gift. In Shamanic terms, this is a totem, an object of power that connects you to the realm it originated from. If the Elemental Guardian of Air gives you an object, it will be associated with the Element of Air, etc. There are many things it could be: a precious stone, a flower, or even a feather. If you receive such a gift, you should try to find a physical token of the same object, as it will help you connect with that realm in future magical working. Many practitioners of Shamanism carry a small bag for such objects. It is commonly known as a spirit bag, which is traditional in many cultures. In ancient Irish magic it was known as a *crane bag*, and in Native American culture, a *medicine bag*.

The Creation and Use of the Astral Temple

Constructing and using an Astral Temple has always been an integral part of the Western magical tradition. The Order of the Golden Dawn, the Ordo Templi Orientis, and all the magical orders of the 20th century made it a major part of their magical practice. The first time the idea of such an Astral construct was published was in Dion Fortune's *The Sea Priestess* in 1957.[14] Prior to this publication, the practice was a closely guarded secret. Dion Fortune's work became an important part of the Gardnerian Wiccan corpus. Over the years, her Moon Temple of Isis has gained more and more form. It has become a permanent construction of symbolism on the Astral Level. Much of this is due to the fact that her writings are still published and read by witches and occultists in general, which has the effect of giving more power to the construct. The method for creating an Astral Temple is really no different from that of consecrating a magical item and the creation of an Astral Double. The major difference is that a physical token is not necessary, although a painting or piece of sculpture may be used for this purpose.

In a working magical coven that has built up a Gestalt or Coven Mind, such a temple may have already been created, although the coven may not be aware of it. The more the coven works in a consecrated circle, the stronger the temple will become. This also applies to the solitary witches who create their own personal Astral Temple in a similar way. The coven may give form to their temple by deciding what it looks like, what materials it is constructed of, and, as previously mentioned, even have someone draw a sketch or paint the joint interpretation of it. This piece of art can then become an important centerpiece of the physical circle when they are working, mounted on the wall behind the altar. Once this is done, they can access it by ascending the Spiral Path into the Astral Realm to ask the Astral Guide to take them there.

The visualization of the temple should be carried out regularly, both as a coven and individually. The temple will gain more power and form on the Astral Level this way. It is important that all the coven members agree to visualize the same temple. The Astral Doubles of the magical tools of the coven should be visualized there, as well as other symbols, such as the statue of the gods and goddesses used by the coven. Once the coven is happy that the temple has been built, it can then be used magically.

One uses the temple magically by visualizing the performance of magical rites within it. An advantage of this is that the coven does not actually have to all meet in the same place to carry out a ritual. Coven meetings can take place on an Astral Level in the Astral Temple. The coven members just have to have a quiet place in which to visualize and meditate upon the temple.

The Astral Temple's primary purpose in the Western magical tradition is to invoke gods and goddesses and the Astral Guardian directly. It acts as a gateway for these entities directly from the Realm of the Divine. Speaking from our experiences with the temple, we can say that it is much eaier to connect with the gods and goddesses directly on this level than on the material. You just have to verbally call them within the temple, and if they are ready, they will appear.

Covens who use Astral constructs all speak of having similar experiences. We have heard many stories from individuals and covens who have met within the temple at a predesignated time. When they have talked to each other afterwards in the material world, their stories of what they have experienced have been uncannily similar, even down to what they talked about. These are common occurrences.

Endnotes

1. Quoted in K. Wilber's *The Spectrum of Consciousness*, p. 24. William James (1842–1910) was an original thinker in and between the disciplines of physiology, psychology, and philosophy.
2. One view is that the divisions between Celtic and Germanic peoples were in fact as much a creation by the Roman Empire for political reasons as anything else. For a long while, the Germanic peoples were simply known as "the Northern Gauls." Nationalism during the 1800s only increased this view of racial divisions.
3. There has always been much debate over the symbols on the entrance stone at Newgrange, which traditionally had to be climbed to enter the chamber. During a visit by Issac Bonewits in 2001, both he and Gavin noticed that the markings on the stones bear a strong resemblance to the eddies of the River Boyne. The stone may, in fact, be a representation of the river.
4. In old Scandinavian myth, only one god, Odin, can sit on this throne. He being "the all father"; the chief of the gods. The only exception to this has been Frey, who surreptitiously mounted the throne. (From *For Scirnis, The Prose Edda*, circa 1200)
5. Irish mythology was in fact a fusion of many different regional mythologies, which became fused at the time of Christianity. There are many different names to be found in Irish mythology for the same realm because of this.
6. This one description, from one Icelandic prophecy, has come to shape the whole Asatru view on cosmology. There is no doubt that it is an accurate portrayal of the Northern European Tree of Life, but it is nonetheless just one of possibly many interpretations. What has made it powerful is that fact that it is based on psychic rather than intellectual experience.
7. In many cultures it is believed that man was originally born from the Trees. In Norse, the first man and woman were Ask and Embla (Ash and Elm). It is interesting to note that even in a completely diverse culture, the Australian Aboriginal, they have a similar myth.
8. These five were the Bile Uisnig at Uisneach; the Craobh Daithi at Farbill, Co. Westmeath; the Bile Tartan, an ash tree, located near Ardbraccan, Co. Meath; the Eo Mughna, a yew tree; the Eo Rossa, Old Leighlin, Co. Carlow, also a yew tree.
9. These two realms are Svartalfheim and Ljossalfheim, the realm of the dark elves and the realm of the light elves, respectively.
10. Albert Einstein recorded this need with his Theory of Relativity; that our position and our movement within the universe is really relative to our perception of it. Within

our need to center there is a spiritual truth that we are all, ultimately, at the center of our own universes.

11. In the Sleeping Beauty myth, the Underworld, the Shadow, is the castle and wasteland, and the Bright Shadow is the finely draped room where Sleeping Beauty (the Anima) resides waiting to be rescued. She is, of course, guarded by the Dragon, the Guardian of the Mysteries.

12. According to *Isis in the Graeco-Roman World* (*see* Bibliography), they were sometimes combined in the Graeco-Egyptian Mysteries as Hermanubis.

13. The Lords of the Watchtowers are common in the Gardnerian and Alexandrian traditions. These are traditionally invoked by the use of the Invoking Pentragram Ritual of Earth in these traditions (*see* page 218) rather than the use of visualising the Guardians themselves.

14. Dion Fortune's Moon Temple is unusual in many ways, as it connects all the realms of the Axis of Consciousness in one place. Over the years, Janet has regularly performed the Journey to the Moon Temple with dramatic results. It has been not unusual for the spirits of passed loved ones to appear, as well as personal messages from the gods and goddesses.

Chapter 8

Sorcery:
The Magical Art of Witchcraft

Real magic is energy-based; not ceremony-based.

—Skirnir Freyassonn[1]

The word sorcery tends to cause a negative reaction, mainly due to the stereotyping that has occurred in fictional literature and films. In the average person's mind are images of wizards with flames coming from their fingers and enchantresses glamoring knights in shining armor. The word *sorcery* is therefore unpopular among Neo-Pagans, who find that this fantasy portrayal of the word has demeaned it in some way.

By the Middle Ages, sorcery had come to mean alchemy and High Magic. The magical word sorcery has origins in the French word *sorcier*. It is traditionally used in that language to describe a witch. But even this word has its origins in an older word which we derive the word *source* or *to source* from. This suggests the idea that sorcerers or witches source their power from the Divine Spirit, regardless of whether it is called *Great Spirit, God,* or *Goddess*. This is important, as it is no different to the way contemporary Eurasian Shamans claim to derive their magical power. A good example of this in ancient Pagan practice is the Norse runes, which are actually a system for representing the different energies of the universe that were magically directed by the *Vitki* (magician). The Welsh and Irish Celts had a similar system called Ogham, where the energies of the universe were symbolized as trees. In this chapter, we present a combination of certain received traditions like these with new innovations developed in response to the requirements of our time.

What is this energy? From the perspective of the witch, it is the very energy of life itself. When someone interested in witchcraft comes to us, we have a simple test. We get them to close their eyes, ask them to put their hands out in front of them with their palms up. We then ask them if they wish to see some magic. How they react to what happens next is important. When they open their eyes they discover that we have placed a simple houseplant in its pot on their outstretched hands. We look for the recognition in their eyes, for the understanding that magic is not separate or supernatural, but is life itself.

The idea that magical power and the energy of life are one and the same is not new. It is well known in the spiritual practices of Taoism, and more importantly to us, in the Indo-European magical practices of Hinduism, commonly known as Tantra.[2] It has appeared even in science fiction, which can be perceived as modern mythology.[3] Almost everyone is aware of the idea of *the Force* in the *Star Wars* films—the Jedi are, by any definition of the word, sorcerers! This puts the stereotyped images into better perspective. When we see the wizard with flames coming from his fingers, we are seeing power, the controlled use of energy—his aura. In the enchantress, we are seeing the use of both the aura and the energy centers in the body to create a perceived image and create an appropriate response.

So what is the difference between power and energy? Energy is the raw unmolded material, as opposed to power, which is controlled and put to use. In her second book *Dreaming The Dark: Magic, Sex and Politics*,[4] Starhawk talks about power in several ways. Her discussion is about political power, but it applies to magical energy as well. *Power-over*[5] is the manipulation of another person's energy in order to control him or him, whereas *power from within* describes the witch's role as one who helps individuals come into their own power. This is a perfect description of a Priestess or Priest. While we agree with Starhawk, we would like to add another complimentary perspective. Ultimately, it is not our power, as it derives from the Divine and will eventually return to it.

The energy of life is dynamic. It does not stand still. The energy of the aura and the seven chakras is no different: It is transient, always moving. It is like running water. You may try to hold on to it in your cupped hand, but it will eventually seep through your fingers, go back into the Earth, and make its way back to the great sea that it came from. It is not possible to hold on to it, so to make any magical use of it, it becomes necessary to work with the tide of this energy, allowing it to flow in the direction it wants to flow in. In traditional Anglo-Saxon magic, this is conceptualized as the idea of *Wyrd*, where this flow is also seen to affect the whole course of your life in microcosmic/macrocosmic fashion (for more on this see page 188). This philosophy has strong similarities to the ideas found in Far Eastern Taoism, which we previously mentioned. To work against this flow, to coax the creative energy into a direction it would not naturally go, can be perceived as the misuse that Starhawk refers to as *power-over*. In popular terms, this is commonly known as black magic, although we consider this a misleading term, as magic and energy are neither black nor white.[6] Because this energy is effectively on loan to us, we have a responsibility to use it wisely and ethically or face the karmic consequences.[7]

Being of divine origin, its use does of course connect us with the gods and goddesses in a more direct way. By practising magic correctly, we are using this Divine Energy and allowing it to direct us in its use. By doing so, it will, in the fullness, of time bring us face to face with the mysteries, as "The first thing magic changes is the self" whether we intend it to or not (see pages 63-64).

The Chakra System

The Hindu/Buddhist chakra system was introduced into Western occult thinking at the end of the 19th century, almost certainly by Madame Blavatsky and the Theosophy movement. In Indian philosophical thought, the chakras (or *chakrams*) have been known as they presently appear since at least the 7th century, the time of the first transcription of the Vedas. An early form of the system probably existed well before this date, and there is some circumstantial evidence that a proto-chakra system was known throughout the earlier migratory Indo-European culture. This would have brought this bodily energy system into pre-Christian Germanic, Celtic, and Greek mystical thought.

The significance of the caduceus in Greek myth bears a striking resemblance to the chakra system. The serpents may represent the path of Kundalini, and the place where they cross represents the centers themselves. The caduceus is also the symbol of Hermes, who as Hermes Trismegistus is equated with Anubis as the Guardian of the Mysteries.

This was cited by the Theosophy movement as evidence of a similar system in Europe, and notes on this relationship were first published in C. W. Leadbeater's *The Chakras: A Monograph*[8] as early as 1927. Thus, around the end of the 19th century and into the 20th century, many occultists started using chakras.

Within Western occultism there has always been a belief that it is dangerous to mix magical systems, which has resulted in the idea that Western philosophical thinking does not always readily combine with Eastern. This dogma has its origins in ceremonial magic rather than Pagan philosophy, which has always been ready to adapt to new ideas due to its polytheistic philosophy. Regardless of whether you believe the evidence for the existence of a Western system of energy points of Indo-European origin, it did not stop occultists from working with them. It soon became apparent to them that the chakra system and the energies it represents are as real as the physical organs of the body. In some magical orders they were an important part of mystical doctrine, but their use was kept well hidden. Aleister Crowley and his Ordo Templi Orientis used them extensively, but Crowley refers to them only fleetingly in several of his works as *The Seven Seals*. In his poem *"Aha,"*[9] he describes opening "The Great Gate," the access to the Astral levels through the crown chakra:

> There are seven keys to the great gate,
> Being eight in one and one in eight,
> First, let the body of thee be still,
> Bound by the cerements of will,
> Corpse-rigid; thus though mayst abort
> The fidget-babes that tease the thought.
> Next, let the breath-rhythm be low,
> Easy, regular, and slow;
> So that thy being be in tune
> With the great sea's Pacific swoon.
> Third, let they life be pure and calm,
> Swayed softly as a windless palm.
> Fourth, let the will-to-live be bound
> To the one love of the profound.
> Fifth, let the thought, divinely free
> From sense observe its entity.

Watch every thought that springs; enhance
Hour after hour thy vigilance!
Intense and keen, turned inward, miss
No atom of analysis!
Sixth, on one thought securely pinned
Still every whisper of the wind!
So like a flame straight and unstirred
Burn up they being in one word!
Next, still that ecstasy, prolong
They meditation, steep and strong,
Slaying even God, should he distract
Thy attention from the chosen act!
Last, all these things in one o'erpowered,
Time that the midnight blossom flowered!
The oneness is. Yet even in this,
My son, though shalt not do amiss
If thou restrain the expression shoot
Thy glance to rapture's darkling root,
Discarding name, form, sight, and stress
Even of this higher consciousness;
Pierce to the heart! I leave thee here:
Thou art the Master, I revere
Thy radiance that rolls afar,
O Brother of the Silver Star!

—First published in The Equinox,
vol. I, no. III, 1919

Other occultists of this period warned against their use, including noted occultist and author Israel Regardie, but this was more of a warning against mixing the chakras with other magical systems such as Cabala. This would certainly be inadvisable, although it has not stopped Cabalists from adapting the idea of energy centers into Cabalistic rites such as the Middle Pillar exercise, due to the lack of an extensive body/spirit system in Western occultism. Francis King and Stephen Skinner even adopt chakra symbolism in the form of the *tattwas*, the symbols representing the chakras.

In *Techniques of High Magic: A Handbook of Divination, Alchemy, and the Evocation of Spirits*, they use the tattwas of the four lower chakras to represent the Elements, plus a fifth, Akasha representing Spirit.[10] They conveniently miss out the symbols for both ether (the throat center) and mind (brow center), as they do not fit into general Western occult thinking.

Chakra is Sanskrit for "wheel," and is used to signify the idea of a turning center of energy within the body. To the gifted psychic, chakras manifest as revolving discs of light emerging from the body, sometimes described as funnel-shaped when viewed from the side. These centers are normally arranged within the human body in a vertical fashion. It is important for anyone studying them to realize that there is more than one descriptive system. This will well help to prevent confusion while researching the subject. Different systems quote different numbers of centers, positions, and functions. These range from seven major chakras up to 10, and up to 21 minor chakras. The most commonly used system is the original seven-centered one, and we feel this is the best system for witches to concentrate on until they sufficiently understand the nature of the energy they are working with.

The chakras act as connection and transferral points for the energy of the body. It is vitally important for any student of the occult to understand that the chakras are not objects, but expressions of the flow of energy. Just as the elements exist in the physical body, so they must also simultaneously exist in the etheric, mental/emotional, and spiritual aura. The first four lower chakras are dedicated to the elements. The next three upper chakras are for the purpose of generating the aura bodies. The result of this is a complex, interwoven system of energy, which is sometimes seen by the clairvoyant as a web of colored energy enmeshing spinning colored vortices.

The energy does not exactly spin out from each chakra as first suggested. Rather, the force actually pours into each center at its rear and is then pushed out by the spinning motion at right angles to itself at the front of the body. This action has been described as the same effect as when a bar magnet is pushed into the field of an induction coil, resulting in an electrical current that flows around the coil at right angles to the direction of the magnet.[11] One effect of this action is to cause the formation of "petals," formed of the undulating primal energy as it passes through the chakra. The number of petals within each center increases as you move up from the root center, with the exception of the brow center (see page 161).

In most individuals, the chakras remain in a semi-dormant state, and each center is only opened more fully when its action is required in everyday life. Normally, only three to five centers are clearly open at any one time. They enlarge as spiritual development increases. When all the centers are opened simultaneously, in perfect balance, and have reached their full development, each center spins in the direction opposite to its two adjacent chakras. This effect has been likened to the transferral of energy by series of cogs.

This action is responsible for moving two flows of energy—one positive, one negative—up and down the whole system from the root center to the crown, when the centers are consciously opened in various spiritual exercises, such as in yoga. This is the mystical Kundalini, the Serpent Fire, which the Eastern yogis attempt (though only with full understanding and control) to raise through the other chakras to bring about psychic enlightenment. If aroused early in the unprepared, the Kundalini is potentially highly dangerous, and we recommend that those interested in these practices find a competent instructor.

One interesting aspect of the system is its relationship with the physical body's endocrine system.[12] Chakric meditation seems to act as a color-coded trigger system for controlling these glands and the release of their hormones. There is certainly a correlation between the action of each chakra and its corresponding endocrine gland. A good example of this is the sacral center, which is governed by the Element of Fire. This center is responsible for governing the body's vital energy. It can be no coincidence that it is positioned over the adrenal glands, which are responsible for stimulating energy for the bodies "fright and flight"[13] reflex.

The Seven Major Centers

1. **The Root Center—Earth** (Vedic name: *Muladhara*): This is the seat of the mystical Kundalini, which in Hindu culture is traditionally believed to be a goddess.[14] There are differing views about its actual position. If the body is in the lotus position, it is certainly at the base of the spine (the fourth sacral bone). There is also the view that the normal position of this center is at the base of the feet. This makes sense to us, as it is the center that links us with the Earth. While dowsing, this center picks up energies within the Earth and allows dowsers to detect what they are searching for. It is normally seen as a rosy red color when at rest and fiery orange-red when active. It is divided into four segments or petals, representing the four elements in the material world.

As the center is principally related to the Element of Earth, it is responsible for the disposal of unwanted, impure energies that pollute the three bodies of the aura and the other center. It is therefore of vital importance in the act of grounding. Within the physical body, it governs the spinal column and the urinary system, including the kidneys. This chakra is also associated with physical sensations, such as pain and pleasure.

2. **The Sacral Center—Water** (Vedic name: *Svadhistana*): This is positioned in the genital area. Early Theosophists and practitioners of Laya Yoga worried that concentration on this center would result in the awakening of sexual feelings, and therefore they replaced this chakra with the minor spleenic center, which was described as several inches off-center and to the left of the others. Sexual impulses were considered inherently "black" in nature, as much of the Theosophist literature of the period testifies.

This chakra appears orange in color and relates to the Element of Water. It is traditionally divided into six petals (the four Elements plus "above and below"). It has obvious associations with sexual love, as it controls the flow of energy to the reproductive organs and the endocrine glands in the gonads. Psychologically, it is associated with the emotions and is actively involved in all forms of intimacy, interpersonal feelings, and one's emotional well-being.

3. **The Solar Plexus—Fire** (Vedic name: *Manipura*): Early literatures gave a blend of several shades of green and red for its color, divided into 10 petals, but modern writers tend to portray it as yellow, as do many psychics and healers. We also prefer yellow for this chakra, as yellow fits the color sequence for all the chakras best.

Because of its association with Fire, it is sometimes referred to as the "survival" center. Physically, it is related to the digestive system and the adrenal glands (although some relate these endocrine glands to the first center). This center therefore governs the lower gastrointestinal tract, including the stomach, liver, and gall bladder, probably because this is the system responsible for producing the body's energy.

4. **The Heart Center—Air** (Vedic name: *Anahata*): This center relates to the heart, which in Western culture has been traditionally associated with love and the emotions. This chakra is responsible on the etheric level for our capacity for sympathy and compassion with the pain and pleasures of others. It is hence of great importance for those

involved in the healing arts to study this center in depth. It is also responsible for metabolising the energy of love that we receive from others.

For those on the spiritual path, this chakra is the first center to deal with the concept of *"Self."* For this reason, some have placed this center with the higher chakras, despite its elemental nature. On the physical plane, it governs the heart and the associated vagus nerve and circulatory system. This center is also positioned in the same area as the thymus gland, connecting its actions to the immune system of the body.[15] It is related to the Element of Air, and modern practitioners tend to see it as green or turquoise in colour. Early Theosophical works gave it a golden color and divide it into 12 petals.

5. **The Throat Center—Ether** (Vedic name: *Vishuddhi*): This is the first of the upper centers, positioned at the throat. It relates to the concept of ether, and is therefore the center responsible for generating and connecting us with our etheric body. It is positioned over the larynx and has obvious associations with communication and speech, the power of the word, listening to others, and taking responsibility for what we say.

    Physically, it is related to the respiratory system, the upper alimentary canal, and the vocal apparatus. The throat center also affects metabolism due to its relationship with the thyroid and para-thyroid glands. All traditions agree on its blue color, and it is divided into 16 petals.

6. **The Brow Center—Mind** (Vedic name: *Ajna*): This is the mystical Third Eye, positioned on the brow. It rules the mind and is responsible for generating the mental body. It is well-known as the center that controls clairvoyance and psychic experience. For this reason, it is referred to by some as "the doorway to eternity."

    Within the physical body, it affects the lower brain, ears, eyes, and nervous system. It is positioned perfectly over the pituitary and hypothalamus glands, which control the whole endocrine system. Again, there is no dispute among traditions about this center's color, which is violet or indigo, although there is debate regarding the number of petals. There are two differences in thought. According to the Rev. C. W. Leadbeater[16] there are 96 petals, but according to most Hindu and Buddhist traditional writings, there are two.

From the perspective of the seeker of the mysteries, this chakra has two petals, for the brow chakra governs the psychological processes. The idea of two lobes therefore gives us polarity: positive/negative, right brain/left brain, yin/yang, etc., and of course, Jung's concepts of Anima/Animus and Ego/Shadow, which are of prime importance in understanding the mysteries (see page 63–65).

7. **The Crown Center—Spirit** (Vedic name: *Sahasrara*): This is the final center, known as the crown because of its position at the top of the head. It is the ultimate link with the person's spiritual body and is where the soul enters. It is therefore governed by Spirit. It is the abode of what is often referred to as the Higher Self, or Holy Guardian Angel. This is the Astral Guardian, who monitors and protects us when we venture into the spiritual realms (see page 141).

Its color varies, depending on the individual's spiritual development. It is generally visualized as white, which is made up of all the colours of the spectrum. In a spiritually developed person, it becomes quite large, and when fully open, covers the whole head, producing the classical halo effect. This effect is also produced by its staggering 972 petals.

In Oriental pictures and statues, this chakra is often shown quite prominently, as it is in early Christian iconography. This is considered to be the highest chakra, as it connects the individual to divinity, which is Kether (the crown) in Cabalistic terms, or God and Goddess in general Pagan terminology. In the physical body, it controls the nervous system and the higher functions of the brain.

8. **The Eighth Center:** Spiritualists tend to work with an eighth center, for which they have no name. This is the center Aleister Crowley refers to in his poem, "Aha!" It is located from 18 to 24 inches above the crown center. This puts it outside of the physical body, but within the aura. It is said to act as an intersection between the body's aura and the soul's energy, and as such, can be considered to be nothing more than an extension of the crown center, and related to the remnants of the pineal gland.[17] We suggest it is in fact the crown center as manifest in the spiritual body, and not a separate center.

Visualising the Centers

To have an understanding of what the chakras are, it is necessary to visualise them. This is best done in a semi-meditative state, with eyes closed, in a relaxing atmosphere.

First, visualize a bathtub, then visualize it in the shape of a person. Imagine there are not one, but seven plugholes and place them appropriately in the positions of the seven centers.

Secondly, fill the bath with water. Imagine the water spiralling down the plugholes in a clockwise fashion as it normally does (if you are in the Northern Hemisphere). Now visualize that this flow alternates with each chakra: root center turns clockwise; the sacral turns counterclockwise, and so on up the body.

Third, imagine this process in reverse, as if watching a film backwards, with the water spiralling out of the plugholes into the bath. Now take away the bath, but keep the water there.

Finally, imagine the water coming up out of each plughole in the appropriate color for the chakra. Now imagine the water flowing from the front of each center, and being pulled into the other centers from the back and being pushed out the front.

What you are visualizing is the flow of energy around the aura as it comes out of each center, resulting in a cascading flow of color around the body.

Opening the Chakras

Opening the chakras is an essential exercise if you are going to work with magical energy. Many Pagans who work magic in a circle, and who raise the cone of power, find this quite easy. We would recommend using the following opening and closing exercise on a daily basis until you are adept at the processes involved. It takes approximately 20 to 30 minutes. We would recommend having somebody present who is sensitive and able to see the chakras the first few times you do it. Your helper can confirm when the centers are open. With practice it takes less and less time to open your centers, and you will eventually find that you can discard this exercise completely and open them by willpower alone.

The first stage is to find somewhere quiet and comfortable to sit. The best position to sit in is the well-known lotus position, used in Eastern yoga, because it has the effect of bringing the muladhara, or root center, into line with the other chakras. If you are not supple enough to use this position, sitting cross-legged or kneeling will have the same effect. The important thing is to stay comfortable for a reasonable period of time.

The next stage is to breathe regularly. There are various breathing patterns used, but we have found that breathing out for seven seconds, holding for two seconds, breathing in for seven seconds and finally again holding for two seconds is the most effective. It is important to breathe from the base of the lungs, by expanding the stomach first and then the ribs. It will take a while to get used to this, so give yourself time to master it.

The next stage is to visualize that you are breathing in light—initially this should be white light—before going on to the next stage.

Energizing the chakras, one by one, is the third stage. Continue the breathing pattern that you began with, which by now should be natural and rhythmic. Visualize the root center at the base of the spine as a red, glowing, spinning ball. As you breathe in, visualize the color of your breath as the same color. This should have the effect, after several minutes, of making the chakra expand while spinning faster and brighter.

Finally, imagine the energy from the center you have just energized moving up to the next chakra (in this case, the sacral center), but change the color of the light you are breathing to that of the new chakra (in this case, yellow). Again it should take several minutes to energize the chakra, which should behave in the same way as the first center. You simply repeat the process until you reach and energize the Third Eye or brow center. Then visualize all the colors from each of the energized chakras moving swiftly up to the crown center at the top of the head. Allow the energy to leave the top of the head like a fountain and bathe your aura.

The Aura

The aura is the visual expression of the seven layers of energy that surround the physical human body. There is one for each chakra, but in practice, most only manage to see three of these levels: the etheric, the mental/emotional, and the spiritual. The other four are related to the Elemental centers that manifest the physical body. The inability to see all the different levels is mainly due to cultural perception. Western thought tends to confuse the mental/emotional body, although in fact it is not distinctly divided. Some advanced psychics are able to see all of the seven levels within the aura, but generally most are only able to see the three main levels we have mentioned here.

Chakras

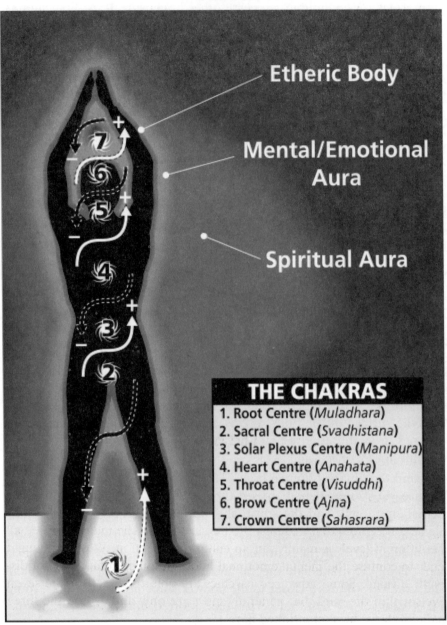

Etheric Body

Mental/Emotional Aura

Spiritual Aura

THE CHAKRAS
1. Root Centre (*Muladhara*)
2. Sacral Centre (*Svadhistana*)
3. Solar Plexus Centre (*Manipura*)
4. Heart Centre (*Anahata*)
5. Throat Centre (*Visuddhi*)
6. Brow Centre (*Ajna*)
7. Crown Centre (*Sahasrara*)

Figure 6

The various levels of the aura also act as a psychic shield and a form of interface for communication with other organisms. It can indicate the emotional and mental state of individuals, as well how spiritually developed they are. Every living organism has an aura, and with practice, it is quite possible to see it. The easiest aura to see is that of a tree at dawn or twilight. It normally manifests as a misty grey field around the topmost branches. In humans, the aura is generated by the action of the chakra centers spinning. The result is that three distinct levels of the aura exist, layered like the skin of an onion (see Figure 6 on page 165).

The etheric body

The grey misty area closest to the body is generally referred to as the etheric body, which normally extends about one to three inches over its surface. The term ether refers to a state between energy and matter. Gifted psychics often describe the etheric body as being composed of energy lines forming a sparkling translucent web along which sparks of bluish white light move. This gives a pulsating effect. The first four chakra centers, these being related to the Elements of Earth, Air, Fire, and Water, generate it. This is important to realize when doing any magical work, as we shall explain later.

The action of these four centers in conjunction with the fifth, the etheric chakra, results in the formation of this part of the aura. The etheric body vibrates at the same frequency as Spirit and acts as a vehicle for it. It therefore helps to shape and anchor the physical body, which is why it hugs the surface of the body so closely. For this reason, it is sometimes referred to as the etheric double. Its main purpose is to feed the body with life force, or *prana*.

The mental/emotional body

The second part is the mental/emotional body, which is generated by the sixth chakra. It made up of even finer energy than the etheric body, and unlike that body, it is normally ovoid in shape. How far it projects depends on the immediate mental and emotional state of the individual. The aura will withdraw closer to the body of someone who enters a room full of strangers. When that person feels more comfortable with the others around, it will begin to return to its normal size.

The aura of an extroverted person can project out as far as several feet, but that of an introvert may remain always close to the body, almost withdrawing into the etheric body. A trained psychic sees this part of the aura as made up of a variety of colors. These, like the size of the aura, indicate the mental, emotional, and (occasionally) the physical state of its owner.

The spiritual body

The last body, and the least easy to see even for someone sensitive, is the spiritual body. This connects with the last of the chakras, the crown. In a spiritually developed person, it can extend from the body for some distance. It is said that the spiritual body of the Buddha Gautama, in his last incarnation, could be seen for six miles. This part of the aura exists on the Astral Plane and is the individual's connection with the world of Spirit.

The individual's consciousness moves in this body, combined with the mental/emotional body, during Astral travel in the higher planes. But during out-of-body experiences on the physical material plane, it is only the mental/emotional body of the aura that detaches from the physical body. This can happen involuntarily, sometimes during sleep, giving what is often referred to by scientists as lucid dreaming or rapid eye movement (REM) sleep (for more on this see page 205).

Because of the etheric body's responsibility for continuing the life functions, it remains attached to the body until the moment of death. As with the mental/emotional body ,there are colors present, but these indicate the character and personality of the individual rather than just his or her present emotions. After physical death, the consciousness leaves the physical body and withdraws into the Astral.

The Auras and Chakras in Magical Work

It is important for a witch to have a true understanding of what is happening with their body's energy system even when performing some of the most basic acts of Wiccan practice. In fact, all of the magical practices utilized in Wicca stimulate the chakras and aura, using their flow of energy as a source of power. The application of the knowledge gained from studying the chakra system and the aura grants this understanding better than any other system we have come across, as it is intrinsically a holistic system, incorporating both a physical and spiritual understanding of occult practice.

When setting up a temple, the most common magical practice in Wicca, we can see the chakras and auras at work:

- **Consecration of salt and water**: Blue energy is visualized cleansing these elements. It derives from the etheric (throat) chakra. The color for this center, of course, is blue.

- **Casting the circle:** The circle is visualized as a globe of blue energy coming down the arm into athame/sword. This energy is, again, coming from the etheric center. Blue is seen as a both a protective and cleansing color because it strengthens the etheric body.

- **Calling the Elemental Watchtowers (Pentagram Ritual):** This actually opens the appropriate chakra in the individual/coven members. For example, if you call the Western (Water) Quarter, you will also open the sacral chakra.

It is noteworthy that the system at work here relates directly to the chakras. When you look at calling the quarters, for example, the centers are opened in sequence: East (heart/Air), South (solar plexus/Fire), West (sacral/Water), and North (root/Earth). We do not believe that this is a coincidence, as the act of using the throat center to previously cast the circle would open this chakra, just as the act of concentration and visualization would open the brow center. Finally, the invocation of deity would open the crown center. What we see in the circle casting and calling of the quarters in general magical practice is a ritualized act of opening the chakra centers and extending the aura for protection.

The etheric energy from the throat center is the most common form of energy used. In the act of consecrating salt and water, it is used for purifying and activating these two elements (salt representing Earth). The consecration results in the formation of an Astral double, a thought-form on the higher planes, from the life force itself (*prana*). In consecrating a magical tool, all four Elements are used in sequence. This is based on the occult idea of the four Elements creating Spirit. The energy from the four Elements comes from the appropriate lower chakra, activated by the symbolism used. In reality, it is actually creating life force, ether. It is this that creates the Astral double as there must be a reflection of all life on the Astral Planes—"As above, so below" in reverse, so to speak. This is symbolised in the Celtic cross, rather than the pentagram, which represents Spirit controlling the elements, rather than the creation of spirit.

This use of the four Elements and ether is also important in other magical acts, such as creation of thought-forms or spell work. In thought-form creation, the process is the same as consecration except that mental/emotional energy is added to create an entity. A common way of creating thought forms is using a jar filled with samples of the four elements: consecrated water, incense (Air), candle wax (Fire), and Earth. Traditionally, "life" (etheric energy) is then breathed into it, and the user gives the thought-form a name, appearance, and charges it with an objective. These latter actions give it energy from the brow center responsible for mental/emotional activity. The result is the creation of an entity on an Astral level.

It is also worth looking at energy-raising rituals to understand what importance the bodily systems play. The cone of power is raised by the use of the energy from the coven. This is generated by physical activity, such as dancing. This increases mental/emotional energy flow, as well as etheric. Chanting also increases energy as it increases flow from the throat center more fully, the center related to communication and pranic flow. Circle casting is not just done for protection: It is also cast to "maintain the energy raised within thee." It acts as a barrier to hold the combined aura of the coven, as individual auras of the coven members not only increase, but merge with each other. The circle symbolically represents the group's aura and to what limit it can extend on the physical and etheric levels. Such rituals of course strengthen the Coven Mind, as the use of ether creates an Astral double of the coven on the higher levels.

Practical Exercises

The following exercises are designed to help the witch feel the flow of magical energy. First of all, you will need to be aware of which of your hands produces energy, and which hand receives it. One easy way to find out is to clasp your hands together and then to see which thumb is on top. Normally this is the primary hand, and, we should point out, is in no way related to whether someone is right- or left-handed. Some find that if they repeat this exercise several times, the thumb changes. This is not unusual and means they can use either hand. Because magic generally goes clockwise in the magic circle, the left hand usually gives energy and the right receives it. This is important to know because if you send and receive with the opposite hand, you will need to practice using both hands. There is a commonly used phrase related to the use of aura energy in magical or healing work: "Energy follows thought," or "Where thought goes, energy flows." It is possible for the mind, working of course through the brow chakra, to direct the energy flow from the hands. To help understand the magical use of energy we have included two exercises.

Two-person exercise

This exercise is very useful in helping to form the magical polarization between working partners.[18] The first stage is for both of you to open your centers (see page 163) and sit comfortably facing each other. You can be sitting either on chairs, or cross-legged on the floor. The important thing is that you are of roughly equal height. You should place the palms of each of your hands facing each other at chest height, and about 12 inches apart. It is important that your hands do not touch at this stage, as the object is for each of you to feel for the other's aura. After a period of time sitting in this position, you should both begin to feel the energy emitting from the minor chakra centers in the palms of your hands. This normally feels like heat to most people, but some individuals may perceive it differently.

Once both of you have felt the flow of energy, you should signal to each other and simultaneously close your eyes. Very slowly, you should move the palms of your hands together, slowly entering each other's aura, and then touch fingertips to fingertips. You should then visualize the energy flowing from your heart center in a circuit going clockwise, from your left hand to your partner's right hand, through your partner's heart center, and back through your partner's left hand to your right hand.

After a period of time visualising and sitting in this position, you may get the sensation that your partner's hands are moving ever so slightly in a circular motion. You should try to follow these movements, but on no account should either of you try consciously to lead these movements. You are feeling the flow of energy within your partner's aura, as it emerges from their chakric centers.

At this point, you and your partner should try to see what effect concentrating on various significant words, colors, and concepts have on the flow of energy. For example, concentrating on the word "love" will probably increase the flow of energy because of is associations with the heart center, which is being used in this exercise. This is the perfect opportunity for you and your partner to find what triggers the flow of energy for you personally, and for you to develop the correct frame of mind for healing. Developing this will enable you to flow with the energy of the coven in magical work. You should repeat this exercise using the crown and the root chakra, but remember to pass this energy through the heart center.

Group exercise

This is really an extension of the two-person exercise. It is useful for attuning the whole coven to each other's energy and understanding such processes as the cone of power. This should preferably be done in a cast magic circle. The coven sits in a circle. Where possible, sit alternately male and female, although, if this is not possible, it will not make any major difference. The Priestess or Priest, or whomever directs the exercise, talks everyone through the opening of the chakras. When this is completed and everyone is happy with the results, all the members of the coven hold hands— left palm down, right palm up. The person directing this exercise then tells them to visualize blue etheric energy flowing from one person to the other in a clockwise direction. He or she encourages the coven to visualize the energy coming down from their crown chakras (white/silver/gold), through the brow (violet) and to the throat center, where it changes to blue, and then down and around the heart center (color remains unchanged). It then goes down their left hands. At the same time, they receive energy from the person to their right. This increases the energy flowing around the circle. When the person directing the exercise feels the energy has built up enough, he/she encourages the coven to visualize it going from them into the center of the circle to form a glowing ball of etheric energy, spinning and growing as they feed it. The color of the energy can be changed as it is passed around the circle. The easiest colors to change into are the colors of the chakra centers that the energy has already passed through.

At the end of the exercise, the energy can be dealt with in two ways. The Priestess or Priest can visualize and release the energy in the same way as in the cone of power (once a worthy recipient of the magical energy is decided upon), or the energy can be taken back into the coven and grounded. We would recommend the former method, until the coven are all thoroughly adept at grounding themselves.

Closing chakras and magical grounding

It is important to ensure that your chakras are closed after you have finished any form of magical work, particularly after the previous exercises. This is commonly called grounding. Leaving them fully open can result in a loss of vitality, higher risk of disease, and mental stress. Most people who are not grounded describe a feeling of disconnection with the world, a feeling of light-headedness. The easiest way to close them down is to eat. This is the purpose of Cakes and Ale ceremony found at the end of most Wiccan rituals, as the ingestion of food closes the chakras while replenishing any energy loss (modern witches are renowned for their fondness for chocolate!).

One other method commonly used is to place the palms of the hands flat on the ground to remove any excess energy left in the system. It is then visualized going into the ground. This is commonly used while visualizing the root center.

If you are new to magical practice or to doing any form of intensive magical work, we recommend the following technique. Visualize the energy draining back down from one chakra to another. Once you have drained the energy from each chakra to the one below it, you visualize a shutter closing it from vision. You repeat this center by center. When you reach the root center, remember that it is the only one you leave open all the time because it acts as the body's grounding point and helps to prevent mental and psychic overload.

Endnotes

1. Pseudonym for a little-known Anglo-Saxon practitioner. He regularly lectures on traditional English magical practices. Taken from his London talk of July 2003.
2. We would like to point out that this word is often misused to mean purely sexual magic. The correct word for sexual magic is Shaktiism.
3. Most science fiction bases its story lines on old mythological precepts. *Star Wars* is one example given, but also the series *Star Trek: Voyager,* which follows the pattern of Homer's *Odyssey.* They very much follow the theories put down by Joseph Campbell in *The Hero With A Thousand Faces.* Science fiction is therefore no more than the modern development of mythology. It is not surprising that so many witches are science fiction fans!
4. *Dreaming The Dark: Magic, Sex and Politics* (*see* Bibliography). Chapter 1, pages 1–14.
5. The continual use of *power-over* practices within Wicca has also contributed to the continual rebellion-dogma-rebellion and acceptance patterns that continue to occur in the Wiccan movement (*see* pages 53–54).

6. This idea of there being two forms of magic, black and white, is derived form monotheistic thinking rather than polytheistic. This is a concept examined carefully by Isaac Bonewits in his seminal work *Real Magic* (*see* Bibliography), where he talks about magic being multicolored.

7. It is important to note that these karmic consequences are not the Judeo-Christian idea of "divine retribution," but a natural process of rebalancing in accordance with magical law (*see* Appendix III).

8. The Rev. C.W. Leadbeater's work has become the standard source material on chakras for most writers on the subject. Unfortunately, it is full of the Victorian prejudices of its time, resulting in this information being relayed into modern works for example, the position of the root center being at the anus or perineum due to the belief that the physical universe was by its very nature corrupt. This is a belief not held within the Hindu/Vedic religious belief system.

9. Published in *Magick* (*see* Bibliography), page XXIII.

10. This use can be found in Chapter 6, pages 54–59 of *Techniques of High Magic: A Handbook of Divination, Alchemy, and the Evocation of the Spirits* (*see* Bibliography).

11. This action is clearly described in Leadbeater's work, as well as in recent editions on chakras including Anodea Judith's *Wheels of Life* (*see* Bibliography).

12. The endocrine system is a series of ductless glands in the body responsible for releasing hormones directly into the blood stream.

13. "Fright and Flight" reflex is the release of adrenaline and noradrenaline into the blood stream in times of danger, resulting in increased awareness and energy levels for the purposes of physical protection.

14. According to Anodea Judith in *Wheels of Life: A Journey Through the Chakras* (*see* Bibliography), "all the Chakras were originally first associated with the Goddess Kundalini. She is described as a sleeping serpent coiled three and a half times around the first Chakra at the base of the spine. Her name comes from the word kundala which means coiled."

15. Until recently, doctors believed that the thymus went dormant after puberty, but recent research now suggest that it remains active, stimulating the production of white blood cells when required.

16. The Rev. C.W. Leadbeater lists 96 petals in his work *The Chakras: A Monograph* (*see* Bibliography). His rationalization for this number of petals relates to energy rather than symbolism.

17. For a long while it was considered to be an inactive organ, but now it is believed to be responsible for controlling the various biorhythms of the body. It works in harmony with the hypothalamus gland that directs the body's thirst, hunger, sexual desire and the biological clock that determines our aging process. It has long been thought by mystics that it was the "seat of the soul."

18. In Wicca, magical polarization was traditionally between couples, a linking of the chakras between two people on an Astral level. The act of polarisation creates increased magical energy between a couple. In later magical development, the individual polarizes with his or her own Anima/Animus complex with the same effect. This is an essential part of the mysteries.

Chapter 9

The Wheel:
Cycles of Time and Fate

Change is the constant, the signal for rebirth, the egg of the phoenix.

—Christina Baldwin[1]

M any years ago, we had a strange experience that caused us to seriously question the nature of time. Like most people, we had always seen and perceived time as linear, but this experience challenged that deeply ingrained idea. Gavin had learned hypnotic regression as a technique from a Buddhist he knew in Portsmouth, and had been regressed by her several times himself. Janet wanted to explore some of her past lives, so he went through the process of taking her back. First Gavin relaxed her, putting her into a light trance state. He then took her slowly back, initially by asking her what happened this day last week, and then last month, the last year, and so on until he started working on memorable events, such as birthdays, Christmas, etc. Finally, Janet was taken back beyond birth. At this point, things did not go as we had expected.

Janet began to recall a past life. She described sitting in front of an expectant crowd. She described them singing and chanting, and she described slowly entering a trance state. "What are you doing here?" said a voice that was definitely not Janet's! "Be gone foul spirit!" A rapid question and answer session opened up between regressed and regressor. Gavin tried to work out exactly what had happened, as Janet, or rather the seeress, became more agitated! In the end, Gavin decided the safest course of action was to bring Janet back to the safety of the living room, so he slowly brought her out of the trance state. She had no memory of the events that had come to pass.

There is no doubt in our minds that this incarnation of Janet's was that of a seeress, a prophetess, possibly in Northern Europe,[2] who entered trance for the benefit of her community (see page 202). We keep an open mind on what had happened, but we believe one possible reason why the incarnation started to question Gavin was that she perceived him as an unfamiliar entity or spirit. We believe this happened because Janet was in a trance within a trance, so to speak, which opened up a bridge between two lines of time—one past, one present. At this time, Janet knew nothing about these trance practices, except of course Drawing Down the Moon, with which she was very familiar. It was to lead us into a whole new field of study, some of the fruits of which can be found in this book.

From the moment humanity first became sentient and self-aware, we have been preoccupied with time. By dividing it, logging it, cataloging, and pondering on it, man has attempted to control the uncontrollable passages of birth, growth, decay, and death that have come to represent time. This need to control time comes out of fear and apprehension about tomorrow, stimulated by our primordial need for survival. It is so strong that even one of the first science fiction novels ever published was about time travel: H. G. Wells' *The Time Machine*. The idea of time travel continues to be a favorite subject amongst science fiction writers and pulp sci-fi on television because of our inherent fascination with the passage of every second, minute, and hour.

Many aspects of magic itself have been about this attempt to control time. The magic circle is cast in the direction of the sun, for the first unit for measuring time was the passage of the day into night. Each quarter has become not only associated with the time of the day (the position of the sun), but also with the season (North: Winter, East: Spring, South: Summer, West: Autumn). As many witches can testify, our perception of time changes when we are in the magic circle. For some, it seems to speed up, for others, it seems to slow down. To quote from one ritual; "This is a time that is not a time, in a place that is not a place, on a day that is not a day, between the worlds and beyond..."[3] Time is, at the end of the day (excuse the pun!), about our own perceptions. There are physical markers; the movement of the sun dictates our whole perception of time, but we decide what markers to use, and this is very much guided by our spiritual beliefs.

From antiquity, time was always connected to the steady movement of the stars, the planets, and the sun. The great Greek philosopher Plato confirms this association in his major work on cosmology, the *Timeus*. He identifies time with the movement of the celestial bodies; the cosmology of *wheels within wheels*, or the *Crystal Spheres* as it was known. Although his student, Aristotle, tried to separate time from our movement through space, it was the Christian scholar St. Augustine who finally started to separate the two in people's thought at the start of the Christian era. He considered time to be purely subjective, an internal sense, and outlined this belief in his work *Confessions*: "What, then is time? I know well enough what it is, provided that nobody asks me; but if I am asked what it is and try to explain, I am baffled."

Divination, prophecy, and soothsaying are all magical arts associated with witchcraft. They are attempts to foretell the future and to discern our fate within the rigors and uncertainty of time. Janet has noticed over the years that the number of customers coming to her for tarot readings increases at times of social stress and world upheaval. In recent years, this has been particularly noticeable during times of war.

Foretelling the future was important to the spiritual practices of the ancient world. In ancient Greece, the Pythoness of Delphi would sit over a chasm believed to be the entrance to the realm of the dead. She would sit on a tripod over the chasm and inhale the fumes that rose from the abyss below her. Her consciousness would be overcome, and she would enter trance and communicate in cryptic images to the gathered dignitaries. It was believed that she was inspired by one of the serpents of the staff of Apollo, the deity to whom she was dedicated. The same process can be found throughout Europe, although the method of inducing trance may be different. The practice of Seith and of Drawing Down the Moon are both methods of true divination, for they enable contact with the Divine to understand the future. From a sociological viewpoint, it can be said that these practices came about to allay people's fears and apprehensions, allowing them to function without stress in the world around them. Prophets thereby assisted the requirements of survival not only for the individual, but also of the society they lived in. They promoted order and structure within the society and thus became a method of social control.

It is interesting that the staff of Apollo is none other than the same caduceus carried by Hermes, who as Hermes Trismegistus is the psychopompous, the guide who takes us to the mysteries. The staff can represent not only the energy centers of the body (see page 155), but also the Axis Mundi of the spiritual cosmology (see page 134). It also bears a startling similarity to the basic structure of DNA, which biologists now know causes our ageing process.[4] Something to consider is this: Is it a map of time? Our usual belief is that time is linear and we move only in the direction of the future. This is opposed to ancient thought that observed the circular movements of the heavens, stars, and planets, and concluded that time is cyclical.[5] This is also why the standard week has seven days, each with a planetary association. Our ancient ancestors believed that time would repeat itself, but this was, of course, a spiritual rather than a scientific belief.

For anyone on the spiritual path, it is impossible to separate our perception of time from our spiritual practices. Many believe that religion's main purpose for coming into being is to allay our fears of death.[6] We say that religion's main purpose is to prove that there is more to our existence than just death, more than oblivion and nothingness. Our spiritual perception of time tells us that life and time are cyclical and that our soul will return. This enables us to realize that there truly is meaning to life.

The Eight Sabbats—The Wheel of the Year

The witches' year is traditionally divided into 13 lunar periods called Esbats and eight solar festivals called Sabbats (see Figure 7 on page 179). Each week is divided into seven days, one for each visible planet plus the sun and moon. This is repeated in the day, which was also traditionally divided according to the planets in medieval magical thinking. The origins of the modern Pagan year can be found in the folk festivals of Europe, as well as academic works of the 19th and 20th centuries. There are many books on these festivals, indicating their importance in the theology of modern Paganism. With her late husband Stewart, Janet wrote one of the most influential works on the subject, *Eight Sabbats for Witches* (see Bibliography). It remains one of the standard source books for information on this subject. It is not our intention to repeat that material, but to supplement it with more spiritual insight. Yet, it is still necessary to run through the basics of the eight festivals of the witches' year.

The Wheel of the Year

Figure 7.

Imbolg:　February 2nd. Also known as Oimelc, Brigantia, and Christianised as St. Bridget's Day and Candlemas. Imbolg means "in the belly," a reference to the seed growing in the ground. It is the quickening of the year, the first foetal stirrings of spring in the womb of Mother Earth. Agriculturally, it was the time when the ground was prepared for planting. In Wiccan ritual practice it is marked by the banishing of winter and the welcoming of the Goddess into the cycle of the year; "Brid is come, Brid is welcome."

Spring Equinox: March 20th (or thereabouts). Also known as Ostara, for Eostre, the Anglo-Saxon goddess of spring, and Christianized as Lady Day and Easter. In the Mediterranean practices associated with this festival, there were strong sacrificial mating themes linking it to the mysteries, particularly those of Cybele, which involved death and resurrection of her lover Attis. It is clearly apparent why Christianity chose to place Easter near this festival (on the Roman Catholic calendar, Easter Sunday is always the first Sunday after the first full moon after the Spring Equinox).

Beltane: April 30th. Also known as Bealtaine, May Eve, Walpurgis Night, Cyntefyn, and Roodmass. In Wicca, Beltane very much embraces the same theme of the Spring Equinox, the resurrection of the Oak King, the god of fertility. In traditional folk custom, the lighting of the Bel-Fires marked this occasion. It was also a traditional festival of unbridled sexuality. Sexual rites were an important part of the agricultural cycle as a form of sympathetic magic to fertilize the crops for the coming harvest. These rites continue today in folk custom as May Day with the erection of the phallic May Pole. This tradition continues in Wiccan ritual, such as the jumping of the Baal Fire, or the Great Rite, which symbolically or literally reenacts sexual intercourse. Beltane was also traditionally the time for Greenwood marriages, which lasted a year and a day.

Summer Solstice: June 20th (or thereabouts). Also known as Litha, Alban Hefin, and Christianized as St. John's Day. The Solstice marked the sun at its height, with the nights now beginning to draw in earlier. In Wiccan ritual, it is the end of the rule of the Oak King and his death. The Goddess now gives birth to the Holly King, who rules from this point onwards, symbolically marking the waning of the year.

Lughnasadh: July 31st. Commonly known as Lammas (Loaf Mass) and Lady Day Eve. This is traditionally the Harvest festival celebrating the end of harvest of cereal crops such as wheat, barley, etc. In times of old, it was the time of sacrifice in thanks for the food crop that would sustain the tribe during the coming year. Once it may have been an act of real human sacrifice. But even before the advent of Christianity, it changed into a symbolic act, and as a symbolic act it continues in modern Wiccan ritual.

Autumn Equinox: September 20th (or thereabouts). Known as Mabon in Wicca, as well as Alban Hefed. After Autumn Equinox, night starts to become longer than day. It is the second Harvest festival when berries appeared on bushes.

Samhain: October 31st. Called Halloween, All-Hallows' Eve, and Calan Gaef. This was the time of year when domesticated livestock was either brought into the homestead for feeding and protection or slaughtered and salted for the winter months. It is the latter that gives it one of its associations with death, as well as the fact that most deaths occurred at this time of year due to the change in weather conditions. It is also the third Harvest festival when fruits, such as apples, were ready to collect from the trees. In agricultural Pagan practice it is the New Year, the time to honor the ancestors. This is done in Wiccan ritual by calling back the dead, and then celebrating this connection with the past.

Winter Solstice: December 20th (or thereabouts). Known as Yule, Modranacht, and Alban Arthan, this was the original New Year in the hunter-gather cycle, the occasion when the days started to become longer. For the Anglo-Saxons and the Norse, it remained so even with the advent of agriculture; hence it became known as Modranacht, the night of the mother, when the Goddess gave birth to the god of the New Year. This is one of the principle reasons Christianity originally placed Christmas on this date. In Wicca, it marks the birth of the Oak King.

The Witches' Wheel of the Year

Pagan Name	Common Name	Date	Saints/Holy Day
Imbolg (Oimelc)	Candlemass	February 2nd	St. Bridget's
Ostara	Spring Equinox	Approx. March 20th	Easter
Beltane (Bealtaine)	May Eve	April 30th	St. Walpurgis's
Litha	Summer Solstice	Approx. June 20th	St. John's
Lughnasadh	Lammas	August 1st	Lady Day Eve
Mabon	Autumn Equinox	Approx. September 20th	Michaelmas
Samhain	Halloween	October 31st	All Saints'/All Hallows' Eve
Yule	Winter Solstice	Approx. December 20th	Christmas /St. Stephen's

The solar festivals: the hunter-gatherer cycle

The first festivals recognized by man were the solar festivals, particularly the Equinoxes. For some witches, this may be a revelation, but for anyone living in Ireland who has explored the landscape, this is patently obvious. The first hunter-gatherers who came to Ireland settled and started to build the monuments, the passage tombs and mounds, which exist on many of the hills of Éire today. Most of these monuments are lined up to the Equinoxes rather than Solstices. Slieve na Callaighe (The Hill of the Witch) in County Meath, Four Knocks in County Lough, and the great passage tombs of Knowth and Dowth in the Boyne Valley are all aligned to the Equinox. Sites such as Brú na Bóinne (Newgrange) and Stonehenge in England, which mark the Winter and Summer Solstices respectively, are in the minority. This is really quite logical, for the Equinoxes are the easiest to recognize, due to the equal lengths of day and night—a powerful time magically, being a balance of polarized energy. Their recognition by ancient peoples would have divided the year into two; they may even have perceived the existence of two years, each six months long.

The Goddess of Life and Fertility ruled spring and summer starting on the Spring Equinox, while the God of Death and the Hunt ruled autumn and winter, beginning on the Autumn Equinox. Even today, some witches still divide the year between these two deities. The God of Death and Hunt is of course, the Horned God of witchcraft, Cernunnos or Herne (see page 89). His importance was self-evident to a culture that relied on hunting during the winter months to survive when basic agriculture and the gathering of berries and fruits had come to an end. His worship ensured the success of the hunt, and he was believed to have taught man the first skills of hunting, the first male mysteries. Modern witches refer to this festival as Mabon, a reference to the Welsh Celtic male deity who rode on horseback and who was believed to hunt with a hound of unsurpassed ability.

The Goddess of Life and Fertility ensured the arrival of the spring, the warmth of the summer, and the fertility of crops and plants, marking the beginning of the pastoral year. From her came the fertility of the tribe and the power of the tribes' women to bear children. She was the first Mother Goddess, and as such, was responsible for teaching the first female mysteries. The Anglo-Saxons named the Spring Equinox after Ostara, the Goddess of Fertility. This is the word from which we derive Easter.

The Solstices began to take on more importance as early agriculture developed. It became necessary to mark the mid-summer and mid-winter positions to calculate the right times to harvest and plant. Eventually, the lunar cycle was to take precedence over these festivals, but they were still important as they marked the points where the year started to wax and wane.

The fire festivals: the lunar agricultural cycle

What are commonly referred to as the Celtic Fire festivals date back prior to both the Celts and the Northern European peoples. They date back to the first agricultural practices of our early ancestors. They have become associated with specific dates of the modern calendar, since they were absorbed by Christianity into saint's days. Hence, they tend to have several names; for example, Lughnasadh is also commonly known as Lammas, or as it was originally known before being shortened in speech, Loafmas, the Christian name for this Harvest festival. The original festivals of Imbolg, Beltane, Lammas, and Samhain were originally lunar celebrations, falling on new, full, or waning moons. Not only early on, but also until quite recently, man planted his crops according to the phases of the moon. Agricultural festivals would have been reflected in the time of the celebration. This can again be found in the Old English Church calendar, where the festival closest to Imbolg was also known as Plough Charming Day or more importantly, Plough Monday.[7] Monday is, of course, the day related to the moon. These were practical festivals as well as spiritual ones. They related directly to the everyday survival activities of the farming communities that celebrated them.

Each month, or "moonth" as it was originally known, was directly related to a full moon cycle. Each moon had a different attribution:

The Names of the Lunar Months[8]

January	Snow Moon	**July**	Lightning Moon
February	Death Moon	**August**	Harvest Moon
March	Awakening Moon	**September**	Hunters' Moon
April	Grass Moon	**October**	Blood Moon
May	Planting Moon	**November**	Tree Moon
June	Rose Moon	**December**	Long Night Moon/ Ice Moon

Of course, before the introduction of the modern Julian and then Gregorian calendars, there were 13 moons in a year and therefore 13 months; hence Long Night Moon and Ice Moon are both in December. Many of the names of these "moonths" relate directly to the festivals that fall in them, particularly Samhain and Lughnasadh; Blood Moon related to the need to butcher livestock before the Winter, and of course Harvest Moon related to the Harvest festival of Lammas. Beltane falls on Planting Moon, indicating that the festival would have been a celebration of the completion of this agricultural task and the asking for blessing on this act. Imbolg would have been Death Moon, a name that may seem odd at first unless you take into account that Imbolg is about rebirth from death.

One theory we have developed is that the lunar cycle and the Fire festivals were originally directly related to each in the following way. Imbolc would have been held on the dark moon/new moon towards the end of January or beginning of February. This is logical, as the Goddess was hidden from view, and preparation of the soil traditionally takes place at this time. Beltane would have been on the new moon, marking the beginning of summer. Lughnasadh, the Harvest festival, was traditionally held at full moon, the time of completion and birth; hence its name, *Lady Day*. Samhain, traditionally associated with the hag on a broomstick, would have originally fallen on the waning moon, the moon associated with the Crone. The Christian Church placed the lunar orientated agricultural Fire festivals on saint's days, and in one stroke managed to remove the worship of the moon and the Goddess from the calendar.

Many Pagans and witches are in fact still worshipping on these saint's days rather than the original dates for the Fire festivals. Many covens find themselves working on the closest weekend due to the commitments of work and modern living. There is nothing wrong with this, as in a fast modern world it is necessary for witches to be adaptable. They are flexible festivals related to the activities of man rather than astronomical cycles, before the advent of the fixed calendar. Even the lunar associations are in fact a side issue, as very few modern farmers now sow, plant, or harvest according to the moon. In practice, this means that a good witch needs to look at the activities of the countryside (or even the town) for guidance as to when to hold the festival. We do this ourselves. We wait to celebrate Lughnasadh until the crops are in before celebrating the harvest, an eminently more sensible way of doing things when you think about it. We teach our students that if they want to know what a seasonal festival is all about and conduct a ritual with appropriate symbolism, the answer is to "look out the window" and draw your inspiration from nature, not a book!

The inclusion of the Holly King/Oak King cycle into the Wheel of the Year was very much a medieval invention. Its inclusion into Wicca is really quite modern, with Robert Grave's *The White Goddess* as the major source. Prior to its inclusion in Janet and Stewart's *Book of Shadows*, and then into *Eight Sabbats for Witches,* its use was non-existent within the standard Alexandrian *Book of Shadows* or within any of the copies of the Gardnerian *Books of Shadows* that we have seen.[9] It was included because it worked, for it was based on an observable cycle within nature. Additionally, to quote Stewart, there were "very little bones" in the existing Sabbat rituals. From a progressive viewpoint, we see no reason why others cannot do similarly, looking at the cycles of nature where they live and adapting their seasonal festivals appropriately.

In *The Witches Way* Janet and Stewart pointed out that the seasonal festivals in the Southern Hemisphere were 180° out of position in the year acording to the Northern Calendar (spring starts in September as opposed to March).[10] This is now completely accepted by the Pagan communities of Australia and New Zealand who have adjusted their festival dates accordingly. For example, Beltane is celebrated on the 31st of October rather than the 31st of April. The debate now is focused on the position of the Elements and circle casting.[11] The question is, should the circle be cast counter-clockwise, the direction of the sun in the Southern hemisphere? Also, should the Element-to-Direction correspondences be changed due to the fact that the sun rises in the West, is at its mid-point in the North, and sets in the East? The existing Elemental/cardinal point correspondences in the Northern hemisphere have always had these attributed to them because of the sun's position at time of day (see page 133). A good example of this is the West's association with the Element of Water, death, and rebirth, because it is the quarter of the setting sun. From the viewpoint of the mysteries, we would say that it is necessary to look to nature rather than dogma, and to change appropriately. Others would of course disagree, arguing that these associations are set in stone on the Astral level. We do not believe this to be true. Our counter argument is that the occult law of "As above, so below" applies here, implying that the physical movement of the heavens in the Southern hemisphere would be reflected on the Astral level if you are working in that hemisphere.

This flexibility of location does bring up another issue. How relevant is it to work an agricultural cycle in a location where that actual cycle does not exist? It seems logical to us that any connection with nature means connecting with the natural environment around you. We believe that, for example, it is pointless to work with symbolism such as the Corn King if corn does not exist as a crop in your location. We feel it would be better to echo the local environment in your seasonal workings. By doing so, you will connect with the season cycle on a deeper level by reflecting the "As above, so below" law (see Appendix III).

Spirituality, the Mysteries, and the Power Tides

By connecting to nature directly, we realize that we are in fact physically affected by these cycles, particularly those of the sun and moon. If you have ever come across anyone who suffers from "Winter Blues," or as it more correctly known, Seasonal Affective Disorder (SAD), you will be aware of the effects the yearly cycle has on him or her. SAD is in fact not a disease or a disorder, but a memory of the time when our metabolism, the speed of our bodies, slowed down due to the decrease in certain frequencies of light during the autumn and winter months.[12] This was necessary as food became short in supply, and a slow metabolism requires less energy—food—to sustain it. Of course, in the modern age, with abundant food and warm houses, this is redundant, but in the past it was a necessary physical reaction needed for survival. Unfortunately, evolution has not caught up with some people and they still have this mild hibernation reflex. They are directly affected by the change of seasons. What is interesting to note is that the most effective cure for SAD is hypericum or, as it is more commonly known, St. John's Wort. Obviously, our ancestors were aware of its effects, as St. John's Day was Summer Solstice, the day when the sun was at its height.

The purpose of recognizing the yearly cycle in magical practice is to connect us with the ebb and flow of nature's energies, which are called the *power tides* (see Figure 7 on page 179). This is a highly important aspect of witchcraft, as it firmly grounds Wiccan spirituality in the cycles of nature. Without connection to these energies, we would neither be able to connect with our own true selves, nor with the gods and goddesses as manifestations of the Divine. The cycles of sun and moon affect all other cycles of life, including the seasons, the tides of the seas, and ultimately, the cycles of life on Earth, including those of man. From this, we can see why such occult sciences as astrology became so important, as well as the later development of biorhythms, which gained acceptance in the 1970s.[13] There are four power tides in the year:

- **Tide of Destruction:** Winter Solstice to Spring Equinox.

- **Tide of Renewal:** Spring Equinox to Summer Solstice.

- **Tide of Completion:** Summer Solstice to Autumn Equinox.

- **Tide of Preparation:** Autumn Equinox to Winter Solstice.

The ebb and flow of creative, transformative, and recessive energy are directly related to the Equinoxes and Solstices. It is at these times that they reach their peak. Some of the most magical times to work are when these powers are in a balance, equal polarity, a state of Yin and Yang—not just in basic magical work, but also in self-transformative work related to the appropriate energy. The four Fire festivals are the celebration of the use of this energy in conjunction with the feminine energy of the lunar cycle for agricultural and fertility purposes. But the most magically important festivals to this cycle are the Solstices and Equinoxes.

The mysteries are therefore directly related to this energy as well as the deities associated with each of the festivals. Each Sabbat is also named after a deity; for example Ostara, or Imbolc, is also known as Brigantia, the British name for Brid. The spiritual attributes of the energy present were personified[14] as gods and goddesses. It is therefore possible to connect with these energies via Deity itself and use this energy in experiencing the mysteries. Our ancestors saw the passage rites of birth, death, and life as magical rites. They would have orientated such rites to the power tides. Hence Beltane was seen as a time of marriage and procreation, being at the height of the Tide of Renewal.

The Gods and Goddesses of Fate and Wyrd

Even today, we still personify time. The old Greek god Cronus, for instance, is still with us as "Old Father Time," holding his sickle and hourglass. He appears at every New Year, but few realize his true name or origins. At the strike of midnight, he dies and Horus is born, the child of hope for the forthcoming year. Our need to personify time goes back even further than these primal deities. The Triple Goddess of modern witchcraft, the Maid, Mother, and Crone, relates to the cycles of the moon. The waxing, full, and waning moons are also the Moirae, the Greek goddesses of Fate. They were the daughters of Zeus by Themis. Clotho was the spinner of the web of life. Her sister Lacheisis wove the threads. Finally, the last sister Atropos would cut the thread. Their will was carried out by the Keres, "the dogs of Hades." It was said that they would pounce on the dying at the appointed hour. The myth is almost identical to that of the Norns of the Norse and the Wyrd Sisters of the English. It has a common origin in Indo-European culture.

It was Wyrd or Urd who was responsible for spinning the thread of life, while Verdandi wove this as the thread of fate, and finally Skuld would tear the thread. It as said that they were the Guardians of the sacred tree of Yggdrasil (see page 134). They remain with us today in Macbeth as the three witches, "these three weird sisters," and as the much-sanitized modern Wiccan concept of the Triple Moon Goddess. The Triple Goddess does of course reflect time, but on the much smaller scale of one lunar month. The Moirae and Norns are eternal, reflecting the cycles of life. In both Norse and Greek myth, it was believed that even the goddesses and gods of the ancient world were at the mercy of the three fates. Even they could not escape the ravages of time. This is a prominent theme in Norse/Icelandic poem *The Lay of the High One*[15] when Odin hangs on the World Tree to discover the Runes. In this classic description of a Shamanic initiation, Odin goes through the process of sacrificing the self, by descending into the Underworld through the Well of Urd. In Norse myth, the base of Yggdrasil the World Tree is guarded by the three Norns. Odin corresponds with Wednesday in the weekly cycle, which is governed by the planet Mercury (in France Wednesday is known as Mercredi, Mercury's day), who as a god is of course none other than Hermes Trismegistus, the psychopompous of the mysteries. Here we have a clear link in mythology between the ideas of fate, time, and the classical idea of the mysteries.

Our modern word *weird* does in fact have its origins in the word *Wyrd*. Wyrd is often used to describe our ancient ancestors' concept similar to fate. We have all had "weird" things happen to us; for example, just when we require help in someway, someone appears from our past to miraculously help us. Possibly a series of events seem to strangely come together in such a way, causing a thing of monumental importance in our lives to come to pass. This is Wyrd at work. To our ancestors, our fate was not fixed. They perceived that our lives were like a web, a web of Wyrd, and that we slowly worked our way from the outside of the web to the center—the strand spun by Urd or Clotho, to the moment of our death—when Skuld or Atropos would cut the thread.

As we move forward on the strand to the center, the strand of development and growth, it is inevitable we will have to cross the weft of the web, woven by Verdandi or Lacheisis, the concentric strands that she wove around the web. This signifies that there are some things we cannot avoid. They are generally karmic and carry on from previous incarnations. Some things in our lives are destined, such as meeting an acquaintance from a past life, be it a positive or negative experience. The general outcome of one's life is not fixed: For instance, what happens after you meet that person is in your hands! There are many different ways of reaching the center of the web. One can move sideways along a weft onto a different strand to the center. You can even move backwards, particularly if you do not learn an important lesson. You therefore become destined to repeat the pattern in a cyclical fashion until you break free from it. Sometimes this breaking free from a cycle can in fact be a form of initiation and can break a cycle that may have existed through many lifetimes. If we do not, the cycle is destined to repeat itself into our next lives, for the cloth on Verdandi or Lacheisis's loom remains unfinished.

Our ancestors believed strongly in cycles. They saw cycles around them in the movement of the sun and moon. This idea is carried over in modern astrology where it is believed that our lives go in a 29-year cycle called the *Saturn return*. It is important to note that Saturn as a god is none other than the Romanization of the previously mentioned Cronus, the Greek God of Time and Fate. In astrology, the Saturn return is believed to be a time when we come into our own as controllers of our own destiny; an important goal of magical practice.

The Mysteries in the Wheel of the Year

From Imbolg, when we emerge from the womb, to Yule (Winter Solstice), when we return at death to the Earth, we experience the seasonal tides both internally and externally with each passing year. Every spring, like Persephone, we rise to greet our own new season of life; from our Underworld of Winter depression we wake to new growth, optimism, and an enthusiasm for our future challenges. By the time Mabon (Autumn Equinox) is upon us, we become more aware of how our lives have progressed during the warm months of Summer, digesting and storing away for the Winter months things to be worked on to better our future after the Winter Solstice. We digest all those glorious memories of the long, lazy days of Summer, intuitively knowing that after the crisp frosts of Autumn, when our senses become sharper, we inevitably have to face the dark Underworld days that lie ahead of us.

With each year, our awareness of identity becomes more complete. From the angst of teenage years, when our bodies are budding and our brains are still struggling to reach full maturity, to the early adult years when the desire to reproduce takes precedence, we become self-absorbed, full of free Spirit and inner desires. By the midsummer of our lives, we are formulating future security, learning from the lessons of those early years. We have gained a modicum of wisdom and maturity. Although we embraced the Maiden in our physical existence, it has been the Crone of Wisdom from whom we have desired to learn as we grew, and she is slowly replaced by the Mother Goddess, who holds the scales of life and balance within us. This is the time of nurturing years of our lives. Caring for our young and finding ways to provide for their future adds to our personal library of knowledge and wisdom. If one is a healthy individual, by now we should have the confidence to have learned from the mistakes we inevitably made during those formative years and be gracious enough to admit to not always being right.

As we enter our middle years, the Crone replaces the Mother physically, and from the Crone's wisdom, we learn to psychologically embrace the Maiden, and a sense of freedom and peace begins to descend upon us. Our offspring are nearly fully independent, forming lives of their own, and once again, we are free to explore our inner world. It is "time out" for ourselves. The middle years are the time to harvest the fruits of our lives, and to enjoy a newfound freedom. We explore all the possibilities that life now offers to us. We can look back on the mistakes we have made on our life journey. Some we will view with sadness, others we will find humorous and, like Persephone, we will throw caution to the wind and laugh with joy at all life has to offer. Yet deep inside we are aware that the Underworld cave is coming more into focus with each passing day. Like the Spring Goddess, we must eventually enter that cave and explore the great winter mystery—the Mystery of Death. To the witch, however, this is not viewed with cold terror but more with a sense of dejá vu. We know that, like the sun at Newgrange during the Winter Solstice, light will penetrate the realm of Hades and we will return again to this earthly cycle to renew the mysteries within each of us. With each rebirth, we acquire more knowledge and spiritual strength; the cyclical mysteries of life and death are the very foundation stones that will be our guides upon the path of existence.

Endnotes

1. Christina Baldwin is a writer and lecturer on the subject of spirituality and the spiritual journey. She has several books to her name including: *Seven Whispers: Listening to the Voice of Spirit* (New World Library, 2002) and *Calling the Circle: The First and Future Culture* (Bantam, 1998).
2. This is the practice of Seith or Seidr we have mentioned previously in Chapter 7.
3. From *A Book of Pagan Ritual* by Ed Fitch (*see* Bibliography).
4. It is interesting to note that the structure of DNA was discovered because of a dream by one of the scientists.
5. This is a view proposed by Mircea Eliade, one of the world's foremost authors on mythology and religion, known by most Pagans for his seminal work *Shamanism: Archaic Techniques of Ecstasy.*
6. A theory of the philosopher Frederich Neitzsche.
7. This is a traditionally Anglican (Church of England) festival, although now rarely performed.
8. It is important to remember that there are several systems of names for the lunar months.
9. We have little doubt that since the 1960s much of its material has been incorporated, either from the primary source or as handed down "traditional" material.
10. Chapter 25, pages 269–272 of *A Witches' Bible* (*see* Bibliography).
11. This is a debate fueled by several talks and articles by Julia Phillips, a well-known Wiccan writer and lecturer. She outlines her argument for the quarters being also affected by the Southern Hemisphere in the on-line magazine *Shadow Play*, #25.
12. SAD is caused by the lack of light during the winter months. Light is necessary for stimulating the production of seratonin, a neuro-receptor, within the brain.
13. In the 1890s, a highly respected doctor from Berlin, Wilhelm Fliess, did pioneer work involving the 23- and 28-day cycles of some of his patients—biorhythms. The statistics he gathered led him to believe he had discovered certain rhythms that were fundamental to life. These rhythms related to the occurrence of illness, as well as emotional, mental, and physical agility. He developed two theories based on the principle that nature bestows "master internal clocks" on humans that begin counting at birth and continue until death, and that these clocks are responsible for regulating a 23-day cycle that influences the physical condition while another regulates a 28-day cycle influencing the emotions. From a Pagan viewpoint, it is interesting to note that this 28-day cycle seems to be directly related to the cycle of the moon, particularly as the moon is said to govern the Element of Water, the element of emotion. As interest grew in Dr. Fliess' theories, Sigmund Freud, as well as many other noted scientists, began showing an avid interest in the studies. In the 1930s, a very successful study was done that related accidents to the critical days in the cycle. These are the days when the cycles drop from highs to lows. Although there is plenty of evidence for their existence, many more mainstream scientists and doctors still debate their existence, but certainly they fit in with the cyclical nature of both the lunar and power tide cycles.
14. The Church, of course, slowly merged aspects of saints with those of deities, making it easier to absorb the lunar fire festivals.
15. From *The Poetic Edda* by Snorri Sturluson (*see* Bibliography). Also known as *The Saying of Har.*

Chapter 10

Priesthood:
Connecting With and Serving Deity

*We should take care not to make the intellect our
god; it has, of course, powerful muscles, but no
personality.*

—Albert Einstein[1]

It is the role of the Priestess or Priest, not only to commune with the gods and goddesses as the manifestation of The Divine, but more importantly, to serve them for the benefit of humanity and the world. The Priest or Priestess has traditionally throughout the world been defined as someone who acts as a conduit for deity, the ancestral gods and goddesses of the people talking through them to guide or help them in some way. To quote the well-known witchcraft writer Gavin Frost, the New Age faces us with, "a religion that cuts out the middle man." Witchcraft has become a religion that does away with the old Christian idea that only the Priest connects with The Divine. In this situation, the role of the witch as a Priestess or Priest becomes more important, as it now becomes his or her responsibility to teach people how to connect directly with the old gods and goddesses of the people.

There is a difference between connecting and serving. While connecting with deity should be at the core of all religious practice, serving as a

Priestess or Priest of deity is a vocation, a religious calling, and therefore not suited to everyone. Some might say that this is elitist thinking. But that argument confuses *connecting to deity* with *serving deity* as if they are the same process. We would say they are not, as no one would accuse a doctor of being elitist for following his vocation, nor say that only he was responsible for your health and well-being. Any good doctor would say you are ultimately responsible for your own health. Likewise, the Priesthood's role is to help connect the individual with divinity, but not do to it for him or her.

The witches' role, we believe, stretches beyond the boundaries of what is referred to as "Pagan community." It has been the nature of Neo-Paganism to be insular due to fear of discrimination and prejudice. In some areas, this has resulted in the attitude that we should only be concerned with acting as a Priesthood within the coven and the Pagan community, but not beyond. This attitude is very much influenced by the doctrine of secrecy (see page 46) and the fear of prejudice and discrimination. Speaking from experience, when you connect with divinity, you cease to see the world with such limited tunnel vision. Even labeling oneself *witch* or *Wiccan* becomes secondary to the idea of being a Priestess or Priest of a specific god or goddess. Connection with The Divine enables one to realize how arbitrary religious divisions are. Many witches and witchcraft-based organizations have put their hands out in friendship to other religious groups, realizing that The Divine is present in every perception of spirituality. Witches can now be found on ecumenical councils both in Europe and in the United States.[2] We are pleased to say that this has had an important beneficial effect, both for the Pagan community and the world in general.

The witch must serve everyone in his or her community, not just the Pagans. We do this ourselves, as do many other witches. Janet counsels local people with the use of tarot cards; Gavin acts as a healer when called upon. We have also found ourselves performing rituals for non-Pagans, particularly passage rites such as handfastings (wedding ceremonies). Sometimes these have been secular with very little in the way of religious overtones; sometimes these have even included some Christian symbolism if, due to a previous divorce, the couple have been unable to marry in the Catholic Church. We see all of this as part of our role as a progressive Priesthood of witchcraft. In recent years, we have found ourselves doing rituals for our community at local events, such as a blessing for a twinning of two towns and a harvest thanksgiving festival for our local Chamber of Commerce.[3] We see this as part of our roles as Priest and Priestess. By doing so, we are not only overcoming prejudice and creating a better understanding of what witchcraft is about, but also truly serving the Divine as a Priesthood, returning witchcraft to its origins as the spiritual leadership of the community, the village.

We are certainly not the only ones doing this. It has become a trait of those who are progressive in their approach to witchcraft. We would credit Starhawk as a progressive Priestess in both her internal work with the Reclaiming Collective[4] and her political actions (whether you agree with them or not). Neither she, nor the collective, separate their magical lives from their everyday lives. They seek to serve the Divine, the Goddess, in everything that they do. They have strong convictions, which can only come about from having strong connections with deity. But it is always important to remember that as a Priesthood to different gods and goddesses, we may serve in different ways.

Connecting With Deity

Connecting with Deity is one of the primary mysteries in witchcraft practice. It is therefore both subjective and experiential. We also believe that you do not find your deity: Your deity tends to find you. In this respect, it is very similar to finding your power animal in Shamanic practice. The same process of "meaningful coincidence," which Jung would call *synchronicity,* tends to occur[5]. First you are brought to the attention of the god or goddess concerned. This could be in ritual or in something you do in everyday life. A good example of this happened while Gavin was working on our previous book, *The Healing Craft*, and working on reclaiming the Hippocratic Oath as Pagan. This caught the attention of the primary deity mentioned in the script, Aesculapius. We had several occurrences related to the deity around our home, including physical manifestation. Gavin did not continue the connection through any practice, mainly because he already had Freya as his primary deity to whom he was dedicated as a Priest. But those experiences leave him able to work with Aesculapius in future.

The idea of taking a specific god or goddess for one's *primary life guide*[6] is important. This is the deity you connect with fully, and becomes your face of The Divine. It is this deity who will guide you through your work as a witch and help you understand the nature of your spirituality, and as the name suggests, will act as guide for you in everyday life. For this reason, the deity should be the one you dedicate to as a Priestess or Priest, as it servant, if you decide to do so. We should point out that this is a reciprocal arrangement. The deity needs you as much as you need it. You are not its slave. Consider yourself its employee, and remember that this means you have union rights! We have found that life guide deities look after you, if you look after them.

You can recognize your life guide because it possess aspects that relate to you in someway. Not surprisingly, many witches find that they have goddesses who are linked to witchcraft (see Appendix I). A healer may get a deity of healing if this is their calling, while a blacksmith may get a deity related to Fire or smithcraft. The deity may be linked to your career or vocation. Bear this in mind, as you may be disappointed if you think you will necessarily get a goddess of witchcraft! But we have found, more often than not, that there is an ancestral link between yourself and your deity.

The idea of ancestral deity is at the root of ancient Pagan practice. Many of the gods and goddesses that we know have their origins in ancestral worship, a form of Paganism we can still see practiced in Japan today as Shinto. This comes about through a deification process of an "honored ancestor." A good example of this is the Northern European god Odin. He was originally a tribal leader who gave his people a code of conduct to live by, the *Havamal* or *Sayings of Har*, as well as the runic language that Pagans are more familiar with. Initially, he became a mythical hero, mentioned in song and prose by the skalds, the Northern bards. Offerings would have been made to him, strengthening the process. The result is that he became deified, not just in the minds of his people, but also on an Astral level. This was a process well-known to the Romans who tried to accelerate it for political reasons on several occasions, initially by granting godhood to the Emperor Augustus and then to later emperors.

We have found that strong genetic links with the primary life guide tend to come to the seeker. In our case, both of us have a mix of origins for our ancestors, but the strongest is our English (Norse/Anglo-Saxon) origins. It is hardly surprising then, that we have made a link with our goddess, Freya. There may also be links through reincarnation. You may have not had the genetic link in this life, but you may have had one in a past life, as we have found with those using Egyptian and Middle Eastern deities.

The gods of the locality may also make a claim. We once did a talk in a shop in New York City on this subject. A young lady wanted to know why she had made a connection with an orisha (Santeria spirit/deity form), which was now an important part of her life. She had no genetic or past life connection as far she knew. It initially left us dumbfounded, and we were unable to explain why this had occurred. We believe that this orisha had been drawn to her through her locality, for she lived in an area of New York City where there were many practitioners of Santeria. The invocation of the orishas had, over a long period of time, installed them as the genus loci, the deities of the land or area. We actually owe a debt of thanks to that young lady as she had made us think carefully about why this had happened and made us challenge our preconceptions. It has made us examine the possibility that a localized deity form may be able to take on this role as life guide to a Priestess or Priest.

Generally, you find that primary life guides fit into one of three categories, although it is not unusual to find a deity, which fits into two, and very rarely all three:

- **Primal:** These are deity forms that represent natural forces both macrocosmic and microcosmic; for example the sea, the wind, or even the natural human drives, such as sexuality, and fertility.

- **Ancestral:** Deities that you are genetically linked to, as well as the deities of craftsmen and craftswomen—those deities that manifest human skills. The goddesses of witchcraft fit into this category, such as Aradia, as do the gods and goddesses of smithcraft—Brid, for example.

- **Genus loci:** Translated this means "the spirits of the place," deities who are connected to a specific place. They may also *be* the locality; the Goddess Boann is the River Boyne, and the Goddess Pele is the volcano Kilauea.

Once you have found a primary life guide (or rather, once the deity finds you) you need to research it, both intellectually and psychically. There is plenty of material written about the many gods and goddesses who exist, but they may not always be correct. You will also need to connect with them psychically by using some of the techniques we have mentioned below.

Reinforcing the Bond

It will take time for you to be certain that you have found your god or goddess. Be aware that this can take years! As with Gavin's experience with Aesculapius, it may not necessarily be the only god or goddess you have an experience with. You may connect with others, intentionally or unintentionally, if you decide you need their help for specific magical work. This does not necessarily mean that they are your primary life guide.

We have given here techniques that help you not only connect with your god/goddess, but also reinforce that connection:

1. Make a shrine or altar, inside or outside your home. It needs to be decorated appropriately to the deity, so some research will be necessary. Regularly leave offerings appropriate for the deity on the shrine. Janet leaves flowers of specific colors on our shrine to Freya every Friday, her day of the week. Of-

   ferings of other sorts may also be required. Make sure you "feed" your god or goddess, leaving offerings of their favorite drink and foods, particularly if you are asking for assistance of some form.[7] They will also be more than happy to tell you what they need!

2. Every god or goddess has its own festival date. Some of them fall on the traditional Wiccan calendar of eight Sabbats, but others don't. Make sure you are aware of your deity's festival and the customs related to it. Always make sure that you leave some sort offering on that date, even if you can't mark it with a full ritual or celebration.

3. Meditate on your god or goddess. Visualize the deity in front of you. Talk, ask questions, and ask for guidance. This is one of the first stages of learning the processes involved in deity assumption or Drawing Down the Moon. Remember that your god or goddess is there to guide you through the difficulties in your life. Listen to its guidance.

4. Dress appropriately in everyday life, as well as in ritual. You may find the inclination to dress in a certain way naturally. For example, followers of the love goddesses (Aphrodite, Venus, etc.) tend to dress provocatively. Wear the colors associated with your god or goddess, even if only on a scarf. Most goddesses of witchcraft have black associated with them,

which is why witches often wear black. This is often a subconscious decision. Deities of healing prefer their acolytes to wear white, while some deities have taboos on certain colors. Make sure that you have researched this fully, so as not to offend.

5. Work with the culture of that deity magically. Understand its specific symbolism, magical practices, and mythology. It makes no sense to work in a Celtic style of ritual if you are working with a Greek deity; ritual is language, therefore use the language your deity understands. It is important to note that you do not have to work this way all the time, but only when you are working with your god or goddess.

6. Be aware that there will be some deities that you will not be able to work with once you have dedicated to your god or goddess. For example, followers of the Norse god Thor will not be able to work with Loki, as this would be offensive to him. Make sure you know the mythology surrounding your deity.

Priesthood: Dedicating to Deity

Once you are certain that you have found your life guide, consider the need to dedicate to it as its Priestess or Priest. This is a serious commitment. We cannot understate this in any way. We would recommend that at least a year should pass, if not more, between finding your life guide deity and dedicating your life to it as its Priestess or Priest. What makes being a Priestess or Priest of a deity special is the level of commitment and the nature of the relationship. A deity is for life, not just for Yule! When you dedicate to your god or goddess, you agree to let it direct your life completely. You are committing yourself to being as its servant. Likewise, it commits itself to look after you. As we can testify, you never do without. But you get what you need, not necessarily what you want. It is a reciprocal arrangement. You are giving it "the tiller" of your life, rather than just asking for directions as you would have done before. It will now intercede directly without asking and will put you in the direction that it feels is necessary for you to serve it. We always warn that these can sometimes be negative rather than positive experiences. The question in the Wiccan initiation, "Art thou willing to suffer to learn?" becomes highly relevant in such circumstances.

The results of dedication to a specific deity are life-altering. How you view and relate to the world can change dramatically. Becoming a Priestess or Priest of a deity is one of the mysteries in its own right, closely connected with the Wiccan second-degree initiation. It can therefore take you on a descent into your own Underworld, your Shadow, to face the darker aspects of yourself that most would prefer to ignore. There is no place for personal ego in this process. For this reason, we would not recommend this dedication until you have already been through this mystery. If you do not wait, you may find yourself being used by deity in a way you could not have foreseen. We have seen deities use their dedicated Priestesses and Priests as negative example, for the benefit of others.

Any dedication should be done in the cultural fashion of that deity, as previously mentioned. You may also want to have a new set of robes as part of the dedication ritual, as well as a piece of jewelry connected with that deity that you consecrate and wear permanently after your dedication. The ritual can be simple: anointing and purifying yourself, making an oath to serve the god or goddess you have connected with as Priestess or Priest, and then adorning yourself with new robes and newly consecrated ritual jewelry. It can be done privately, or as part of a coven ritual. If possible, it is always useful to try to find someone else who has been through this form of dedication even though it may not be to the same deity. Their advice will be invaluable.

The service you give to the deity as Priestess or Priest will differ according to the god or goddess you have agreed to serve. A Priest or Priestess of a healing deity will devote his or her life to healing, while a Priest or Priestess of a deity of smithcraft, such as Brid, may make beautiful things as part of the devotion to that deity. Bear in mind that deities rarely have just one aspect, so you may find yourself learning new skills. It is also not unusual for the Priestess or Priest to take on some of the personality traits of the deity that he or she serves, particularly if the deity is drawn into the Priest or Priestess during ritual.

Drawing Down the Moon and the Assumptive Process

In both modern and older Pagan traditions, the ultimate expression of connection and service to a deity is to "assume" the deity in trance. The term and practice of Drawing Down the Moon as found in the

Gardnerian and Alexandrian traditions of Wicca is firmly rooted in Charles Godfrey Leland's *Aradia; The Gospel of the Witches*. There is little historical doubt that such a rite in Etruscan religious practice existed, but little is known about the psychological processes involved and what effect they actually had on the Priestess. We can be sure that the ritual used in modern Wicca probably has little in common with the original Etruscan practice. In the modern Wiccan Drawing Down the Moon, there are elements of ritual High Magic and Cabala in the rite. For example, the Five-fold Kiss is said to be the enactment of the Center Pillar ritual,[8] which performs the same role as opening the chakras. Regardless of its mixed origins, as most Wiccan High Priestesses can attest, it works and has become the central ritual of Wicca, the communion with the Goddess through the High Priestess.

Drawing Down the Sun, the male equivalent of Drawing Down the Moon, was created by Janet and her late husband Stewart. They felt a need for sexual balance. They created the ritual and first published it in *The Witches' Way* in the early 1980s following discussions with Doreen Valiente. Doreen then went on to produce a *Charge of the God* to supplement her earlier work. There is no reason why a man cannot assume a male deity form, just as a woman does the Goddess. It is seen all the time in religions such as Voudon, and according to Ray Buckland, who has studied their practices for many years, it is also not unusual for the loa to manifest contra-sexually (a female loa "riding" a male adherent and vice versa), something he told us he once witnessed. There should be no surprise in this, as spiritual mediums have always been able to do the same thing.

Generally, Drawing Down the Moon is an act of prophecy that can work in several ways or may progress through several stages, according to the Priestess' adeptness.

1. The Priestess may meet the deity in a trance state in another level of reality, such as the Astral Plane, who then relays important but sometimes cryptic messages to them. This is a prophetic act of clairvoyance or clairaudience.[9]

2. The deity speaks through her, she feels the deity enter, but she retains her control and memory of the entire event.

3. The deity form completely overwhelms the Priestess, sublimating the Priestess' personality completely. She loses complete control and memory of the events that transpire.

We do not know which of these the Priestesses of old experienced, but we do know what is happening today from our own experience, which we feel is of more importance from a progressive perspective. From illustrations of the time there is evidence that the Etruscans used much more hypnotic techniques in their rites than we do today. One such illustration on the side of a piece of pottery shows the use of a bowl to reflect the moon into the eyes of the Priestess. On one occasion, we mimicked this ritual with surprising results. While the full moon was reflected into Janet's eyes by Gavin and strobed (he tilted the bowl up and down), he also invoked the Goddess Diana. She came through Janet, taking over her whole demeanor as well as changing her voice. She then went on to prophesize for everyone in the circle, one by one. This was no different than her experience with the traditional Alexandrian and Gardnerian style of Drawing Down the Moon, except that a specific deity was invoked and a different technique was used. In Doreen Valiente's *Charge of the Goddess*, the invocation is not aimed specifically at one deity, but at the broader Archetype of the Great Mother. We believe this indicates that Doreen Valiente was well aware that the Gardnerian method for invoking the Goddess was not intended to bring through any one goddess in particular.

Drawing Down the Moon is an act of mediumship. This description covers all the stages mentioned previously, which are commonly experienced by Wiccan Priestesses. But the possession of the Priestess in trance by a deity has a specific name: the *assumptive process*—the assumption by a recipient of the deity form's personality. The assumptive process is not only found in Wicca. Traditions using it can be found right across the world in many other cultures. The first to come to mind is Voudon, in which participants of a ritual may be "ridden" by a loa. But it can also be found in other traditions close to home, such as ancient Norse and Anglo-Saxon culture in the practice of *Seidr* or *Seith*.[10] This Northern European practice is witchcraft in the true sense of the word, and would no doubt have been practiced in England. In Seith work, the seeress or seer is traditionally seated on a small hill if outdoors, or on a high chair if indoors. He or she descends into the Underworld by means of a hypnotic chant, while visualising the route to the Underworld. The spiritual cosmology used is well recorded in the "Voluspa" or "Song of the Seeress" in *The Poetic Edda*[11] (something we have already talked more fully about in Chapter 7).

After the descent, the seer or seeress then enters the gates of Helheim, the Underworld, Jung's Shadow. It is here that they recount what they see to those present, who may ask questions about the future. What they see is generally in symbolic form, just like a dream. ("I see you walking along a wall with a drop on either side, but you are close to the end of the wall and will soon be able to walk on firm and safe ground again.") It is generally left to the person receiving the information to translate the cryptic imagery.

In recent years, trailblazers such as Diane Paxton[12] have reconstructed the practice of Seith. We are honored to have been present at such an event. Although there is no mention historically about deity forms assuming the seers or seeresses, this very quickly began to occur with quite dramatic results. The gods and goddesses had a voice again and wanted to use it![13] The process parallels Drawing Down the Moon as found in Wicca, but with a Northern European slant. Unlike Wicca's Drawing Down the Moon, a cosmology is actively applied in the process.

As Janet can attest, no instructions were given for Drawing Down the Moon when she trained within Alex Sanders' coven. No visualization or trance techniques were taught, nor was any advice given. The technique relied purely on the dogmatic following of ritual with no understanding of the metaphysics involved. When it was successful, the Priestess got either one of the two results we have described: a descent into the Underworld to gather symbolic information, or a trance possession, an act of mediumship. We believe the latter should be the desired result of Drawing Down the Moon. The former should be an intermediate stage, the first experience of those who are new to the technique.

The metaphysics of deity assumption

When a Priestess or Priest has successfully had the moon (or sun) drawn down on them, they generally describe the same feeling. They are sitting in the back of their mind, seeing and hearing everything that is going on, while the deity speaks through them. They often feel as if descending in a counter-clockwise spiral. Those witnessing the rite often comment that they see what appears to be a physical change in the face of the Priest or Priestess, seeing their face shape shift into that of the invoked god or goddess. There can also be a change in voice, and noticeably, in temperament. This clearly describes an overlaying of the Priestess' or Priest's aura or mental/emotional body with that of the deities (see Figure 8 on page 204).

For this to take place, several things must happen. The first is that the chakras have to be opened. In the traditional Wiccan ritual of Drawing Down the Moon, this is done by the Fivefold Kiss, which is carried out by the magical partner of the Priestess. This rite should have this opening effect on the chakras, but we now use a Sevenfold Kiss[14] to ensure their full opening during this rite. This also assists in creating an exchange of polarized energy, emanating from the throat center (ether) of the Priest performing the rite on the Priestess whom the moon is being drawn down upon.

There are three chakras that specifically need to be open during this rite if it is to be successful: the root center (Muladhara), the brow or Third Eye (Ajna) and the crown chakra (Sahasara). The root center ensures that there is grounding, so there is a free flow of energy during the process.

Drawing Down the Moon

Figure 8.

If this is not opened, then there will be no flow of energy, and the deity's aura will not flow into the Priestess' aura. It also keeps the actual Priestess grounded and able to witness what is happening, hence most Priestesses or Priests describe the feeling of "stepping back" within themselves. If not, they will have problems re-aligning their own mental/emotional body of the aura after the deity has left.

The brow is the key to the whole process. It not only generates the mental/emotional body but, more importantly, it is the center responsible for psychic connection. It enables trance state to be achieved, but only when it is fully opened.

The crown chakra, the center that generates the spiritual body, is the gate through which the deity's mental/emotional body descends into and overlays the Priestesses own aura. It is here that our Astral Guardian[15] resides. This aspect of our higher selves prevents unwanted entities from gaining entry, resulting in what is commonly called *demonic possession*. In all our experiences of trance techniques, we have never seen this form of possession occur.[16]

Polarised energy draws the deity form through the Priestess' spiritual body and into the mental/emotional body in the usual rite of Drawing Down the Moon. In normal Wiccan practice, this is done by the Priest's use of the Invoking Triangle of Water. But if the person is in balance with his or her own Anima/Animus complex, then this exchange of polarized energy will not be necessary, as they will be able to generate it themselves through their own chakras. This is what happens in ecstatic Shamanic techniques, where ecstatic dance and rhythmic drumming are used. This technique not only opens the chakras, but also increases the energy of the aura, making it more accessible to the deity.

It is also important to understand what is happening from the viewpoint of brainwave activity[17]. This is normally measured by electroencephalogram (EEG). In our everyday waking lives, our brainwaves are in a state psychologists called *Beta*, but when we relax our brainwave activity slows and enters a stage called *Alpha*. The two most important brainwave activities relevant to the process of deity assumption are *Theta* and *Delta*. When a Priestess goes into the lighter prophetic trance states we mentioned earlier, she enters a *Theta* brainwave state, the next slowest stage from *Alpha* (which normally occurs just after we enter a sleep state), but as and if she goes deeper, she enters the least brainwave activity stage, *Delta*. This is the same state that we enter in lucid dreaming or rapid eye movement (REM) sleep, when we connect to the Astral levels.

Studying the processes related to the auras and chakras (see Chapter 8), brainwave activity, and spiritual cosmology (see Chapter 7) make it possible for us to clearly understand what is happening in the rite of Drawing Down the Moon and allows us to create techniques that assist in the process of deity assumption.

Assisting the process of deity assumption

- ⚜ **Calling specific gods or goddesses by name:** The first deity you assume should really be the one to whom you are connected or dedicated as a Priest or Priestess. This will be the easiest one to bring through. Once you have worked with this deity, you can move on to being open to others, as you will have experienced the feeling of the process. This is important, as it is a subjective experience and no two Priestesses or Priests have the same experience.

- ⚜ **Visualisation techniques:** The Priestess or Priest visualizes descending downwards, to the left, while the invocation to deity is called. At the end of the journey, she visualizes the god or goddess standing in front of her and asks the deity to enter into her. To use this method, it is necessary to have an understanding of spiritual cosmology, particularly the use of The Spiral Path (see page 143). This method can be practiced beforehand in meditation, up to the point of calling the deity.

- **Masks:** This is an ancient technique used in ancient forms of Shamanism dating back to the Stone Age. It is where the myth of shape shifting comes from. A mask or veil, as well as appropriate dress, removes the everyday Persona of the Priestess or Priest and replaces it with a magical one. This is particularly effective if the mask is of the face of the deity being invoked. By using this method, the Ego can be sublimated, so it ceases to be a hindrance to the process.

- **Rhythmic Music:** Drumming is a traditional method for causing trance states, or as Michael Harner[18] calls them, *Shamanic states of consciousness* (SSC). Music with a strong rhythm of about 220 beats a minute stimulates *Theta* wave activity. Tapes or CDs of drumming music can also be used if drumming is not practical. Such tapes for this purpose are now easily available from occult bookstores.

- **Chanting:** Another ancient method, instead of having just the magical partner invoke the deity, the whole coven does it with the use of a chant (*"(name of deity),* come to us!"*) repeated rhythmically as the coven circles around the Priestess or Priest.

The God or Goddess arrives!

What happens after deity has entered the Priestess or Priest during a trance process such as Drawing Down the Moon depends on both the deity concerned and the coven. In normal Wiccan practice, the deity speaks through the Priestess, initially reciting the *Charge of the Goddess* or something similar. Emphasis may be put on specific aspects of the *Charge* by inflection or by the addition of extra speech. The deity then prophesises in a general way and directs the magical work of the group. After this, the deity slowly leaves the Priestess. If the deity remains for a longer period than expected, it may be necessary for the magical partner to ask her to leave the Priestess. This should always be done politely. It is also not unusual for the Priestess to feel physically drained, particularly if the assumption has continued for a prolonged period. The usual cure for this is food, especially foods high in sugar. It is also common for the Priestess to loose any memory of what was said during the experience. What is happening is the same as when we loose the memories of a dream; the dream is fresh in our memory first thing in the morning when waking, but by midday, we have only fragments of it left. This is hardly surprising, particularly if there is full assumption, as the mind will be in *Delta* wave activity, the same level of brain wave activity found in REM sleep.

There can also sometimes be a residual effect in the Priestess where some of the goddesses' mental/emotional body may be left behind, and some of the deities' personal traits intermittently reappear in the Priestess. This can sometimes last, in our experience, for several days, particularly if the Priestess is not grounded correctly through her root center.

There are other variations and departures from the standard Wiccan practice that work. One of these is for the deity to go around the coven, one by one, prophesizing to each individual. There is also no reason why members of the coven should not individually ask questions. When we have done this, we have prepared for it by having a chair for the Priestess to sit on during the rite. One can also make libations, offerings, and requests to the deity. To do this, though, it is really necessary to invoke a specific deity rather than do a generalized goddess invocation, as is the norm in Gardnerian and Alexandrian Wiccan ritual.

When the deity has manifested through the Priestess, it should be treated with respect. As we have said, it is a personality in its own right. It will consider itself a guest in your circle, but will still expect to be treated with reverence. Be prepared for it to act according to its personality; on several occasions we have had people shocked by the behavior of the god or goddess who has come through. Expect a deity of love and fertility to act in a flirtatious way, and a god of a beer to go on a drinking binge! Always remember after the ritual that this is not the fault of the Priestess or Priest hosting the deity. They are not the ones responsible for the behavior of the deity.

But what happens if the goddess or god called doesn't come through? Don't be downhearted. This is a spiritual discipline that takes time to learn. It also may be an indication that you need to do more study of the processes involved. This is not something you can learn overnight, and some may never be able to draw deity into them in this way. Finding the right technique for you may be a process of trial and error. Drawing Down the Moon is a spiritual experience that, by its very nature, and regardless of the metaphysical explanations we have given, is a subjective experience.

Endnotes

1. Better known as a physicist, responsible for formulating the Theory of Relativity, Albert Einstein also saw The Divine at work in the Laws of Physics.
2. The Aquarian Tabernacle Church based in Seattle, Washington, is very active in promoting Ecumenicalism in Wicca, as are several other Wiccan organizations.
3. These are done under the guise of *Ancient Ceremonies Theatre*. We see no dichotomy in doing this as theater's origins are in Greek ritual and ceremony.
4. Reclaiming is a tradition of witchcraft that began in the 1980s in Northern California, and by the year 2000, had adherents throughout North America and in parts of Western Europe. The community has no formal membership. It is a community of women and men working to unify Spirit and politics (abridged from *www.reclaiming.org*).
5. Jung defines *synchronicity* as "a meaningful coincidence in time," but specifically in connection with deity, "The coincidence of a certain psychic content with a corresponding objective process which is perceived to take place simultaneously." From *Synchronicity: An Acausal Connecting Principle* (*see* Bibliography).
6. This is our own definition. In the spiritualist sense, it is no different from the Holy Guardian Angel.
7. This is a common practice in Santeria with the feeding of orishas. The same principles apply to western deity forms.
8. The Center Pillar Ritual is the opening of the energy centers related to the Cabalistic Tree of Life (see Figure 1). They are opened, from the feet: Malkuth, Yesod, Tiphareth, Da'arth, and Kether. In *The Witches' Craft: The Roots of Witchcraft & Magical Transformation.* Raven Grimassi points out that these are also in Freemasonry as "The Five Points of Fellowship." (*see* Bibliography).
9. As in Anglo-Saxon/Norse Seith, sometimes a Priestess may have no contact at all in this first stage. What in fact happens is pure prophecy with the Priestess relaying the cryptic derived from images that she perceives.
10. *Seith* is the word our modern words *sooth* and *soothsayer* derive from.
11. *The Poetic Edda* was written between 1178 and 1241 by Snorri Sturluson. It has the most complete description of an act of Seidr/Seith prophesy, as well as the most complete description of a Pagan cosmology, described by a seeress herself (*see* Bibliography).
12. The biggest exponent of this practice in Neo-Paganism has been Diane Paxton of Berkley, California. She has toured the United States giving demonstrations of this Northern European form of prophetic trance. She has been a major influence in our work in the areas of Wiccan trance work.
13. There is no historical evidence that deity assumption occurred in Seith or Seidr practice. In recent years, Diane Paxton has discouraged this process to occur because of this lack of historical evidence.
14. This goes in the order: feet (Root Center), genitals (Sacral Center), abdomen (Solar Plexus Center), upper chest (Heart Center), Mouth (Throat Center), Forehead (Brow Center) and top of head (Crown). During the kissing process, the person performing the rite breathes prana into the appropriate center.
15. Often referred to as the Holy Guardian Angel.

[16] Such forms of possession only normally occur in people who are already psychologically disturbed. *Demonic possession* is a symptom, not the cause of the problems the person has. The possession takes place due to disconnection with Higher Self on the Astral level. The entity that comes in simply fills the existing void.

[17] Research taken from Dement, W.C. *Some must watch while some must sleep*. New York: W.W. Norton (1978), and Pinel, J.P.J. *Biopsychology*. Needham Heights, MA: Allyn & Bacon (1992).

[18] Professor Michael Harner is considered to be the "father of modern Shamanism." His core Shamanism techniques were the first published in his work *The Way of the Shaman* (*see* Bibliography), the first book of its kind.

Chapter 11

The Liber Actios:
A Training Manual

*Learning without thought is labour lost; thought
without learning is perilous.*

—Confucius[1]

The purpose of *The Liber Actios* (Book of Actions) is to teach the witch how ritual actually works. It is a suggested course of study that should take twelve months or more to complete. In many previous books on the subject of Wiccan ritual, including our own, much emphasis has been put on exact words for rituals. Here the emphasis is on the feeling, understanding, and knowledge that are important to create successful ritual. To do this it is necessary to have read the other chapters in this book, particularly the section "Knowledge-based ritual" (see page 127) and the chapters on spiritual cosmology (see Chapter 7) and chakra and aura energy (see Chapter 8). In this way, the student can learn ritual both as a skill and as an art form while avoiding the dogmatic use of phrase. They can also add their own words and cultural overlay to any magical work (whether Celtic, Norse, Greek, Roman, Faery, etc.) with a bit of research. Quite simply, this is a blueprint for creating your own unique *Book of Shadows* and personal (or group) magical tradition. This is in keeping with the ideals and *Tenets of Progressive Witchcraft* we have listed in Chapter 2 (see page 56).

Creating Your *Book of Shadows*

The *Book of Shadows* (*BOS*) is the witch's magical diary and note-book. Of course, this is the traditional Wiccan name, but other names are also used, such as *Book of Lights, Book of Light and Dark*, and *Liber Umbarum*[2] (The Black Book) to name a few we have encountered. What is important is its function as a record of what you are doing and what you have done. It is a magical notebook and diary combined. Traditionally, the *BOS* is passed on. In this way, knowledge could be accumulated over a period of time and added to by the new generations of witches.

Most people imagine a leather bound, black, dusty old tome of knowledge when you talk about the *BOS*. The reality is something different. Most witches who have been around a while, including ourselves, prefer to use ring binders. These are popular as you can move material around very easily, which is particularly useful if you wish to update rituals. There are some quite fancy ones for sale nowadays, particularly from occult shops. In the last 10 years, even the ring binder has been superseded: We are now in the age of the CD *BOS*, with all the necessary material being kept on personal computer.

Your *Book of Shadows* is the first thing you need to acquire, even before being initiated. It should include the following material:

- **The magical and occult laws** (see Appendix III). The first stages of a new witch's training generally cover ethics and magical and spiritual Laws. In a coven this also includes the coven rules and craft laws (see page 97).

- **Magical and spiritual cosmology**: List and draw out a diagram of the realms. Mark out any paths you find between them as you explore them. Make a diary of your experiences within each realm.

- **Magical Exercises:** These include working with the elements and the other exercises included in this book, such as the chakra exercises (see page 169). These should be included after you have done them, not before. You should include personal notes on your experiences—how you felt, and what you visualized.

- **Rituals:** Circle casting, seasonal festivals (Sabbats), and other magical workings. Like the magical exercises, these should be included after you have done them, *not* before.

⤶ **Correspondence tables:** Instead of just copying out the correspondence tables as you have found them in this and other works, you should also include the correspondences you have discovered from working with the Elements in the exercises, and from magically working with the seasons and power tides (see page 187).

The Magical Tools

The most important magical tool that you have is your mind. Without the skills and knowledge of their use, your other magical tools are useless props. With practice, a good witch should be able to cast a circle or do a magical act purely with energy and without any tools at all. Magical tools exist purely as aids, which is particularly useful when you wish to focus a group of people on a complicated magical task. It is true that a well-consecrated magical object exists on an Astral Level (see page 168), but it is still just a tool, nonetheless.

The personal tool of the witch is often referred to as the athame,[3] a small knife blunted for safety purposes. It may have other names, such as the sax in the Seax-Wicca tradition. It can be decorated with magical sigils appropriate to your belief. It represents the Element of Fire, just like the sword, of which it is the smaller equivalent. It is a memory of humanity's first truly crafted tool, the knapped flint, and his mastery of the elements in creating it.[4]

There are four magical tools related to the elements, as previously mentioned. Their purposes are related directly to the elements they represent:

⤶ **Pentacle:** The tool for banishing through grounding and for consecration to cause physical/Astral link.

⤶ **Wand:** The tool for invoking higher forms of Spirit (gods and goddesses, etc.).

⤶ **Sword/Athame:** The tool for invoking and controlling through the use of will the lower forms of Spirit (Elementals). It is important to note that its traditional use at the quarters is not to control Guardians of the Quarters,[5] but the raw element they bring into the circle.

⤶ **Chalice:** The tool for evocation from within. For instance, the chalice is used to evoke the emotions of love and trust.

There are also three other magical tools,[6] which are rarely discussed as such:

- **Cauldron**[7]: Represents ether (see page 166), life force. It is placed in the center of the circle during the raising of energy.

- **Stang or staff**[8]: Represents the power of the mind; an extension of the power of Air. It is traditionally pointed at its bottom end, so it can be pushed into the ground in the center of the circle, where it represents the Axis Mundi (see page 134).

- **Altar:** The altar represents the Spirit of the individual practitioner(s) of the ritual, as well as of the Divine. Normally, it would consist of a small table with a cloth and a representation of deity placed centrally on it. Outside, it could be a tree stump or even just a cloth on the ground. For a group or an individual, it should have on it representations of the sacred, such as a statue of the God and/or Goddess. Traditionally, it is placed in the North[9] or in the center of the circle, although there is no reason it could not be placed at any of the other quarters if you are working with that quarter's element. On it should be the elemental tools, censer, candles, etc., as well as the athame ready for use.

Working With Your Aura and Chakras

It is a good idea to understand how your bodily energy system works before starting any of the following exercise, particularly those related to circle casting and working with the Elements. Read the chapter on sorcery (Chapter 8) carefully, and start a regime of practice related to your chakras and aura:

- Open and close your centers on a regular basis for a period of a month, ensuring that you ground properly.

- Practice expanding and retracting your mental/emotional body on a regular basis.

- Be aware of how your chakra centers and your aura react to the presence of with others.

- After a period of time successfully opening your chakras, hold one hand in the other and visualize a circuit of energy flowing around from heart center to your hands and back to heart center. If you are working with a partner or group, work through the chakra exercises together.

Creating the Temple: Basic Magical Practice

The general method of creating sacred space in witchcraft is to cast the circle. There are generally three reasons for doing this before performing any magical work:

1. To put up a protective etheric barrier against spiritual intrusion.

2. To act as a vessel to prevent any magical energy from dissipating.

3. To create a sacred consecrated space, which reflects on to the Astral Level.

A circle can be cast for any or all of these reasons. The reason for casting the circle is more important than any particular method of working. To perform any kind of magical working, the following are required:

- **Preparation:** Having everything you need to perform the magical task. This includes basic knowledge of ritual, magical tools, correct environment, etc.

- **Intention:** Being clear in your mind about why you are performing ritual, and being able to focus on what you want to achieve. One should, for example, know what a Quarter Guardian is if you will be calling one.

- **Visualization/Vocalization:** The ability to fix an image in your mind of the magical energy/spirit forms you are working with, and then verbally express what you are doing.

- **Action:** Implementing all of the above, including the correct physical actions for each magical tool (for example, an invoking pentagram using the athame).

These guidelines were originally summed up as the occult maxim, "to know, to will, to dare, and to be silent." They relate to the Elements Air, Fire, Water, and Earth, respectively.

Casting the circle

The first stage is preparation, as mentioned previously. You will require a quiet place where you can work undisturbed. Set up what you require:

- ❧ The altar with lit incense in a censer (or even just joss sticks), lit candles, and your magical tools, etc. as previously described.

- ❧ Place lit candles in holders at each quarter. They may be colored for each element and quarter (see Appendix II for correspondences).

Sit in the space you are going to work in and relax facing the North quarter. Ground and center by visualizing yourself surrounded by the magical realms: the four elemental realms around you at each quarter, and the worlds above and below you (see page 135).

Pick up your athame from the altar and hold it in front of you, facing the North. Think about casting the circle, what its purpose is, and why you are casting it.

Slowly draw the circle with this energy by walking around the circle clockwise. Visualize a blue sphere surrounding you as you do it. Speak the reasons why you are casting the circle. What words you use are not important, but the intent certainly is.

Calling the quarters

The purpose of calling the quarters is to bring the Elements into the magical circle on a spiritual level. By doing so, you also assist in bringing them into balance within the self ("The first thing that magic changes is the self." See page 63). For this reason it is not the element that is called, but the spirit of the element, often referred to as the Lord or the Guardian (see page 143). It is a common mistake just to call the Element itself. The Spirit of the element regulates the flow of Elemental energy into the magical circle, rather like a valve. This action protects the practitioner against elemental forms that may intrude on the sacred space being formed. This action also has the effect of opening the appropriate chakra related to the Element (although the normal process of opening the chakras is from the root center up, we have found that opening from the heart center down ritually has the same effect. See page 167). This action is generally verbalized as "witnessing and guarding the circle."

We have used archetypes to represent these Guardians. This is how we see them. You may find that the Guardian you call may appear differently than the ones that follow. There is nothing wrong with this, and we recommend that you work with the form that manifests for you. In fact, there is no reason why you cannot invoke deities to perform this role.[10]

Traditionally in Wicca, the Lesser Pentagram Ritual of Invoking and Banishing (see Figure 9 on page 218) is used to call the Quarter Guardians. This is only one method that can be used. You can also create your own ritual action to serve the same purpose. To give an example, we have created the Celtic Cross (see Figure 9). What is important is that it is reversible, so it can be used for banishing as well as invoking. Ritual stances can also be used (see Figure 10 on page 219), and we highly recommend these for the calling method used below.

- Go to the Eastern Quarter. Think about the Guardian of the Element of Air. Vocalize this to reinforce your intention. Use a ritual action to reinforce the process. During this process, visualize the Elemental Guardian. He is an old man, a sage, or wizard carrying a staff, walking towards you and then turning his back to face outwards. Become aware of your heart center opening.

- Now go to the Southern Quarter. Repeat the ritual process used above. Call the Guardian of the Element of Fire and visualize him as a young man, a warrior with sword, walking towards you and then turning his back outwards. Become aware of your solar plexus center opening.

- Now go to the Western Quarter. Repeat the ritual process as before. Call the Guardian of the Element of Water and visualize her as a young maiden, fertile and bearing a chalice. She walks towards you and then turns her back outwards. Become aware of your sacral center opening.

- Finally, go to the Northern Quarter. Repeat the ritual process. Call the Guardian of the Element of Earth and visualize her as an older woman, a mother figure holding a pentacle or something else representing Earth. Become aware of your root center opening.

Invoking Pentagram of Earth

Banishing Pentagram of Earth

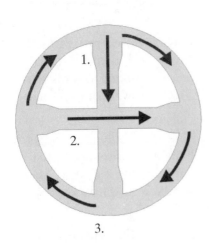

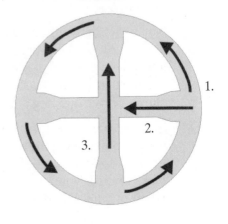

Celtic Cross of Invocation

Celtic Cross of Banishing

Figure 9.

Osiris Slain

Osiris Risen

Ritual Stance—Invoking

Osiris Risen

Osiris Slain

Ritual Stance—Banishing

Figure 10.

After calling the Quarters, stand in the center of the circle facing North with legs apart. Hold your arms out to your sides. Now visualize the worlds around you. Vocalize this by saying something like: "Before me is the Realm of Earth, behind me is the Realm of Fire. To my right is the Realm of Air and to my left, the Realm of Water. Below me are the Realms of the Underworld and my ancestors, and above me the Astral Realms and the abode of the Gods."

Banishing the quarters

This reverses the process of invoking the Guardian of the Element. Remember to use your *intention, visualization/vocalization,* and *action.*

- Stand in the Eastern Quarter. Visualize the Guardian protecting the Circle. Thank him for being present and ask him to return to his realm if he wishes. Carry out the ritual action for banishing. Visualize him nodding to you in acceptance and walking away until he fades into the distance. Become aware of the appropriate chakra for the Element closing. Repeat this process for each quarter, each Guardian, and each Element.

- Now ground and center yourself. Ensure that all your chakras are closed (see page 173).

You may sense that a specific Guardian has not left. If this has happened, do not worry. This means that there is some residual energy present related to that Element. Allow them to leave when they have finished their task.

Finally, always remember when doing any form of invocation (be it Guardian or Deity) that the two most important magical phrases are "please" and "thank you"!

Working With the Elements

In most Wiccan, as well as other magical traditions, working with the four elements is the first stage of practical training after learning the necessary meditation and visualization techniques (see page 217). Traditionally, the newly initiated witch learns this when she is presented with the magical tools after initiation[11]. The next stage was to learn what the correspondences of each Element are. Correspondences are a way of understanding how the Elements are present in the world around us and how we can see them. It is, of course, an intellectual approach, and most witches absorb this information from the many correspondence tables that are available in books. In fact, there are whole volumes dedicated to this function, such as Aleister Crowley's *777*, and we have included some basic tables in this book (see Appendix II).

Mastery of the Elements is important for two specific reasons. In the journey to experience the mysteries, balancing the elements within the self is essential to truly understand them. Secondly, the Elements are the key components used in all of the witch's practical magical work, such as spellcraft and the creation of thought forms. These two reasons cannot be divided from one another because of the simple occult law, "The first thing that magic changes is the self." It is unavoidable that magical work will effect how the Elements behave within the individual magical practitioner. It is therefore necessary to understand the Elements not just intellectually, but also on the physical, emotional, and spiritual levels as well.

After learning about the correspondences and intellectual attributions of each Element, it is necessary to feel the Elements if you are to be one with them. They will "talk to you," and by doing so, you will gain more knowledge about them, directly from the horse's mouth, so to speak. The first stage is always to connect with the Elements physically, in the natural environment. You are connecting with each of them through the Element of Earth. Witchcraft is traditionally said to be an Earth-based tradition of magic. This is followed by connecting with the Elements on an Astral Level.

It is possible to access the elements by use of the Wiccan cosmology we have outlined in Chapter 7 (see page 137). By travelling up the Spiral Path (see page 143) in a meditative state, you can ask each Elemental Guardian for access to that realm and to guide you within its boundaries. What you see and experience in that realm will help you to understand that element. When we do such an exercise with our students, we take them to these realms and encourage them to explore them at their leisure; by doing so, they will gain the benefits of connection with these Elements in their everyday lives.

We recommend that certainly no less than a month should be taken to work on each element, and that all of these exercises, be carried out in a properly cast circle.

Connecting With the Elements

The Element of Earth

⊱ Intellectual Connection: The traditional magical tool of the Element of Earth is the pentacle. This is usually a round metal or wooden disc with the pentagram, the symbol of Spirit over the four elements, graphically portrayed on it. It may also have other symbols related to specific Wiccan tradition, but these are really superfluous to its function; what is important is its roundness, which represents the 360-degree view of the world we live in. There are alternatives to it. Some use a bowl of Earth, and we have even seen an apple, freshly cut to expose the five pointed star formed by its seeds. All are valid, as they express the physicality of the universe, and the cycles of birth, life, death, and rebirth, which are at the center of our understanding of the mysteries. It is considered to be feminine in gender, and its archetype is the Mother to Crone in aspect.

⊱ Physical Connection: It is necessary to find a place that represents the Element of Earth. Find a quiet piece of woodland or forest where you know you will not be disturbed. After dark or at Winter Solstice are good times, due to their associations with this Element, but always put personal safety first. It doesn't necessarily have to be in the countryside. Many towns have parks where there are useful tree plantations. Find a tree that appeals to you. It should be large enough for you to sit with your back to it. Feel it, touch it with your hands. Put your face up against it. Try to feel what it feels. Now sit with your back to the tree in a cross-legged or similar comfortable position. Go through the process of opening your chakras (see page 163). After your chakras are open, become specifically aware of your root center. Keeping your eyes closed, feel the ground beneath you through the chakra. You should become aware of the sensation of being able to pull heat up from the Earth into your body. What else do you feel? Do any particular images come into your mind? Now put your hands into the soil around you and pick up a handful. What is it you are actually holding? What is its texture? What is "Earth" really made of? Finish by closing and grounding (see page 173).

- **Astral Connection:** Follow the exercise on page 144, Ascending the Spiral Path. On meeting the first Guardian, the Guardian of Earth, ask her to take you into the Realm of Earth. Allow her to lead you off the path into a forest or a similar place. She will then take you to a clearing where you find a stone circle, tree circle, or similar place (be aware, it can be a different place for each person). This is a place of peace and tranquillity, a place where you can go if you are stressed or facing problems. It is a place of grounding where you will find clarity of thought. It has obvious connections with the Root Center (see page 159).

The Element of Air

- **Intellectual Connection:** The magical tool of Air is the wand. Air is the element of the mind, governing the intellect, knowledge, and ideas. Traditionally made of wood, the wand is therefore the perfect tool to represent this Element. Air is the Element that governs spiritual cosmology, which is of course an intellectual construct allowing travel and communication (both governed by Air) between the different realms of reality; hence the associations with Mercury (Hermes Trismegistus) who of course carries the caduceus (see page 155), which is a wand or staff. It is considered to be a masculine Element, with the sage or wizard figure carrying his magical staff ("Merlin") as its archetype.

- **Physical Connection:** Find a high, windy place, preferably in the natural world, such as a hillside, cliff, or mountain, but even a tall building where you can safely stand on the roof would be good. At dawn or at Spring Equinox would be a good time to do this. Get yourself comfortable, as you did when you explored the Element of Earth, by sitting in a cross-legged position. Now open your chakras. Be aware specifically of your root center and also your heart center. Breathe in deeply and listen. Now stand up, facing the wind, and open your arms wide. Visualize that you are breathing directly into your Heart Center. What do you hear? What do you feel? What do you smell? Let all your senses come into play. When you breathe in, where is the air going? What is it doing in your body? Finish by closing and grounding.

- **Astral Connection:** Repeat the process similar to the Element of Earth, but this time follow the path up to the next Guardian, the Guardian of Air. Ask him to take you into his realm, and allow him to guide you to a building with large doors. This is the library. Knock on the doors and wait for entry. When the doors open, enter the library and explore the contents. The library is a useful place if you have questions about magical or spiritual matters, as the answers can sometimes be found amongst the books that sit on the shelves, but only if you look hard enough. You may find a large table with the book you need on it only after visiting this place several times. This is your book, your Akashic record. In it is recorded your past lives and built-up karma from those incarnations. Very few are able to read the whole book.

The Element of Fire

- **Intellectual Connection:** Fire is the most active of the elements, being both creative, if handled properly, and destructive.[12] Its magical tool, the sword,[13] sums up its nature perfectly, as it is a double-edged weapon, forged in fire. Fire is the element of will and of desire, be it positive or negative. The sword has always traditionally been associated with law, so Fire also governs the will for justice. The sword is born by the young warrior, an archetype that suits this element perfectly.

- **Physical Connection:** Build an open fire outdoors, preferably at midday or at Summer Solstice. Sit in front of it as with the other elements, but at a distance so that you can comfortably stretch your hands out in front of it. Now open your chakras. Be aware specifically of your root and solar plexus centers. Keeping your eyes closed, put your hands out in front of you until you can feel the heat on the palms of your hands. What is it you actually feel? What do you smell? What do you hear? Now open your eyes. Look into the heart of the fire. What do you see? Are there any images forming in the flames? Finish by closing and grounding.

  ❧ **Astral Connection:** Repeat the process as you did for Earth and Air, but this time proceed up the Spiral Path to the next Guardian, the Guardian of Fire. Ask him to allow you to enter his realm, and let him guide you into it. Let him take you to the smithy. You will hear it before you see it. You will hear the pounding of the hammer on steel and smell the hot coals on the air. Watch the activities there, but do not enter the smithy; this is a place of both creation and destruction. Only enter the smithy if there is an aspect of your inner self that you wish to have removed from your personality or re-worked. This is the job of the smith who works here.

The Element Water

❧ **Intellectual Connection:**
The chalice or cup traditionally represents the Element of Water. This vessel holds the chaotic nature of the fluid within, just as we hold the emotions within ourselves in check. It can also be seen to represent "the vessel of the Universe," creation itself. The chalice is the universe held in place by the spiritual, the goddess energy of the Divine, and the womb. Water is traditionally the element of "death and initiation;" in other words, rebirth. Its archetype is therefore the fruitful and fertile maiden.

❧ **Physical Connection:** Find a river, a stream, or even a coastal inlet. Autumn Equinox and twilight both have associations with this element. Go through the same process as you did with connecting with the other elements, getting comfortable and opening your chakras. Be specifically aware of your root and sacral centers. Breathe in and out rhythmically, and open your senses. What do you smell? What do you hear? Allow yourself to drift with the sound of the water for a while and allow images to form in your mind. Now open your eyes and carefully go to the edge of the water and scoop up a handful.

What does the water do in your hands? What does it feel like? Finish by closing and grounding.

Astral Connection: Repeat the process as with the other Elements, and allow the Guardian of Water to take you into her realm. She will lead you to a place of water, a stream, river, or even a well.[14] These are all access points to the Underworld. By looking deeply into them, you can see not only your Shadow, and other aspects of yourself, but you can also divine future possibilities and events.

Exploring the Outer Realms: The Astral and the Underworld

After successfully exploring the Elements, the next stage is a course of exploration of the Wiccan cosmology (see page 137), specifically the Astral Realm and the Underworld. There should be periods of rest between each exploration: We recommend at least a month. Exploration of these realms is a lifetime's work. The student should bear this in mind. The first stages are to find both your Astral and Underworld guides.

Finding your Astral Guide

This is already explained in "Ascending the Spiral Path" (see page 144). Once you have found your Astral Guide or totem animal, you simply ask them to show you around the Astral Realm. You should also ask your guide his/her name. This is important, as it is a way of calling your guide during future exploration of the realms. Once you have your guide, you can do the following things:

- If you have already practiced casting and creating sacred space on a regular basis, then you will have already started to create an Astral Temple (see page 149). Your guide will take you to your temple if asked, and if you haven't started this process, they will take you to the place best suited to create one.

- Within your Astral Temple, you can invoke your personal god or goddess.

- You can ask your guide to show you the different ways of accessing the various realms on the Tree.

Finding your Underworld guide

This process is very different than finding your Astral Guide, although you initially use the same pathworking technique described in "Ascending the Spiral Path." The only difference is that you stop at the Tree of Life and descend into the tunnel between the roots of the Tree. One then descends from the Astral Realm into the Underworld. On the way, you will pass through the Realm of Experience, the abode of your Id, your animal self.

> Slowly, as you approach the base of the tree, you become aware of a dark patch between two of the larger roots. This circle of darkness grows as you get nearer to the tree, and seems to suck in the light around it.

> You can now make out that it is a hole: a large animal burrow. You crouch in front of it, and peer into its darkness. You realize that, with a bit of effort, it is large enough for you to enter.

> You push your head into the hole, then your shoulders, wriggling to get them in completely. The hole is tight, but not tight enough to prevent you from moving your body and pushing yourself into it.

> You begin to push more of your body into the hole: Now your hips are in, and with a bit more effort, your knees, and finally your feet leave the outside world.

> You are in darkness, complete darkness. You smell the earthy scent of the soil around you and feel the tendrils of small roots touching your head.

> You push yourself down the hole, wriggling like a snake.

> Down and down you descend, down and down. Pushing with your shoulders, your hips and your feet, down and down into the unknown.

> You descend further down into the darkness, down and down, down and down.

You feel a root brushing your shoulder, but continue to descend, down and down, down and down, into the blackness.

The tunnel you are in begins to feel tighter as you go deeper, but undeterred you descend further, pushing with all your strength. Down and down, down and down you go.

The tunnel is now becoming so tight that you have to squeeze all your effort out of your muscles to move. Down and down, down and down you go.

Very slowly, you begin to make out a faint point of light: a greyness within the absolute blackness of the tunnel. You continue to head down, down and down, and nearer and nearer to this point of light.

The tunnel has now become tighter, but the light has become nearer, and you push yourself towards it.

You become aware that it is an opening to a dimly lit cavern, and you finally push your head through, and the whole of your body tumbles into the dimness that is beyond.

You look around and become aware that the light you could see was the phosphorescence of the cave walls. There is light enough just to see the ends of your arms and no more.

Suddenly you become aware of a presence apart from yourself: the noise of movement, but nothing else.

You feel something brush past part of your body, and then a second later it happens again.

Slowly, as your eyes adjust to the light, a shape begins to take form in front of you, and then it disappears into the dark shadows of the cave.

Suddenly it is in front of you again, and you can make out the eyes of a living creature staring back at you.

Then it is gone again into the shadows, but it returns: This time you can see not only its eyes, but also its shape—and you recognize what sort of creature it is.

This happens several more times: the creature passing you, brushing against you, staring at you, and then finally it disappears into the shadows, and you become aware that it does not intend to return.

You decide it is time to return with this experience. You find the entrance that you came into the cave through, and push yourself up into it.

The tunnel is tight, but you push yourself up with your shoulders, hips, and feet. Up and up, up and up.

Up and up, up and up you go, retracing your journey.

The tunnel does not appear as tight as it was, and you push yourself up. Up and up, up and up.

The smell of the woods wafts down the tunnel, but you can see nothing but darkness. Up and up, up and up you go.

It has now become much easier to move in the tunnel, and you can see a bright point ahead of you. You push yourself up towards the light, up and up, up and up.

The daylight is now much brighter and you can now see the entrance hole to this tunnel. You push yourself up and up, up and up, towards it.

Up and up, up and up you go.

Finally, you push your head out of the tunnel.

When you are ready, slowly return to this world by opening your eyes, and return to it with the experience of meeting your kindred animal Spirit for the first time.

Although in traditional forms of Shamanic working you "dance your power animal" after finding it, we recommend after you have completed this exercise that you ground and center yourself. You may want to collect items that connect you with your Underworld Guide. These are often referred to as totems. These can be feathers, fur, small representations of the animal concerned, etc. You may want to create a small pouch to keep them in and bring them out before doing any magical work so that you make a connection with your Underworld Guide. This is particularly important when doing Underworld descents.

Once you have found your power animal, your Underworld guide, then you can start to do the following:

    ❧ You can ask your Astral Guide guide to take you down the Left-Hand Path of the Tree of Life into the Underworld. This path is the reverse of the Right-Hand Path. You will pass the Elemental Guardians again on the way down starting with Water, then Fire, Air, and finally Earth. After Earth, you enter the Cave of the mysteries.

    ❧ At the entrance of the Cave of the Mysteries, you call your Underworld guide. On no account commence this journey without it. Ask it to guide you as to where to go. You can then explore the Underworld Realm and the mysteries.

Once you start to explore both the Astral and Underworld Realms, you will meet other entities, such as the Guardian of the Mysteries (see page 142). They, with your Astral and Underworld Guides, will prevent you from entering any realm or experiencing anything that you are not ready for. They do this to prevent you from causing damage to yourself, so heed the advice or warnings that you received from the guides and Guardians that you meet on your journeys. They are real personalities, so treat them with as much respect as you would anyone who is teaching you.

Endnotes

1. From the Confucian Analects (551 BC–479 BC).
2. This term was used by Doreen Valiente in *Witchcraft For Tomorrow* (*see* Bibliography). It is probably a more traditional term than *Book of Shadows* as it can also apply to the Grimoires of the Middle Ages.
3. The origins of the word *athame* are still debated. One view, remarked upon in Doreen Valiente's *An ABC of Witchcraft*, was that it derived from *arthana*, a term found in *The Clavicle of Solomon*. Idres Shah claimed that its name derived from *al-dhamme*, an Arabic name meaning "blood-letter" (from Ronald Hutton's *Triumph of the Moon*, page 273).
4. It is for this reason it is equated with *will.*
5. In Gardnerian and Alexandrian practice, these are referred to as "The Lords of the Watchtowers."
6. With the four elemental tools related to the elements, it can be seen that all seven tools also relate to the chakras, as well as the accessible magical realms.
7. In Celtic myth, the cauldron was a symbol of rebirth, the return of the life force. A good example is the Dagda's cauldron of Irish myth.
8. The stang is traditional tool in Anglo-Saxon magical practice. Reference to its use can be found in several books, including Valiente and Jones' *Witchcraft: A Tradition Renewed* (see Bibliography). Its use in modern Wiccan practice is very much connected to Robert Cochrane.
9. This placing of the altar in one quarter is an adaptation from ritual magic, where the altar is placed in the East.
10. These deities would, of course, be associated with the appropriate elements.
11. *The presentation of the magical tools* is an important part of the first-degree ritual in Alexandrian practice.
12. Even this destructive aspect of fire is sometimes positive, cleansing in nature.
13. According to Francis King, the Golden Dawn set up a "blind" (a deliberate attempt to mislead) related to the sword and the wand, exchanging their Elements of Fire and air. The sword is traditionally associated with fire, being forged in a smithy.
14. The well is believed to traditionally be an entry point into the Underworld and a place of divination. This myth can be found in both Irish and Welsh Celtic mythologies as the Dagda's cauldron of rebirth and Cerridwen's cauldron.

Chapter 12

First Steps on the Path:
Finding a Progressive Teacher or Coven

Let us watch well our beginnings, and results will manage themselves.

—Alexander Clark[1]

Janet initially became involved in witchcraft to get someone out of it. But this was in 1969, and things were very different. Even though the anti-witchcraft law was repealed in Britain in 1951,[2] there was no protection under European law[3] and the general public found it the very difficult to cope with the idea that witchcraft and Paganism was not connected with Satanism, let alone the concept that it was a religion. Witchcraft therefore remained underground, which resulted in two major hurdles for anyone trying to find a way in. The first one was finding a coven, as there were no advertising or Pagan magazines widely available, and the second was learning how to find genuine witches who were not out to exploit you.

There were a couple of ways of finding covens at that time. One of these was to approach an occult bookstore to see if they knew of one. The other was knowing someone who knew the existence of a coven. Even up to the mid-1980s, this was still a problem, as Gavin discovered. It was still a situation where you were more likely to find the egotists who were more interested in exploiting others for the purposes of self-aggrandisement or worse, rather than teaching magical or spiritual practices.

Janet was introduced to the Sanders and their coven through a friend who was reading June Johns' *King of the Witches,* a biography of Alex Sanders. Janet went along with her friend because she was worried about her. At the time, Janet was a Sunday school teacher with a strict Christian upbringing. But this was not her first excursion to see some witches, as she had previously gone along to visit an all-girl coven in Tooting, South London, a group Janet still refers to as "the red knicker coven" because of a strange rule requiring the members to wear red lingerie during ritual. This seemed to confirm in Janet's mind that witches were very strange people indeed! When Janet's friend said she was going to see Alex and Maxine Sanders, she decided that she had better go along too! Janet was quite surprised at what she found. Here was a spiritual path to which she could relate. Rather than dissuading her friend from joining the coven, she joined herself. Ironically, the friend she went to protect decided it wasn't for her after all. Within a year, she met Stewart Farrar, and left with him to form a coven after receiving third degree. Such a quick elevation to this level would be considered unacceptable today, but was not unusual in the 1960s and 70s.

Gavin's introduction was very different. His mother had been very open about religion, regardless of being a lapsed Catholic convert. She had encouraged exploration of all forms of spirituality, including the unknown and the supernatural. She had openly visited mediums on a regular basis. Originally, he had been interested in several different religious paths, and had "picked and mixed" from them: polarity from Taoism, reincarnation from Buddhism, and polytheism from Hinduism. For a while, he regularly visited his local Spiritualist Temple for healing as well as exploring Spiritualist doctrine. He considered his beliefs to be his own and was shocked to find, after getting a copy of Doreen Valiente's, *An ABC of Witchcraft,* that his own unique belief system was the same as that of Wicca.

Over the years, Gavin read more, and slowly met others in his hometown who were interested in Wicca. More books were being published at this time about witchcraft and more people were showing interest. Eventually, in the early to mid-80s, he ended up in the woods one Samhain with a group of friends celebrating the festival. Afterwards, Gavin felt uneasy. The ritual had not gone that well, the circle hadn't been cast properly, and those present had seen inexplicable things in the woods. He set about looking for people with experience, or so he thought!

At this time in Britain, things were still closed off. There was no contact network for witches or Pagans that covered the whole of the country until the end of that decade, and there were still few magazines being published. *The Wiccan,* the journal of the British Pagan Federation, was still a piece of A3 paper folded in half that only gave a few contacts for covens in London and thereabouts. The first group Gavin came across was a magic group working out of the back of an occult shop. It was not a Wiccan group, but a mix of Earth magic, ceremonial magic, Spiritualism, and various New Age practices. It was from this group that the person who introduced him to Seax-Wicca came and helped him and the others form a coven. All the members of this subsequent coven went through several bad experiences with self-proclaimed "experts" and "teachers" who were more interested in control than in expanding the knowledge of the coven members. The climate of the time encouraged such individuals to thrive. Regardless of the setbacks, Gavin continued to look for an established coven to train with while he continued to educate himself on the occult. Eventually, he and his current partner formed their own coven, which ran successfully for many years. Hived-off covens still exist to this day in the South of England

Neither of us regrets the experiences we went through in trying to find a coven. "You have to kiss a lot of frogs before you find a prince," to quote an old saying. We tend to look at them as learning experiences we had to go through to understand witchcraft properly. But that was then, and the situation today is very different.

The Attraction to Witchcraft

There are several reasons why people are attracted to witchcraft. Many have the experience of "coming home." This has been voiced to us on several occasions and seems to be a common feeling. This is mainly due to the fact that witchcraft is a natural spirituality, with free expression as a central part of it. Some become disillusioned with mainstream religion and seek to find something that fulfils their need for mysticism. This important part of Christianity seems to have been lost over the last century. Over the years, we have had contact with several Jewish and Christian witches who saw no dichotomy in being both Pagan and Christian. It may seem odd to some that it is possible to be two religions at once, but this is not unusual in Eastern culture where fusion of such religions as Hinduism, Buddhism, and Shinto are common.

The need to find an explanation for a psychic or occult experience also draws people to Wicca. Witchcraft offers both a good grounding in psychic and occult practices and also a logical explanation of such phenomenon that cannot be found so easily elsewhere. We have initiated at least one person who was a ghost hunter, and it was his need to find an explanation of his first-hand experiences that drew him into witchcraft.

Teenage rebellion is also a common factor. In recent years, television and movies have made this factor even more influential. Many young people go through the phase of challenging the norms and values of their parents and society. Teenagers who played with Ouija boards and tarot cards were almost a cliché when we first came into the craft. Of course, now it is the all-black Gothic/Vampire image that is commonly seen at Pagan Festivals. There is nothing wrong with this. It is part of growing up, and we are the first to admit that this element was (and still is) in us when we first became interested in witchcraft. We expect the same is true of some quite well-known figures in Wicca today.

Many are attracted to the idea of the coven: a small group of people with a similar philosophy. This attraction has very much come about because of the breakdown of the extended family in modern culture. In the past, there were large families with at least three generations interacting. Now we have the nuclear family consisting only of two generations (parents and children), which split when the children come of leaving age (see page 94). The need to belong to a "family" group with its own identity is a strong human instinct. Tribalism can even be seen in the youth culture that has developed since the 1960s. The coven fulfills this need, and many run on this line with the High Priest and Priestess acting as surrogate parents. In fact, one of the greatest complements a High Priestess can receive is when she is referred to as Mom!

We have also come across people attracted to witchcraft because they need healing, be it physical or, more often, psychological. This is called *wounded healer syndrome*. It is a concept known to anyone who is involved in the healing arts. It was known to the ancient Greeks, who personified the concept as Aesculapius, the crippled god of healers. It occurs when a person who needs healing confuses this need with a desire to become a healer. There is nothing wrong with this, as the best healers are those who can empathise due to experience. A good example of this is in rape counselling: Only someone who has been through this traumatic experience can really help others through it. Quite simply, the best healers are those that have been healed. But the "wounded healer" process can only take place if the person recognizes their need for healing.

Of course, the reason for someone's interest in becoming a witch can also be a combination of any of these reasons. But none of them are a reason to turn anyone who is truly interested away. It is easier today to find out about what witchcraft is than at any time in recent history, and the subject of witchcraft has become more publicly acceptable. But for anyone who seriously intends to take up the path of witchcraft, it is important that they understand why they are attracted to it and what their motivations behind this attraction are. They have to ask the question, "Why do I want to be a witch?"

By the turn of the millennium, both in the United States and the United Kingdom, Pagan contact networks had been in existence for more than a decade. The amount of books published on the subject has more than doubled, and there are now even glossy magazines on the market. Finding a coven had never been easier. In the past, you took what you could find, and you had little choice about what tradition or type of coven you joined. Now the seeker not only has this choice, but also can decide to go solitary.

In the past, solitary witches were not accepted on the grounds that they had received no formal training. To be fair, it was a good point, as at that time, there was not the same level of material on witchcraft available as there is today. The publishing industry and the Internet have changed this situation considerably, and we see no reason why a witch shouldn't train him or herself. There are now support groups for solitaries, training courses, and even instructional videos. There are disadvantages, of course, for there is much you can learn about ritual and magic from experienced people that the solitary witch misses out on. Most of the solitaries we have met have learned just as much as they would from a coven, although the process takes longer, and there is a greater chance that they give up. We do recommend that those who wish to become a witch try, wherever possible, to find a good reputable coven to train with, but sometimes this is just not possible when one lives in an area where there are no reputable witches[4] around. It is better to train yourself as a solitary than to join a potentially abusive coven.

Finding a Way In

So what happens if someone has decided that they want to set on this path and want to train with a coven, find an experienced teacher, or get support as a solitary? As we said earlier, this is much easier today than in the past, and there are several options open for the seeker to find. We regularly answer mail from seekers trying to find a teacher or coven, and the options we list below are our most common answers.

- **Local occult/New Age bookstore:** It's not unusual for training groups, covens, support groups, and networks to advertise through these shops, normally with postings on the notice board. You may also talk to any of the staff or to the owner, as they tend to know what's going on in the local area and can point you in the right direction. In our experience, they are always happy to help, as they are normally involved in some form of occult practice. It's also very common for them to be running some sort of group from the back of the shop, particularly if it's an occult bookstore. You may also find that they run workshops, lectures, and have guest speakers at the shop on a regular basis.

- **Magazines and periodicals:** There are several Pagan and Wiccan magazines around nowadays (some of these are listed in the back of this book in the Resources section). They always have a section for advertisements and contacts, normally categorized into covens, training courses, local moots (open meetings), and local events such as open festivals. Of course, you don't see many such magazines on your average newsagent shelf, although some are beginning to appear. You will find them in occult/New Age bookstores.

- **Local moot/support group:** These are open Pagan meetings, not always specific to witchcraft, but you can almost guarantee there will be a few witches present. The useful thing about moots is that you can meet members of potential covens or teachers in an open, non-committal environment, which is good for both parties. Organizers of moots are always quite happy to point you in the direction of people to talk to at the moot, and they often act as go-betweens for magical groups, teachers, and potential members. Most moots have their own mailing lists and can be found advertising on the Internet, as well as on the notice boards of occult bookstores. Moots act as excellent support groups for those who wish to follow the solitary path; they give a feeling of fellowship sometimes not experienced by the solitary, but without the commitment of a coven.

ꙮ   **The Internet:** The amount of information about witchcraft on the World Wide Web is quite staggering, and covens were to quick to realize that they could advertise anonymously through this medium. Many covens and even traditions have Websites outlining their practices, beliefs, structure, etc. This means you can quite literally shop around for the coven that suits you, although you may not necessarily find that your local coven advertises. There are also other sites (such as *The Witches Voice*—see Resources) that have contact pages for covens worldwide. For the solitary, of course, the Web offers an unlimited source of training material, and there are numerous online support groups for solitaries.

ꙮ   **Open organizations:** There are several organizations around that are happy to accept members purely by application. Many of them require a declaration that the potential member has Pagan beliefs and/or ethics. They normally run some sort of contact service, as well having a magazine, Website and/or mailing list, and they organize events such as conferences (for example, The Pagan Federation, Covenant of the Goddess, etc.). They also tend to evaluate covens that advertise through them, and will refuse to list them if there are complaints against them. Such organizations can be found advertising in Pagan/New Age magazines, as well as in more mainstream, newsagent shelf-type astrology magazines.

Approaching a Coven or Teacher

There are no hard and fast rules as to what happens next after you have found someone you want to learn with, as anyone who runs a coven tends to have their own personal rules on such things. If you met them personally at a moot or an open gathering, it is up to you to approach them. Don't do this straight away. Attend several moots over a period of time and try to get to know them. You may find that you don't like them or don't agree with their ideas or philosophy. You need to make sure that they know that you are genuinely interested in learning about Wicca, but don't try to impress them because you won't. Most good High Priestesses and Priests know a yarn when they hear one. Try to find out their views on things that might be of concern to you before asking about coven membership.

If at the first or even the second meeting you are approached by a coven leader and asked if you are interested in joining their coven, walk away! Proselytising is considered to be one of the few witchcraft sins.

There has always been a rule that you don't actively recruit, but allow the seeker to find you. We still feel this holds true, along with the Hindu saying, "When the chela (seeker) is ready, the guru (teacher) will appear." We have found that coven leaders who recruit in such a way do so more for their own needs rather than the needs of the potential member. The same rules apply if you are mailing a coven about membership. You should never receive mail saying that you have been accepted without first some sort of interview.

Asking the right questions

Interviews are normally the second step toward becoming a member of a coven, regardless of how you've contacted them. It gives the coven leaders a chance to meet you more formally and find out if you're serious. These normally take place at the home of the High Priestess and Priest, but they may also meet you at a neutral venue where you can talk quietly. Other coven members may also be present. Expect to be questioned about how you got interested in witchcraft, what your religious beliefs are, and what you understand a coven and a witch to be. Be honest! If you don't know the answer to a question they ask, be unafraid to say that you don't know. It is important that you be yourself. They aren't interested in what you know; they are interested in what sort of person you are, whether you will fit in with the rest of the coven, and if you have a willingness to learn. They should tell you what they expect from their coven members. This will include the level of work they will expect you to undertake, how they expect you to behave, etc. They should also tell you the origins of the coven and how it is organized.

This is also your opportunity to assess your potential teachers. Are they genuinely interested in you and your spiritual development, or are they more interested in getting another coven member? Do they give you a chance to talk, express any concerns, and ask questions? These are all important questions to ask yourself. Good coven leaders are interested in you as a person, not just as a coven member, and will therefore attempt to get to know you. They will also allow you to do most of the talking and will prompt your questions if necessary. Beware of coven leaders who talk at you! This is not a good sign for things to come! They should allow you to ask questions and be comfortable with giving you the answers that you need. Beware of coven leaders who "fudge" answers they don't know. Good teachers will always admit if they don't know something. It is always useful if you bring with you a list of the books you have read and have some idea of questions you want to ask them. Don't be scared to ask the hard questions.

Sexual initiations and skyclad work (naked in ritual) are the most common concerns for would-be initiates in our experience. Some covens still have sexual initiation, although nowadays such covens are rare, as the practice is becoming less acceptable to mainstream witchcraft. There is nothing wrong with sexual initiation as long as the initiate is made aware of this practice within the coven right from the beginning, and that such practices are safe, sane, and consensual. If you don't like the practice, you can look elsewhere. The same applies to going skyclad, which tends to be more common, particularly among more traditional Gardnerian and Alexandrian covens. Find out right from the beginning the practices of the coven, particularly their ethics. It may save you, and the coven that you are considering joining, a lot of future problems. Again, don't be scared of asking such questions. You are more likely to impress a good teacher with your frankness than scare them off, as it shows you have thought everything through carefully.

If you are unhappy with the answers you receive, first try to get them clarified. If you are still unhappy, simply say that you don't feel this is the coven for you. Never join a coven if you have a doubt: You should be completely secure in your decision. A good coven leader will understand this. Not only will she be happy about it, she may even point you in the direction of a coven that might suit you! You should always part on good terms. We, as coven leaders, go out of our way to put people off, as we don't want someone who is going to waste our time and cause problems because our coven doesn't suit them. But that doesn't mean that we necessarily believe witchcraft isn't for them, and on many occasions have passed such individuals on to other covens better suited to them.

Control issues

If things go well, the High Priestess and Priest are likely to say straight away that they would consider you, but they are unlikely to give you a firm yes or no immediately. You will probably be asked to informally meet the coven or even attend a circle. Remember that these are people you are going to have to work with magically and psychically in an intimate environment, and they will also want to get to know you as well. This gives you a good chance to seriously look at the way the group is run and assess whether this is the group for you. With this in mind, we have included a list of considerations[5] when approaching a coven, to assess their practices and whether they are "a safe bet," so to speak.

1. **How much control is wielded by High Priest/Priestess over the coven? Does this include the members' lives outside of the coven, including their sex and private lives?**

   You should look carefully at how much control the leaders of the coven have over the members. Witchcraft is not a cult, with its leaders affecting the whole lives of its members. If a High Priestess or Priest tries to tell the members how to run their lives, then you should think carefully about joining, particularly if this is directed at the members' personal lives. A good coven leader doesn't make moral judgements related to members' sexuality or relationships outside the covenstead. More importantly, they certainly should not see the members of the coven as potential sexual conquests.

2. **Do the leaders of the coven claim to know everything? Do they claim to be infallible in their decisions, or even that their decisions are divinely inspired and therefore cannot be questioned? How are those who question treated?**

   Nobody knows everything. One thing a good High Priestess or High Priest learns is that they never stop learning. Just because someone appears to have a lot of knowledge doesn't mean that they are wise, just that they have read a lot! Wisdom comes from a combination of knowledge and experience. If you come across someone who says that they don't need to learn anymore, this is a bad sign. Such a leader is likely to be dictatorial and will take offense to questions, which they see as challenging their knowledge, and therefore, their authority. They may tell members to avoid or even not to read certain books or visit certain Websites for this reason.

3. **Is the coven run in a dogmatic fashion without creativity? Is it "by the book" so to speak, with the same rituals every circle? Are new ideas discouraged and put down? Does the coven lack a sense of fun and humour, particularly if something goes wrong in circle?**

   Witchcraft is fertility-based spirituality and therefore sees the importance of creativity in everything. A coven that embraces the fundamental principles of witchcraft will therefore be creative in the way it works. There will be experimentation within circle, and its members will be encouraged to experiment with ritual rather than dogmatically follow a system. Any dogmatic or doctrinal coven is likely to continually tell members that show any creativity that they aren't doing things "the right way." Such covens tend to be stagnant and their leaders obsessed with tradition. A lack of sense of humor is a give-away in such a coven. Mistakes by members are likely to be seen as failures rather than experiences to learn from. There will be little room for growth in such a group.

4. **Do the leaders of the coven actively encourage its members to recruit? Do they poach members from other covens? Do they claim to be the only real witches or coven in their area? Do they claim to have "the best coven"?**

As we said earlier, proselytising is unacceptable within witchcraft. Sometimes leaders may get around this by sending out its members to recruit. This is still unacceptable and indicative of a cult-like structure within the coven. High Priests and Priestesses who try to steal members of other covens show a lack of security within themselves and in the coven they run. They may see themselves as being in competition with other coven leaders. This insecurity may manifest as elitism. There is nothing wrong with a High Priestess or Priest being proud of its coven achievements, but there is no competition in spirituality, and a good coven leader knows this. They know that the best way to build a coven is slowly and that they will get more dedication from a coven member who comes to them in their own time.

5. **Do the coven members pay for training, aside from the usual coven dues? How do they rationalize this?**

"You do not charge other members of the craft" is one of the old laws dating back to Gerald Gardner. It still holds true within the coven setting. If you are specifically being charged for attending training circles, then this is financial exploitation. If you join a coven you should expect to train for free, but don't expect the coven leaders to foot the bill for such things as candles, incense, wine, and food for circle. Of course, many coven leaders run beginners courses or even workshops outside of the coven, but this is different from running a coven.[6]

6. **Are members discouraged from leaving the coven? Are ex-members demonized?**

A good witch knows that everyone must ultimately follow his or her own spiritual path, and a good High Priest or Priestess knows that this is also true for their own coven members. For this reason, a coven member should never be discouraged from leaving the coven. They may, in some circumstances, be offered other options, but they should never be told that they can't leave. There should be no paranoia or demonization of ex-members. This happens if the coven is worried that they might reveal a secret that might damage the reputation of the coven or its leaders. If they are worried about this, they probably have good reason to be, particularly if members are told to have no contact with ex-members. It indicates a problem within the coven.

7. **Are members discouraged from being involved in outside activities, such as moots or open circles? Is there a feeling of paranoia regarding outside groups and/or real or imaginary enemies?**

Some covens decide right from their conception to remain secret. Its members may decide that they are quite happy just being within the coven and may not wish to be in contact with the wider Pagan community. This is their personal decision. However, no coven should lay down a rule saying its members can't attend open Pagan events, meetings, or circles. Leaders of such covens are worried that members may discover negative things about them or compare what happens in the coven with what happens elsewhere. Paranoia and the idea of "enemies of the coven" are used by cults as a method of controlling their members, and if this is present within a coven, it indicates that there are more things going on in this coven than first meets the eye.

When you first meet a coven, be it informally or in circle, the first thing that should strike you is how relaxed the members are with each other, particularly when the High Priest or Priestess is present. It should be a family atmosphere rather than that of a religious meeting. There should always be a certain degree of banter and humor going on. The members should always treat the leaders of the coven with respect. They give their time and energy freely to train the coven's members, and deserve this respect. But it should be reciprocal. Good leaders return the respect that they receive. In most covens that have been active for some time, the leaders tend to be seen more like parental figures than leaders.

You're In!

After being invited to several coven meetings, the High Priestess and Priest will decide whether to accept you into the coven. It is likely that they will confer with the other members of the coven on this decision, so be aware of this. The High Priestess and Priest may be happy with you, but if other members are not, then you may still find yourself looking for another coven. Even when you are accepted, you still have the chance to leave if you are unhappy with the coven for some reason.

If you are accepted then you have started with the first footstep on the path to becoming and understanding what a witch truly is. As Stewart Farrar once wrote, "What makes a witch?" The answer he gave was "a sense of wonder!" The long spiritual path of witchcraft makes that sense of wonder one of the most rewarding aspects of being a witch. The enhancing of your personal spirituality and the unveiling of the mysteries behind that spirituality will indeed increase your sense of wonder. Enjoy every step upon the path you have chosen to walk. Honor those who give of themselves to teach, be gracious in your dealings with others, and forgive those who you perceive as doing you wrong, for they are also teaching you. Remember that it is not the end result that is the wonder, but the journey itself—the quest for the Grail.

Endnotes

1. Film and Broadway actor. Died 1995.
2. The Witchcraft Act of 1736 was repealed in 1951, following the prosecution in 1944 of Helen Duncan, a Spiritualist medium. She was from Gavin's hometown of Portsmouth and had, unfortunately, been too accurate for the authorities, informing a mother of her son's death at sea before the Navy could. She was considered a threat to national security.
3. *The European Declaration of Human Rights* (1991) articles 10, 11, and 14, now guarantee European citizens the freedom of religious belief and practice, as does the United States' First Amendment. The United Nations' *Universal Declaration of Human Rights* (1948), article 2, does likewise.
4. Our view of what a "reputable witch" or coven is one that is ethically based, and that does not mean one that necessarily has the "correct lineage" or "initiations."
5. These "considerations" originated from Isaac Bonewits' "Cult Danger Evaluation Frame" (first published in *Real Magic*), which we previously published in *The Pagan Path* (*see* Bibliography).
6. They are not acting as High Priestess or Priestess in these situations. There is no spiritual obligation between them and those attending their workshops, only the obligation to give "value for money."

Appendix 1

The Gods and Goddesses of Witchcraft

We have listed here a selection of gods and goddesses specific to the art of witchcraft. It should be noted that many modern witches worship other deities beside these listed, but due to the sheer number of such deities, we have tried to restrict the entries to those related to magic and sorcery.

Goddesses of Witchcraft

ARADIA: Medieval. Etruscan Witch Goddess, surviving in Italy into this century. Daughter of Diana (Etruscan: Aritimi or Tana) and Diana's brother Lucifer (literally, of the Moon and the Sun). Diana desired her brother, but he fled from her; so she turned herself into the shape of his favorite cat, which slept on his bed. She resumed her own shape while he was sleeping, and when he awoke and found her he was furious; but she charmed him with a song and seduced him, conceiving Aradia. Aradia came to Earth to teach the witches her mother's magic. She was unknown to scholars until Charles Godfrey Leland won the trust of Tuscany witch Maddelena and published the material she gave him in his book *Aradia or the Gospel of the Witches* (see Bibliography) at the end of the last century. She may, however, have spread wider than underground Tuscany during the hidden centuries. The *Canon Episcopi*, a 10th century Church condemnation of witchcraft, gives "Herodias" as a witch goddess name along with Diana, and *airidh* in Gaelic means both "the summer pastures" and "worth, merit." There is some debate as to whether she was an actual goddess or a "Robin Hood" type of figure as indicated by Leland's manuscript. It is very likely that she was "a daughter of Diana," a priestess of her surviving cult.

ARTEMIS: Greek. Nature, Hunting, and Moon Goddess; in Greek-speaking Asia, a Mother Goddess. Daughter of Zeus and Leto, and twin sister of Apollo, though a day older. Known as Potnia Theron, "Mistress of the Animals," Roman equivalent of Diana. She probably absorbed a pre-Indo-European Sun Goddess, and her twinning in classical legend with the Sun God may stem from this. The Greeks assimilated her to a pre-Greek mistress of wild animals. Bears were sacred to her, and she was associated with the constellation Ursa Major. Guinea fowl were her birds. Doreen Valiente (*An ABC of Witchcraft*, 18) says her name may mean "High Source of Water"—the Moon being regarded as the source and ruler of all waters, and of the oceanic, psychic, and menstrual tides. "Hence the moon goddess, by whatever name she was known, was the mistress of magic, enchantment and sorcery" (*ibid*). Invoked as Artemis Eileithyia by women in childbirth, Protectress of Youth, especially of girls. Invoked to bring good weather to travelers. She is depicted with bow and arrows, often with a hound. One of her forms was Callisto. The many-breasted Artemis of Ephesus ("Diana of the Ephesians" of Acts 19) where her temple as a fertility goddess was one of the Seven Wonders of the ancient world, is much closer to her pre-Greek Mother function. Her cult there was said to go back to the Amazons. Festival: February 12, and the sixth day from the New Moon.

BABA: Slavic. The spirit in the last sheaf of harvested grain; a woman bound to it would bear a child within the year. As Baba Yaga, she degenerated in folklore to a frightening witch, Baba Yaga who lived in the forest and scared people to death; she also rode the sky in a mortar, using the pestle as an oar. Skulls were put on fenceposts as a protection against her.

BEFANA: ("Epiphany") Medieval Strega. Italian witch-fairy who flies her broomstick on Twelfth Night (January 6) to come down chimneys and bring presents to children.

BENZOZIA,
BENSOZIA: Basque. Mother Goddess. As Bensozia, also a medieval Witch Goddess name; may mean "Good Neighbor," a common name for the fairies.

CAILLEACH BHEARA, CAILLEACH BUI,
CALLY BERRY (Irish) *also*
CAILLEACH BHEUR

(Scottish): Lake and Weather Goddess who protected lakes from being drained. Beara is a peninsular on the Cork-Kerry border. She dropped the cairns on the hills of County Meath from her apron, moved islands, and built mountains. Originally appeared as a triple goddess, Cailleach Bolus and Cailleach Corca Duibhne. As Cailleach Bui, said to have been a wife of Lugh. The *Book of Lecan* says she had seven youthful periods, married seven husbands (each of whom grew old and died), and had 50 foster children who founded many tribes and nations. In Ireland, a builder of mountains. In Scotland, a warner of storms and bringer of snow; overcome each spring by the appearance of Brighid, she turned into a stone every April 30 and was reborn every October 31. Some scholars identify the Scottish form with Black Annis. One of the most ancient aspects of the Goddess in the British Isles. In Gaelic, Cailleach basically means a wise older woman, and may be applied to anyone from a nun to a witch. Interestingly, *caileach* with a single "L" means "chalice" in Irish—an essentially feminine symbol. In Scotland, the Cailleach was also known as the Carline.

CERRIDWEN: Welsh. Mother, Moon, and Grain Goddess. Wife of Tegid Voel and mother of Creirwy ("Dear One"), the most beautiful girl in the world, and Avagdu, the ugliest boy. She had another son, Morfan, so ugly that no one would fight with him at the Battle of Camlann (at which Arthur and Mordred were slain) because people thought he was a devil. Cerridwen was said to have lived on an island in the middle of Lake Tegid. Owner of an inexhaustible cauldron called Amen, in which she made a magic draught called "greal" (Grail?) from six plants, which gave inspiration and knowledge. She intended to brew a potion in it that would make Avagdu brilliant in compensation for his ugliness, but a little boy Gwion whom she left in charge of it scalded his finger in the bubbling liquid, and sucked his finger in pain, giving him the universal wisdom intended for Avagdu. Cerridwen pursued Gwion, both of them shape changing; first she was a greyhound chasing a hare, then an otter chasing a fish, then a hawk chasing a bird. She finally caught and ate him when she was a hen and he a grain of corn. As a result, she gave birth to Taliesin, greatest of the Welsh bards. This chase may relate to the initiation rituals of a Druid or bard. One of her symbols was a sow. Most of her surviving legends emphasize the terrifying aspects of the Dark Mother; yet her cauldron is the source of Wisdom and Inspiration.

DIANA: Roman. Equivalent of the Greek Moon and Nature Goddess Artemis, and rapidly acquired all her characteristics. Originally from Latium, a Goddess of Light, Mountains, and Woods, and probably first a pre-Indo-European Sun Goddess. Associated with the constellation Ursa Major. One of her sanctuaries was at Lake Nemi, where her priest was an escaped slave who had to kill his predecessor in single combat to take the office—and then hold it against any would-be successor. Like Artemis, classically regarded as virgin, but originally a sacrificial-mating goddess. Under Christianity, she became the Goddess of underground witches, whom the 10th-century *Canon Episcopi* condemned for believing they rode at night "with Diana, the goddess of pagans." In a still-surviving Tuscany witch legend, Diana is the original Supreme Goddess and mother by Lucifer of Aradia—a name that also appears as Herodias in some later versions of the *Canon Episcopi*. Doreen Valiente (*An ABC of Witchcraft,* page 89) suggests that one reason why the name Diana appealed to pagans was that *dianna* and *diona* were Celtic words meaning "divine, brilliant." British legend says it was Diana who "directed the Trojan Prince Brutus, the founder of the royal line of Britain, to take refuge here after the Fall of Troy" (*ibid,* page 91), and St. Paul's Cathedral in London is believed to be built on the site of a Temple of Diana; there is a tradition that bucks were processed up its steps until medieval times. Diana was regarded as the supreme deity by the Gauls as late as the 5th century, and was still worshipped by the Franks in the 7th century. She was identified with Sophia by the Gnostics. She was often portrayed as a mother with a child, and many of her temples were rededicated to the Virgin Mary. Festivals: May 26-31, August 13 and 15; on August 13, she was invoked to protect the crops against storms. Day: Monday.

FREYA ("Well-beloved, Spouse, Lady"),
  VANADIS ("Ancestress-Friend"?):
> Norse, Germanic, and Anglo-Saxon. Fertility Goddess, most revered of the Nordic Goddesses. Daughter of Niord and Skadi, and sister of Frey. Originally of the Vanir (pre-Indo-European culture) in whose legend she and Frey were the children of Niord and his sister. The Aesir welcomed her and Frey and Niord and accepted them; but they rejected incest, so Skadi became Niord's wife in their mythology and his sister disappeared. Sometimes confused with Frigg as wife of Odin, or in some stories, of Od, who is sometimes equated with Odin. Frigg and Freya seem to have been originally the same goddess (or perhaps a Vanir triple goddess with Skadi) then developed as two, finally tending to remerge. Owner of a falcon-plumed robe in which she flew through the air, including to the Underworld to gain information in her role as a

seeress. She was a goddess of sexual pleasure, and was said to have slept with all of the Aesir and with her brother Frey, as well as with giants and mortal men; her priests were regarded as her consorts. She is particularly called upon by women today who wish to regain the strength that Christian patriarchy has so long denied them. Mediaeval songs dedicated to her, called *mansongr*, or in German, *minnegesang*, were suppressed by the Christians, but later troubadours and minstrels revived the tradition, dedicating their songs to the Virgin Mary. Said to have been a mistress of magic and witchcraft. Also a War goddess, commander of the Valkyries (originally her priestesses). She often fought alongside Odin; she claimed half of the dead slain in every battle for her hall, Folkvangr (Field of Folk), Odin taking the other half. She also received the souls of unmarried women. She loved ornaments and jewelry. She rode in a chariot drawn by two cats, and also rode on a boar called Hildisvini ("Battle-Swine") whose golden bristles showed him the way in the dark. May have been priestess of a hawk totem clan. Animals sacred to her included the sow, the cat, the falcon, the swallow, and the cuckoo; and as Frigg the ram, the heron, and the spider. Although a Goddess of Earth, she also had a watery side, and a dwelling in Fensalir ("Ocean Halls"). Her many names included Heidh ("Witch"), Horn ("Flax"), Gefn ("Giver"), and Syr ("Sow"). Her symbols were the spindle and the distaff; she was mistress of the crafts of the home. Associated with the zodiacal sign Leo. Friday was named after her. English place-names recalling her include Freefolk, Hampshire (in Domesday Book Frigefolk, "Frigg's People"); Froyle and Frobury, Hampshire (both the latter Old English Freohyll, "Freya's Hill"); Fryup, Yorkshire ("the hop or marshy enclosure of Freya"), and Friydaythorpe, Yorkshire. Festivals: first Monday after January 6 (Saxon Plow Monday), November 21.

HABONDIA, DAME HABONDE,
ABUNDIA: Medieval. A Witch Goddess name, doubtless implying "abundance."

HECATE: Greek. Originally Thracian and pre-Olympian, and probably even older. At the same time, a Moon Goddess, and Underworld Goddess, and a Goddess of Magic. Daughter of two Titans, Perses and Asteria, both symbols of shining light (a later tradition says Zeus and Hera). Took part in the Olympians' war against the Giants. Dwelt in the Underworld alongside Hades and Persephone. She protected flocks, sailors, and witches. Associated with crossroads, where her three-faced image was placed, called Triple Hecates; offerings of food, called Hecate's Supper, were left there on the eve of the Full Moon to propitiate her; one left them there and walked away without looking back, because no one dared confront her face to face. Of all the Greek Goddesses, she was the most markedly triple. She was also absorbed into the Roman pantheon, where "Diana Triformis" consisted of Diana, Prosperine, and Hecate (in Greek terms, Artemis, Persephone, and Hecate). She was portrayed as three female figures, or as one with three animal heads—horse, dog, and bear, or sometimes of three dogs. Like Herne in the North, she had the reputation of leading a wild hunt of ghostly hounds through the night. The night-calling owl was her messenger, and the dark yew and the willow or osier were her trees; witches' besoms were traditionally bound with osier, otherwise they were said to be useless. Her annual festival on August 13 (also that of the Roman Diana) was a propitiatory one, to avert harvest-destroying storms. She is the Dark Mother, in both the positive and the negative sense. She can send demons to torment men's dreams, and drive them mad if they are not integrated enough to cope with her; but to those who dare to welcome her, she brings creative inspiration. Typically of a Moon Goddess, she has a son called Museos, the Muse Man. For divination, the Greeks used "Hecate's Circle," a golden sphere with a sapphire hidden inside it—the mysterious Moon concealing the bright seed of understanding. Her symbol is the torch, which illumines the Unconscious and reveals its secrets. In Caria (Western Turkey) she was the primary Goddess; she had a sanctuary at Lagina. In Colophon, dogs were sacrificed to her, and she herself could shape-change into a dog. In Samothrace, there was a cave sacred to her called Zerynthos (from which she was also named Zerynthia) where dogs were also sacrificed, and mysteries performed involving orgiastic dances. It is interesting that Shakespeare's three witches in *Macbeth* as worshipping Hecate, at a time when official propaganda had witches worshipping the Devil; growing up in the country, did he know better? Festivals: January 31, March 23, August 13.

HERODIAS: Medieval Strega. She is condemned in the 10th-century *Canon Episcopi* along with Diana as being worshipped by witches—and it is possible that the name is a variant of the Etruscan Aradia. The Biblical reference comes in the story of John the Baptist's execution at the court of Herod (Matthew 14 and Mark 6), and many scholars believe her part in this is a later insertion.

HIR NINEVEH: Assyro-Babylonian. Goddess personifying the city of Nineveh. Roundly condemned in the Bible (Nahum III): "the multitude of the whoredoms of the well-favored harlot, the mistress of witchcraft."

LOUHI: Finnish. An enchantress who is capable of shape-changing and hiding the Sun and Moon. Rune 49 of the Kalevala tells how she sent a bear down to harass the people. She lives in Pohjola, the North, an area associated with magic.

MARI: Basque. Supreme Goddess, ruler of all other deities. Sometimes described as an Earth Goddess, but her attributes seem primarily lunar. She lives in the depths of the Earth but likes crossing the Sky at night; so does her son/husband Sugaar ("Male Serpent"). She rides the Sky in a cart drawn by four horses, or in the form of a burning sickle or crescent, or engulfed in flames, or riding a broomstick in a ball of fire. The Basques appear unique in associating the Moon with the color red and with fire, and Mari has strong fire symbolism. Sugaar also rides as a burning crescent, but to the Basques the Moon itself is always female. They respect her greatly, timing their woodcutting, sowing, and reaping by her phases. The Moon's divinatory animal is the ladybird, known as *Mari Gorri* ("Red Mari"), who is often asked to predict tomorrow's weather. Basques believe it is the light of the Moon that guides the dead to their resting place. Friday is the Moon's day, and Friday night the witches' traditional meeting time. Mari is the patroness of all witches, and a witch herself, with oracular and magical powers. She often appears as an elegantly dressed lady—sometimes crowned with the Full Moon or a burning crescent Moon. She is associated with Akerbeltz ("Black He-Goat"), whom Basque witches invoke and work with at their Sabbats, which are called Akelarre ("Field of the He-Goat"). She also rides a ram, around whose horns she wraps wool to wind into a ball. Other totem animals are the horse, the heifer, and the crow or raven. Mari changes her abode, spending seven years in Anboto, where she is known as Anbokoto Dama ("Lady of Anboto") or Anbokoto Sorgina ("Witch of Anboto"), seven years in Oiz, and seven in Mugarra. Other accounts say she spends time in Aralar, Aiztorri, and Murumendi.

SELENE: Greek (known as Luna to the Romans). Moon Goddess, daughter of Hyperion and Theia, and sister of the Sun God Helios and the Dawn Goddess Eos; though sometimes said to be the daughter of Zeus or of Helios. She was wooed and won by Zeus and by Pan.

TLACHTGA, TLACHTA: Irish. Goddess of witchcraft and the province of Munster. She died giving birth to triplets by three different fathers. Festival: October 31, Samhain Eve. Her sacred site is the Hill of Ward near Athboy, County Meath, where the first of the sacred Samhain fires was lit. She was probably a pre-Celtic sacrificial deity. The Church attempted to obliterate her memory, but she survived the Christian period by becoming merged with the daughter of Mog Ruith, the Arch-Druid of Ireland. This makes her sister of Tailtu, whose sacred site is not far from hers. Some texts say that with her father, she opposed the coming of Christianity to Ireland and joined with Simon Magus in Italy to fight it. Upon returning to Ireland, she brought back the fragments of a stone wheel known as Roth Fáil or Roth Ramhach, which her father and Simon Magus had been using for magical demonstrations in Italy, and placed them near Rathcool, County Dublin, where they may still be seen. Her sacred animal is the cat.

Gods of Witchcraft

AKERBELTZ: ("Black He-Goat") Basque. Goat God invoked by Basque witches at their Sabbats, which were known as Akelarre ("Field of the He-Goat").

CERNUNNOS: Continental Celtic. The only known written name of the Celtic Horned God, appearing on the altar of Nautes, now in the Cluny Museum in Paris. Many other representations (such as on the Gundestrup Cauldron) are clearly of the same God. The name appears to be a Romanization or Hellenization of Herne, which name has survived in tradition and in place-names; *see* that entry.

FREY, FREYR: ("Lord, Spouse") Norse. God of Fertility, Prosperity, and Peace. Equivalent of the Celtic Horned God. Son of Niord and Skadi, and brother of Freya. Originally Vanir; for his and Freya's acceptance by the Aesir, *see* Freya entry. Being an ithyphallic fertility god, it is very likely that he was originally horned; in one myth of Ragnarok it is said that he fought with antlers. His wife was Gerd. His hall was Alfheim, home of the light elves, given to him by the Gods when he cut his first tooth. His horse was Blodhughofi ("Bloody-Hoofed"). His chariot was drawn by two boars, Gullibursti ("Golden-Bristled") and Slidrurgtanni ("Smooth- or Shiny-skinned"), and he often rode Gullibursti, who was said to be able to move over land and sea faster than a horse. Frey was probably originally chief of a boar clan of the Vanir before they merged with the Aesir. His other sacred animals were the stag and the bull or ox. His magical flaming sword could fight of its own accord, and was the only protection against the Fire Demon Surt. His ship, Skidbladnir, summoned up wind as soon as its sail was hoisted; it could hold all the Aesir, but could be folded up and put in his purse. Every year in Sweden, his image traveled the country accompanied by a beautiful girl called "Frey's Wife," who also acted as priestess of his great temple at Upsalla. His titles included "Protector of the Gods," "Ruler of the Hosts of the Gods," and "God of the World." He was a Sovereignty God; many kings who were regarded as his representatives were known as Frodhi ("Fruitful").

HERMES: Greek. Messenger of the Gods, and God of Intellect, Communication, Commerce, and Travel. On occasion also a trickster, bringing good luck to thieves. Originally, like Pan (who was then said to be his son) Hermes was Arcadian, and in that form seems also to have been horned and goat-footed. He was the psychopompous, conducting dead souls to the afterlife. Son of Zeus and the Pleiad Maia. His many reputed lovers included Aphrodite, Hecate, and Persephone. His symbols were the caduceus, the winged cap, and the winged sandals. He was equated with Mercury by the Romans.

HERNE, CERNE: British and Anglo-Saxon. The Horned God, envisaged with stag's antlers. There are traces of him in both Celtic and Saxon tradition, where he was also revered as the god of ale, but like many of the gods of early hunting and agricultural cultures, he was pushed into the shadows by the later and more sophisticated pantheons, particularly those of warrior aristocracies. As Prionsias MacCana puts it (*Celtic Mythology*, 48): "The Cernunnos cult would probably have survived longest among the lower orders of society, where custom died hard and orthodoxy was not easily imposed. Unfortunately this is virtually unknown territory, for it is only in recent times that the usages and beliefs of the common people received conscious recognition in written literature." (Cernunnos has become the generally used name for Herne or Cerne.) The only substantial legend of Herne that has survived is that of Windsor Great Park, where he is said to lead the Wild Hunt of red-eyed hounds, mounted on a black horse. He was associated with a great oak that once grew there. There are many stories of his still haunting the Great Park—one as late as 1962, when a group of youths found a hunting horn there, blew it, and reported hearing an answering horn and seeing the Wild Hunt approaching; terrified, they ran off. His memory also survives in several English place-names, in either the H- or the C- form: Herne Hill, Herne Bay, Hern Drove, Herne Pound, Cerne Abbas, Upper and Nether Cerne, the River Cerne. It has been suggested that the name Herne was adopted from the mating call of a doe for her buck—approximately "Hurrrn!"—on the natural assumption that if that was what she called him, then that was his name.

LUCIFER: ("Light-Bearer") Christian. The Christian use of the name, from its only Biblical mention in Isaiah xiv, 12 is a misunderstanding of the passage, which does not refer to the Devil, but is a satirical metaphor for the tyrant King of Babylon, at that time the occupier of Palestine; it is part of a song, in the traditional Hebrew lamentation rhythm. In Tuscan witch legend, Diana, the first of all Creation, divided herself in two; the Darkness was herself, and the Light was her brother Lucifer. She desired him, but he fled from her as she pursued him round the heavens. Finally, by shape changing into a cat, she got into his bed. He woke to find his sister beside him. From their union was born Aradia, the witches' teacher goddess.

MOSHTO: Romany. Sun God and Horned God of the Summer. He is one aspect of the Great God, the other being Arivell, Horned God of the Winter. Arivell was demoted by Christianity to a demon, possibly because Romany-Gypsies call winter "the little death"; in fact he is entirely beneficent. This one God in his two aspects was son of the Creator Goddess Anusia and the Great God Vista, and brother/consort to the Moon Goddess Doia-Bori. Moshto and Doia-Bori gave birth to the Earth and all life on it.

ODIN, ODHINN: ("Fury, Inspiration") Norse. Chief God, God of War and Poetry, and conductor of the dead. King of the Aesir, which meant in effect he was the God of the warrior aristocracy rather than of the peasants—though he was also a god of fertility, and the last sheaf of wheat at the harvest was left for his horse. Odin was possibly originally a historical person, chief of a powerful raven clan, early becoming a God of winds and nocturnal storms; his most ancient appearance was as a Continental German raging Storm Giant called Wode, who assembled the souls of the dead. Gradually replaced Thor (the peasants' God) as head of the pantheon; though Thor, representing order, remained more popular than Odin, who represented primarily war and violence. His magical number was nine—the number of nights and days he endured Initiation on Yggdrasil in his quest for knowledge. Known as Alfadhir ("All-Father"), and by dozens of other names from Herjan ("War God") and Svafnir ("Luller to Sleep or Dreams") to Gagnrath ("Giving Good Counsel") and Drauga Drottin ("Lord of Ghosts"). Envisaged as tall, gray-bearded, wearing a dark blue cloak, and with only one eye, the other socket being covered by a broad hat or by the cloak as a hood. He lived in Valhalla attended by the Valkyries and with two ravens, Hugin and Munin, who kept him informed on events on Earth—though he visited Earth at will. Leader of the Wild Hunt, in which he rode across the night sky with a pack of red-eyed hounds, souls of the dead. He had an eight-legged horse (Sleipnir), a spear (Gungnir), a magic ring (Draupnir), and two attendant wolves (Freki and Geri). His wife was Freya (Frigg). At Ragnarok, he is consumed by the Fenris-wolf. Identified with the German Wotan (earlier Wodanaz), the Dutch Wodan, and the Anglo-Saxon Woden, and by the Romans with Mercury (also a psychopompous or conductor of the dead).

PAN: ("All, Everything", or possibly "Pasturer") Greek. God of all Nature, the Woods, and Shepherds. Portrayed goat-footed and horned. Originally from Arcadia, as was Hermes, said there to be his father. His worship spread beyond Arcadia, according to tradition, when he gave the Athenians victory over the Persians at Marathon in exchange for honoring him; after the victory, Athens built a temple for him on the Acropolis, and his cult spread throughout Greece. He then acquired a variety of parents. He was said to be the son by Hermes of Dryope, whose father's flocks Hermes tended; or of Hermes by Penelope, wife of Odysseus; or of Penelope by all her suitors in

Odysseus's absence; or of Thimbris or Callisto by Zeus. Another named mother was Amalthea, the Cretan goat goddess who suckled the infant Zeus. The Romans identified him with Faunus, and he tended to merge with the ithyphallic Priapus, also said to be his son. His loves were many, quite apart from his constant pursuit of the anonymous nymphs of his own woodlands. Caves were often dedicated to Pan and a nymph. Nymphs were very much his female counterpart, often memories of primordial local Goddesses, wild beings quite unlike the coy damsels of Victorian art. Beyond his pastoral and musical nature, Pan shared with his father Hermes the gift of wisdom and prophecy—seeming to personify the concept of wisdom through oneness with Nature. His physical appearance supports this—from his animal goat-feet in touch with the ground, through his fertile loins, to his intelligent and music-making head. One story told by Plutarch used to be quoted as confirmation of Christianity's victory over Paganism. While passing the Echinades Islands, a sailor called Thamus heard a voice calling three times: "When you reach Palodes, proclaim that the great God Pan is dead." It is far more likely that what Thamus really heard was the ritual lamentation over the annual death of the Vegetation God Tammuz, mourned as the "All-Great." In Greek, *pammegas* means "Great Pan."

VELNIAS **(Latvian),**

  VOLOS **(Lithuanian**

  and Slavic): God of Death and the Underworld, and of Woodlands and Hidden Treasures. An evil God, of night, darkness, and destructive magic, opposite of Dievas, God of the Shining Sky. Both of them created the world—Dievas the light and beautiful aspects and creatures, Veles/Velnias the dark and cruel ones. Strangely perhaps, while wheat and rye belonged to Dievas, barley, buckwheat, and all root vegetables belonged to Veles/Velnias. Equally strangely, Veles/Velnias was a God of contracts, music, water, and stones, a seer, and connected with cattle and prosperity. Envisaged as one-eyed, horned, and cloven-footed and notorious for lusting after women. A famous example was a young woman picking mushrooms in the forest; when it began to rain in torrents, she took off her clothes and put them in her *kraitis* (hope chest) and stood naked under a tree till the rain stopped; then she put her dry clothes back on and went back to picking mushrooms. Velnias spotted her, and was curious to know how she was dry when everything else was soaked. She told him she had a secret technique to prevent rain from falling on her. She agreed to tell him, if he would tell her all his own magical arts. His curiosity overcame him, and he agreed, telling her all his arts of magic and healing. Then she told him her own simple "secret." He was furious, and flew away screaming that he had been tricked. The woman became the first witch, and passed her knowledge on to others; thus was witchcraft born. Since Christianity made him simply demonic, it may well be that originally the two contrasting Gods represented a natural polarity rather than a confrontation—Dievas personifying Light, Consciousness, promise, and the reward of good deeds, and Veles/Velnias the mysterious Otherworld, the Unconscious, warning, and the punishment of bad deeds.

Appendix 11

Correspondence Tables

Tables begin on page 264.

The Seven Planetary Correspondences

Planet	Sun	Moon	Mars	Mercury	Jupiter	Venus	Saturn
Element	Spirit	(Ether)	Fire	Air	(Mind)	Water	Earth
Magical Tool	Altar	Cauldron	Sword	Wand	Staff/Stang	Chalice	Pentacle
Chakra	Crown	Throat	Solar Plexus	Heart	Third Eye	Sacral	Root
Realm	Gwynfyd/Asaheimr	Annwn/Helheimr	Murias/Muspellheimr	Gorias/Jotunheimr	Abred/Midgardhr	Finias/Vanaheimr	Falias/Niflheimr
Colors	Gold/Yellow *White/Gold/Silver	White/Silver *Blue	Red *Yellow	Orange *Green/Turquoise	Blue/Purple *Indigo/purple	Green *Orange	Black *Red
God/Goddess	Apollo, Baldur, Mabon	Hecate, Diana, Selene	Tiuw, Aries, Lugh	Hermes, OdinAnubis	Thor, Zeus, Taranus	Freya, Aphrodite, Isis	Norns, Morrigan
Day of Week	Sunday	Monday	Tuesday	Wednesday	Thursday	Friday	Saturday
Tree (Ogham)	Birch (Beith)	Willow (Saille)	Holly (Tinne)	Ash (Nuin)	Oak (Dur)	Apple (Quert)	Alder (Fearn)
Rune	Sigel	Lagu	Tyr	Eoh	Thorn	Gifu	Nied
Tarot	The Sun	The Moon	The Chariot	The Hermit	The Emperor	The Empress	Death
Sephira	Tiphareth	Yesod	Geburah	Hod	Chesed	Netzach	Binah
Attributions	Joy, success, advancement, growth, natural power, healing, light	Inspiration, psychic skills, emotions, secrets, cycles	Strength, struggle, conflict, anger, aggression	Communications, intelligence, creativity, science, trickery	Leadership, politics, power, honor, responsibility, wealth, business	Love, harmony, attraction, pleasure, sexuality	Obstacles, limitations, time, death

*Chakra color used for opening/closing

The Four Elemental Correspondences

Element	Air *(To Know)*	Fire *(To Will)*	Water *(To Dare)*	Earth *(To Be Silent)*
Cardinal Point	East	South	West	North
Time of Day	Dawn (sunrise)	Midday	Dusk (sunset)	Midnight
Magical Tool	Wand	Sword	Chalice	Pentacle
Season/Solar Festival	Spring Equinox	Summer Solstice	Autumn Equinox	Winter Solstice
Fire Festival	Beltane	Lughnasadh	Samhain	Imbolg
Archetype	Wizard/Sage	Warrior	Maiden	Mother
Planet	Mercury	Mars	Venus	Saturn
Colors	Blue/Yellow	Red	Sea Green/Blue	Green/Brown/Black
Moon Phase	Waxing	Full	Waning	Dark/New
Attributions	The mind, knowledge, learning, memory	Energy, will, life, cleansing, purification	Emotions, feelings, courage, intuition, the subconscious	Physicality, growth, nature, material gain, birth, death.

Appendix III

Spiritual/Occult Laws

These are our own synthesis and simplification of the magical laws that we have come across over the years. These are not the only ones you may come across. For further information on the subject, we would suggest reading Isaac Bonewits' *Real Magic* (see Bibliography).

1. The Law of Threefold Return.

Also known as the Law of Cause and Effect. This law states that anything you send out magically (or physically, for that matter) will return to you threefold: "As ye sow, so shall ye reap." Threefold does not refer to it actually coming back to you three times, but coming back to you on three different levels—the physical level, the mental/emotional level, and the spiritual level. This law is an expression of exchange of energy on a more subtle level; therefore it is important to ensure balance by returning favors or gifts in some way (see The Law of Balance). In runic lore, this is summed up as "a gift demands a gift" and is symbolised by the rune Gifu (the kiss).

2. Law of Cyclical Return.

If you are unable to overcome a karmic obstacle, or unable to learn from the mistakes in your life; you will continue to face that obstacle until you learn how to overcome it. All other growth in your life will be stunted until you do so. This applies not just to this life, such a cycle can continue over several lifetimes. This is basically the law of karma and is connected to the previously mentioned Law of Threefold Return.

3. Law of Polarity.

In each thing there is an opposite: Chaos/Order, Humour/Grimness, Positive/Negative, Male/Female, Yin/Yang, etc. Both are inherently within each other, resulting in dynamic interaction and power (best visualized as the oyster, and the grit that results in the creation of the pearl). It is for this reason that the use of such polarities is a source of power within magical practice.

4. Law of Attraction.

Following on from the Law of Polarity, such opposites are attracted to each other. Hence, male and female may find magical attraction within circle (something that should not be misunderstood as sexual attraction). There is also another aspect of this law (sometimes known as the Law of Opulence or Law of Synthesis) which states that if you wish to attract something, give away that which you already have of it. Quite simply, by bringing two forces together you create a third. This is summed up in the old Oriental saying, "If you have two loaves, sell one and buy a lily."

5. The Law of Balance.

This law comes into play after the Law of Attraction. Opposite forces will always naturally fall into balance if left undisturbed. "The road to hell is paved with good intentions" is a good way of explaining what happens if this law is ignored. If you do magical work when none is needed, you may cause imbalance, resulting in you causing the opposite of what you were trying to achieve by doing good out of vanity, rather than need.

6. The Law of Magical Accounting (The Karmic Bank Account.)

When any magic that rebalances the natural forces is performed (see the Law of Balance), a karmic payment is due. This payment can be taken in three different ways; it can be used to pay off any karmic deficit; it can be used to pay the universe for a request for magical assistance; or it can be stored in the personal karmic bank account to pay for future deficits (getting in the red). In the latter, it can be transferred after death, to future incarnations. Such a karmic bank account accumulates interest, and with a standing order or cosmic checkbook, can be used to pay off karmic deficits as they occur.

7. Law of Triple Invocation.

All invocations must occur three times to be successful. This triple invocation can either occur in the same fashion, such as vocally ("I invoke you, I invoke you, I invoke you") or on three different levels, such as by visualization, by vocalization, and by action. Regardless of technique, the triple invocation has the same effect, which is to send out the request on three levels: on the Conscious, on the Personal Unconscious, and finally on the Collective Unconscious (Astral) level.

8. The Law of Challenge.

Everything that is experienced and is considered to be mystical— prophetic dreams, visions, clairvoyance, etc.—must be challenged to see if it is a genuine psychic experience. Experiences that are genuine stand on their own merits and are able to withstand such scrutiny; those that do not are potentially harmful if taken seriously, resulting in imbalance and a lack of grounding in the practitioner.

9. Law of Rebound.

A superior force will always rebound a lesser force. Therefore, when approaching an entity on any level of the Astral/Elemental Realms, you will be challenged to your suitability to pass beyond them. If you are unable to pass them, it means that you are not ready and must return to continue your spiritual growth. This is particularly true when approaching the Gate of the Mysteries. To pass beyond such a guardian is to experience a spiritual initiation.

10. The Law of Reflection.

Most commonly expressed amongst occultists by the phrase "As above, so below." Everything on this material level of reality has its reflection on the higher Astral Levels. This is the basis of sympathetic magic, where by using the Elements (Earth, Air, Fire, and Water) it is possible to create an Astral Double and endow it with ability by the use of consecration.

11. The Law of Knowledge (including Self Knowledge).

The basis of this law is that understanding brings control. Knowledge is essential for spiritual growth as well as becoming adept at magical practice. The more that is known about a subject, the easier it is to exercise control over it; the more that is known about the self, the easier it is to control the self.

12. The Law of Names.

A name, by common repetitive use, represents an object or person on an Astral Level. Therefore the use of this name is a link to the object or person through the Law of Reflection. This is one of the reasons that the craft name taken during initiation is kept secret, as such names are an astral link to the bearer and could easily be misused. To know the name of something is to have control over it, particularly spiritual entities. A spiritual entity of good intention will always therefore disclose their name or intention to you.

13. The Law of Connection (or Unity).

Quite simply put, everything in the universe is connected. This means all events past, present, and future are linked. It is only our inadequate senses that perceive separation in the universe. Modern Chaos Theory states that a butterfly beating its wings in South America will cause a storm in Europe. Therefore, all magical acts will affect the whole universe in someway, however minor the effect may be perceived to be. This puts great responsibility on the magical practitioner.

14. The Law of Dichotomy and Paradox.

All workable practices of magic have the idea of the cosmic joker or that the gods have a sense of humor (you may have noticed this in some of the laws). Magic only works because we believe it does; the moment we believe that it doesn't, it will cease to work. This law allows effect to precede cause (time is not linear on the Astral Level); therefore, several days after performing a magical working, an individual or group may discover that it had, in fact, worked several days earlier without their knowledge. It is closely linked to the Law of Attraction, when the forces concerned are at odds with each other, such as grimness and humor. The application of this law can be found in such traditions as Discordia, which works on the aforementioned polarities.

Resources

Organizations

The Pagan Federation
BM Box 7097
London WC1N 3XX
England
E-mail: secretary@paganfed.demon.co.uk
www.paganfed.demon.co.uk

Covenant of the Goddess
PO Box 1226
Berkeley CA 94701
U.S.A.
E-mail: info@cog.org
www.cog.org

Church of All Worlds
960 Berry St
Toledo OH 43605-3044
U.S.A.
E-mail: office@caw.org
www.caw.org

Pagan Alliance (Australia)
GPO Box 2123
Canberra City ACT 2601
Australia
E-mail: i-hamilton@myplace.net.au
www.geocities.com/Athens/Thebes/4320/

Websites

Wicca Na hErin
www.wicca.utvinternet.com
E-mail: wicca@utvinternet.com

The Witches Voice
www.witchvox.com
E-mail: witchvox@witchvox.com

Children of Artemis
www.witchcraft.org
E-mail: webspinner@witchcraft.org

Magazines and Periodicals

Pagan Dawn
BM 5896
London
WC1N 3XX
E-mail: pagandawn@paganfed.demon.co.uk

The Pentacle
Pentacle Magazine
78 Hamlet Road
Southend
Essex
SS1 1HH
www.pentaclemagazine.org
E-mail: subs@pentaclemagazine.com

Pangaea
Blessed Be, Inc.
207 Main Street
Point Arena
CA 95468-0641
U.S.A.
www.pangaia.com
E-mail: info@pangaia.com

The Pagan Times
Pagan Times
PO Box 666
Williamstown
VIC 3016
Australia
E-mail: pagantimeseditor@neogenesis.com.au

Witchcraft Magazine
FPC Magazines Subscriptions
Locked Bag 1028
Alexandria
NSW 2756
Australia

Bibliography and Selected Reading

Adler, Margot. *Drawing Down the Moon.* Boston: Beacon Press, 1979.

Ashe, Geoffrey. *The Finger and the Moon.* London: Heinemann, 1973.

Bates, Brian. *The Way of Wyrd.* London: Arrow Books, 1987.

Blavatsky, H.P. *The Secret Doctrine.* Los Angeles: The Thesosophy Society, 1964.

Bleakley, Alan. *Fruits of the Moon Tree.* London: Gateway Books, 1984.

Bord, Janet and Colin. *Earth Rites.* London: Granada Publishing, 1982.

Buckland, Raymond. *The Tree: The Complete Book of Saxon Witchcraft.* York Beach: Samuel Weiser, 1974.

———. *Buckland's Complete Book of Witchcraft.* St. Paul, Minn: Llewellyn Publications, 1986 Rev. 2002.

———. *The Witch Book: The Encyclopedia of Witchcraft, Wicca, and Neo-Paganism..* St. Paul, Minn: Llewellyn Publications, 2002.

Burland, C.A. *The Magical Arts.* London: Arthur Barker, 1966.

Butler, W.E. *The Magician: His Training and Work.* London: Aquarian Press, 1959.

Campbell, Joseph. *The Hero With a Thousand Faces.* New Jersey: Princeton University Press, 1990.

Crowley, Aleister. *Magick*. London: Routledge and Kegan Paul, 1986.

———. *777*. New York: Samuel Weiser, 1970.

Crowley, Vivianne. *Wicca.* Wellingborough: Aquarian Press, 1989.

Curries, Ian. *You Cannot Die*. Shaftesbury, England: Element Books Ltd., 1978.

Curott, Phyllis. *Witch Crafting: A Spiritual Guide to Making Magic*. New York: Broadway Books, 2001.

Deren, Maya. *The Voodoo Gods*. London: Paladin Books, St. Albans, 1975.

Drury, Nevill. *The Elements of Shamanism*. Shaftesbury, England: Element Books Ltd., 1989.

Eliade, Mircea. *Shamanism: Archaic Techniques of Ecstasy*. New Jersey: Princeton University Press, 1972.

Ennemoser, Joseph. *The History of Magic (Vol.1)*. New York: University Books Inc., 1970.

Farrar, Janet and Stewart. *Eight Sabbats for Witches*. London: Robert Hales, 1981.

———. *The Witches' Way: Principles, Rituals, and Beliefs of Modern Witchcraft*. London: Robert Hales, 1984.

———. *The Witches' Goddess*. London: Robert Hales, 1987.

———. *The Witches' God*. London: Robert Hales, 1989.

———. *Spells and How They Work*. London: Robert Hales, 1990.

———. *Dictionary of World Deities*. (unpublished manuscript).

Farrar, J. and S. and Gavin Bone. *The Pagan Path: The Wiccan Way of Life*. Custer, Wash: Phoenix Publications, 1995.

———. *The Healing Craft: Healing Practices for Witches and Pagans*. Custer, Wash: Phoenix Publications, 2000.

———. *The Complete Dictionary of European Gods and Goddesses*. Chieveley, Berks: Capall Bann Publishing, 2000.

Fitch, Ed. *Magical Rites From the Crystal Well*. St. Paul, Minn.: Llewellyn Publications, 1984.

———. *A Book of Pagan Rituals*. York Beach: Samuel Weiser, 1974.

Fortune, Dion. *Psychic Self Defense*. York Beach: Samuel Weiser, 1982.

———. *The Mystical Qabalah*. London: Ernest Benn Ltd., 1972.

———. *Sane Occultism*. Wellingborough: Aquarian Press, 1987.

———. *The Sea Priestess*. London: Aquarian Press, 1957.

Frazer, J. G. *The Golden Bough*. London: MacMillan Press Ltd., 1974.

Gardner, Gerald B. *High Magic's Aid*. London: Michael Houghton, 1949.

Gilchrist, Cherry. *The Circle Of Nine: The Feminine Psyche Revealed Through Nine Contemporary Archetypes.*. London: Arkana, 1991.

Graves, Robert. *The White Goddess*. London: Faber and Faber Limited, 1961.

Grimmassi, Raven. *The Wiccan Mysteries: Ancient Origins and Teachings*. St. Paul, Minn.: Llewellyn Publications, 1997.

———. *The Witches Craft: The Roots of Witchcraft and Magical Transformation*. St. Paul, Minn.: Llewellyn Publications, 2002.

———. *The Encyclopedia of Wicca and Witchcraft*. St. Paul, Minn.: Llewellyn Publications, 2000.

Guiley, Rosemary Ellen. *The Encyclopedia of Witches and Witchcraft*. New York: Facts on File, 1989.

Gundarsson, Kvelduf. *Teutonic Magic: The Magical and Spiritual Practices of the Germanic People*. St. Paul, Minn.: Llewellyn Publications, 1990.

Halevi, Z'ev ben Shimon. *Tree of Life: An Introduction to the Cabala*. London: Rider and Company, 1972.

Hall, C.S, and Nordby, V.J. *A Primer of Jungian Psychology*. New York: Mentor Books, 1973.

Hampden-Turner, Charles. *Maps of the Mind: Charts and Concepts of the Mind and Labyrinth*. London: Mitchell Beazley, 1981.

Haralambos, M. *Sociology: Themes and Perspectives*. Slough: University Tutorial Press, 1980.

Harner, Michael. *The Way of the Shaman*. New York: Harper and Row, 1980.

Hope-Robbins, Rossel. *Encyclopedia of Witchcraft and Demonology*. London: Spring Books, 1959.

Heselton, Phillip. *Wiccan Roots*. Chieveley, Berks: Capall Bann Publishing, 2000.

Hollander, Lee M. (Translator). *The Poetic Edda*. Austin: Texas University Press, 1962.

Hope, Murry. *Practical Celtic Magic*. Wellingborough: The Aquarian Press, 1987.

Hutton, Ronald. *The Triumph of the Moon: A History of Modern Pagan Witchcraft*. Oxford University Press, 1999.

Jacobi, Jolande. *The Psychology of C. G. Jung*. London: Routledge, 1962.

Johns, June. *King of the Witches: The World of Alex Sanders*. London: Peter Davies, 1969.

Jordan, Michael. *Witches: An Encyclopedia of Paganism and Magic*. London: Kyle Cathie Limited, 1996.

Judith, Anodea. *The Truth About Chakras*. St. Paul, Minn.: Llewellyn Publications, 1994.

———. *Wheels of Life: A Journey Through the Chakras*. St. Paul, Minn.: Llewellyn Publications, 1994.

Jung, Carl Gustav. *Four Archetypes*. London: Routledge, 1972.

———. *Synchronicity: An Acausal Connecting Principle*. London: Routledge and Kegan Paul, 1955.

Larousse World Mythology. Secaucus, N.J.: Chartwell Books Inc., 1973.

Lady Sheba. *The Book of Shadows*. St.Paul, Minn.: Llewellyn Publications, 1971.

Kelly, Aidan. *Crafting the Art of Magic: A History of Modern Witchcraft 1939–1964*. St. Paul, Minn.: Llewellyn Publications, 1991.

King, Francis. *Ritual Magic in England: 1887 to the Present Day*. London: Neville Spearman, 1970.

King, Francis, and Stephen Skinner. *Techniques of High Magic: A Manual of Self Initiation*. London: The C.W. Daniel Company, 1974.

Leadbeater, C.W. *The Chakras: A Monograph*. Eighth reprint. Adyar: The Theosophical Publishing House, 1969.

Leland, Charles Godfrey. *Aradia or the Gospel of the Witches*. London: The C.W. Daniel Company, 1974.

Murray, Margaret. *The Witch Cult in Western Europe: A Study in Anthropology*. Oxford University Press, 1921.

Neumann, Erich. *The Great Mother*. London: Routledge and Kegan Paul, 1963.

Neimark, Philip J. *The Way of the Orisa: Empowering Your Life Through the Ancient African Religion of Ifa*. San Francisco: Harper-Collins, 1993.

Pagels, Elaine. *The Gnostic Gospels.* London: Wiedenfeld and Nicolson, 1979.

Patrick, Richard. *All Colour Book of Greek Mythology.* London: Octopus Books, 1972.

Pennick, Nigel. *Runic Astrology.* Wellingborough: Aquarian Press, 1990.

Perowne, Stewart. *Roman Mythology.* London: Hamlyn, 1969.

Pinsent, John. *Greek Mythology.* London: Hamlyn, 1969.

Powell, A.E. *The Astral Body and Other Astral Phenomena.* London: The Theosophical Publishing House, 1927.

———. *The Mental Body.* London: The Theosophical Publishing House, 1927.

———. *The Etheric Double.* London: The Theosophical Publishing House, 1925.

Reed, Ellen Cannon. *The Heart of Wicca: Wise Words from a Crone on the Path.* York Beach: Red Wheel, Samuel Weiser, 2000.

Roose-Evans, J. *Passages of the Soul: Rediscovering the Importance of Rituals in Everyday Life.* Shaftesbury, England: Element Books Ltd., 1994.

St. Clair, David. *Drum and Candle.* London: Macdonald, 1971.

Starhawk. *The Spiral Dance.* New York, London: Harper and Row, 1979.

———. *Dreaming the Dark.* London: Mandala, 1982.

Sun Bear, and Wabun. *The Medicine Wheel.* New York: Prentice Hall Press, 1986.

Valiente, Doreen. *An ABC of Witchcraft Past and Present.* London: Robert Hale, 1973.

———. *Witchcraft for Tomorrow.* Robert Hale, London, 1978.

———. *The Rebirth of Witchcraft.* Robert Hale, London, 1989.

Valiente, Doreen and Evan Jones. *Witchcraft: A Tradition Renewed.* Custer, Wash.: Phoenix Publications, 1989.

Whitton, Dr. J. and J. Fisher. *Life Between Life.* London: Grafton Books, 1986.

Witt, R.E. *Isis in the Graceo-Roman World.* London: Thames and Hudson, 1971.

Wolfe, Amber. *In the Shadow of the Shaman:Connecting with Self, Nature and Spirit.* St. Paul, Minn.: Llewellyn Publications, 1988.

Index

About the Authors

JANET FARRAR AND GAVIN BONE are practicing priesthood in the old religion of Witchcraft and well-known names internationally within Wiccan and Pagan communities. They have between them more than 50 years experience in the fields of spirituality and the Occult sciences, and are considered to be experts in their field by their peers. Originally initiated into Wicca, they have explored several other paths, including Spiritualism, Spiritual Healing, Voudon, Hinduism, Shamanism, and Ceremonial Magic to broaden their path.

JANET is best known for writing with her late husband, Stewart Farrar, some of the classics of modern Witchcraft: *The Witches' Goddess*, *The Witches' God*, and the best-selling *A Witches' Bible*. To date, Janet has written more than 10 books, including three with her current co-author and partner Gavin Bone. She came into Wicca in 1970, being an initiate of Alex and Maxine Sanders. Since then, she has run several successful training covens and is an experienced coven Priestess, who considers herself just to be a "Priestess" rather than to be of a specific path.

A trained Registered Nurse, GAVIN is a natural Spiritual (empathic) Healer, and came into Shamanism and Witchcraft in 1985, as an initiate of Ray Buckland's Seax-Wicca. Prior to this, he had also explored many of the Eastern paths, looking at their relationship with ancient European Spiritual practices. Alongside Janet and her late husband Stewart, he co-wrote *The Healing Craft*, an exploration of the path of healing within modern Wicca. With Janet, he regularly gives lectures and experiential workshops both in the United States, Europe, and Australia to sold-out audiences.